IMPOSSIBLE PARENTING

DUNDURN

TORONTO

OLIVIA SCOBIE

IMPOSSIBLE PARENTING

Creating a
New Culture of
Mental Health for Parents

Publisher: Scott Fraser | Acquiring editor: Kathryn Lane | Editor: Jess Shulman
Designer: Laura Boyle
Cover image: shutterstock.com/Danussa
Printer: Marquis Book Printing Inc.

Library and Archives Canada Cataloguing in Publication

Title: Impossible parenting : creating a new culture of mental health for parents / Olivia Scobie.
Names: Scobie, Olivia, 1983- author.
Description: Includes bibliographical references and index.
Identifiers: Canadiana (print) 20200278606 | Canadiana (ebook) 20200278738 | ISBN
  9781459746541 (softcover) | ISBN 9781459746558 (PDF) | ISBN 9781459746565 (EPUB)
Subjects: LCSH: Parenting—Psychological aspects. | LCSH: Parents—Mental health. | LCSH:
  Parents— Family relationships.
Classification: LCC BF723.P25 S36 2020 | DDC 155.9/24—dc23

 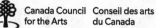 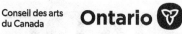

We acknowledge the support of the Canada Council for the Arts and the Ontario Arts Council for our publishing program. We also acknowledge the financial support of the Government of Ontario, through the Ontario Book Publishing Tax Credit and Ontario Creates, and the Government of Canada.

VISIT US AT

∞ dundurn.com | 🐦 @dundurnpress | ✕ dundurnpress | 📷 dundurnpress

Dundurn
3 Church Street, Suite 500
Toronto, Ontario, Canada
M5E 1M2

To my children.
May we always be perfectly imperfect.
And forgiving.

CONTENTS

One	Introduction	1
Part 1	**Naming**	13
Two	The Perinatal Mood Framework	17
Three	Impossible Parenting	37
Part 2	**Hurting**	53
Four	Birth	55
Five	Sleep	75
Six	Relationships	89
Seven	Bodies	105
Part 3	**Healing**	125
Eight	Recovery	127
Nine	Self-Permission	139
Ten	Family-Centred Parenting	155
Eleven	Self-Parenting	175
Twelve	Be Less Alone	191
Thirteen	Final Thoughts	201
	Author's Note	207
	Acknowledgements	217
	Notes	221
	Index	235

ONE

INTRODUCTION

THE DREAM OF THE GOOD PARENT

Before they have children, most parents have a dream of what they think their new life will look like. Some of us focus on snuggling tiny babies, with their sleepy yawns and tiny socks, all nestled into a little blanket burrito. Others think of adorable toddlers with their toothy grins, broken language, and cuddly reading time. A few of us even envision helping school-aged children with their homework or driving them to an early morning sport practice or art class.

In these dreams we usually have quiet, well-behaved, neurotypical, able-bodied children. We have deep relationships with our children where we love and respect each other. Life is good in this dream. It's happy and joyful. We are good parents with good children.

Some anxiety may slip into this dream. We might worry if we will be enough. We might not know if we can afford the vision. We might see other people's children behaving badly and wonder how to avoid such behaviours while convincing ourselves that, somehow, "it'll be different for me/us."

My vision of parenting was patterned on the life of Lorelai Gilmore, the adorable, confident single mother from *The Gilmore Girls*. When I got pregnant with my first-born son, I was young — about a year out of high school. I already knew that the person I got pregnant with wasn't going to be a parent in much more than title, and that I was going to have to figure this out on my own. But that was no big deal. I was Lorelai Gilmore. I imagined going for long walks with my baby in the stroller, coffee in one hand, chatting with friends. I saw us becoming best buds and braving the world together. I knew there would be challenges, but a dynamic team like us? We could handle it.

Then I had the baby.

Becoming a parent was like taking a long series of punches in the face. The birth was traumatic. Nursing was simultaneously a nightmare and a cruel joke, landing us back in the hospital after only a few days because I had an infant so dehydrated that he could barely muster a cry. Once he was nourished with formula, he didn't sleep for more than forty minutes at a time and when he was awake, he cried and cried and cried. I went back and forth, either frantically struggling with a baby that was awake and crying, or stuck under a sleeping baby who could not be put down. He also had a medically complicated urinary system, chronic ear infections, and severe reflux, so we hung out at the hospital a lot. There were no coffee strolls. There were no breaks. We were not friends.

I thought the first year with my baby would be the best year of my life. Instead I found myself praying every day that I would die and that someone more equipped than me would be willing to raise this difficult creature into a lovely human.

Unfortunately, my experience was not unique.

THE GRIND IS UNFORESEEABLE

Once we become parents, most of us realize that our pre-parent selves were naive, or even foolish. To some extent, there's a discrepancy for every parent between what they thought it was going to be like and what it's really like, and there's nothing abnormal about that. When the gap between expectation and reality feels massive, some people adapt relatively easily. But others really struggle.

My partner, Janna, refers to this adjustment as learning to live with the *grind* of parenting, a term I've now adopted as my own. How the grind will feel is simply unknowable before having children. I had two kids when I met Janna, and before we moved in together, we spent a lot of time hanging out as a family. I asked Janna if they were nervous about living with the kids, but they assured me that they had spent enough time with them to get a sense of what it would be like. After a year of living together, we returned to this conversation, and they admitted that while they had a sense of many aspects of parent life, they couldn't have imagined how wearying the daily grind of chores, the irrationality of children, and the never being "off duty" for any more than a few hours at a time would be. It's not one task, one sleepless night, or one tantrum that feels tough; it's the combination of a seemingly endless stream of them, without knowing when you will get a moment to catch your breath, that feels so intense and exhausting. While there are many rewarding parts of parenting, I often liken the early years to waking up with a leak in your energy system and trying to get to the end of the day without letting the grind suck all your energy out of the leak, all the while hoping that there's at least an hour at the end of the day to fix the leak and fill the tank back up, because you have to do it all over again in the morning.

Each parent's experience is different, and it's not possible to understand your own experience of the grind ahead of time. Some people cope better with it. Some babies sleep more than others, and some people are less triggered by crying or whining. But all parents experience a loss of agency and control the moment they meet their kid(s) for the first time. For those who are co-parenting, there's usually one parent, who I call the *primary parent*, who does more of the parenting work in the postpartum period, and they feel the loss of agency very deeply. And while the desire to be in control has a bad reputation and can get you accused of being a "control freak," not having enough control can be disempowering and can make you feel hopeless. And yet much of the advice to new parents is to give in and let go of expectations, with very little discussion about what it's like to live with the serious responsibilities of postpartum life. This leaves parents with little control over their day-to-day lives, because the ever-changing needs of babies and young children often keep us from planning and executing tasks. Establishing a routine feels like a pipe dream, and even when something resembling a routine does emerge, it's almost never set by the parents, and it can be disrupted at any time by teething, developmental milestones, or just plain old off-days. Every day, postpartum parents try to find the balance between moving life forward, by doing basic things like going to appointments and getting groceries, and letting go of it all when their kid(s)' needs take over.

No one teaches us how to navigate this tricky dance of meeting expectations and letting go of them simultaneously, or how to live in a space with conflicting demands. Most of us aren't used to being needed in such an intense way, which makes it hard to understand what kind of resources might help us. Even if we do know what we want or need, resources often feel limited, and some parents have much more access to resources than others. We are taught that to be a "good" parent we must work hard, sacrifice, and be joyful, all of which can sometimes feel more like a performance for others than an authentic experience.

PERINATAL MOOD DISORDERS ARE THE NUMBER-ONE COMPLICATION OF CHILDBIRTH

Adjusting to postpartum reality can have a significant impact on many aspects of parents' lives. When I'm helping clients manage their anxious and depressed moods in my private social work counselling practice, themes related to identity, interpersonal relationships, resurgence of trauma, physical health, and grief come up frequently. It's impossible to know how many people struggle with their mood after becoming parents, but it's so common that perinatal mood disorders are considered the number-one complication of childbirth. The available statistics show varying rates between 12 and 20 percent, but these numbers are likely low because we know not all parents with perinatal mood disorders report it or receive support. This happens because of the stigma around mental illness diagnoses, the feeling among new parents that symptoms are not worth reporting, and the poor understanding among health care providers of perinatal mental health.

Despite significant public awareness efforts over the last twenty years, accessing mental health support is fraught with challenges in ways that getting physical health supports is not. For example, there's no mandatory mental health screening in Canada for perinatal mood, yet all pregnant people are offered a glucose tolerance test, even though gestational diabetes only occurs in about 9 percent of pregnancies. Universal screening of new parents doesn't guarantee that more parents will get the support that they need, because even when health care providers *do* check in with their patients about postpartum mood, treatment options are limited. A patient might be offered medication through their family doctor (if they have one), but it's just as likely that they'll be referred to a long wait-list for a psychiatrist/ hospital mood program or be directed to find their own private therapist, an option that comes with a significant financial barrier for many parents. And that's only if their community has perinatal therapists or public mental health programming; many rural areas and small towns offer no access to these types of support.

Many parents with perinatal mood disorders simply don't have enough help to protect and manage their moods, and solutions to this issue require complex, interdisciplinary, and individualized strategies. My goal with this book is to provide some solutions for parents living with postpartum mood disorders. If that's you, I'm truly glad you're reading this and so sorry that you are having a tough time with your mood. While this book is not intended to replace a therapeutic treatment plan, it's my sincere hope that the information I share provides you a deeper understanding of your experience and leaves you with both a sense of agency to create a personalized support plan and a sense of solidarity: you are not alone.

ROAD MAP TO THE BOOK

The book is broken up into three parts: Naming, Hurting, and Healing. Each part unpacks what it is about parenting that feels so hard for so many people. I outline how the messages, expectations, and structural systems for families with young children in the Western world have created a parenting culture that is so flawed and laden with barriers that it has become impossible to "get right," and how this culture is eroding parental mental health. I walk you through solutions to resisting and thriving within this system.

Naming analyzes four significant influences on perinatal mental health: (1) the biological aspects, such as hormonal changes, genetics, and sleep deprivation, and how they can affect the mood of parents who give birth; (2) thought patterns and thinking styles, and the ways in which they can influence how we interpret our perinatal experiences; (3) the effects of individual and circumstantial risk factors, such as trauma or relational distress; and (4) the community expectations of parents and how this contributes to a positive or negative parental identity. All of these influences exist within a very particular socio-economic environment, which has created a culture of parenting that has such contradictory and confusing messages about how to successfully raise a child that many parents feel like they are damned if they do and damned if they don't. This is the *culture of impossible parenting.*

Hurting explores the culture of impossible parenting and details the ways in which it is eroding parental mental health. Impossible-parenting culture creates complex tensions related to a few very specific topics. How parents become pregnant, stay pregnant, and give birth is often a source of trauma, and I discuss it in chapter four, Birth. Coping with sleep deprivation and the debate over sleep training are covered in chapter five, Sleep, and chapter six, Relationships, digs into the hurt and frustration that many new parents experience when trying to negotiate the work of parenting in their romantic relationships and also with family and friends. Finally, in chapter seven, Bodies, I discuss facing the limits of the control we have over our bodies within the pressure to nurse and lose "baby weight."

Healing provides a light at the end of the tunnel and offers solutions to resisting, enduring, and even thriving during parenting's early years. In these chapters, I support parents in creating their own *recovery plans*, with information to help you make good choices for your unique family, as well as lots of preventive and reactive coping tools to get you through those extra tough moments.

This book may feel different from other books you've read about perinatal mood in a few different ways. In writing it, I took into account four distinct considerations.

Self-Defined Postpartum Period: Although the medical literature often suggests that the postpartum period ends at twelve months, I consider postpartum to extend far beyond that and suggest that each parent gets to define for themselves what it means to be in or out of the postpartum period. I propose that parents are out of the postpartum period when their baby/babies are toilet trained, are consistently sleeping through the night, can communicate and get around on their own (depending on their ability, of course), and, for those who are nursed, are fully weaned. These transitions are more or less complete at around age two for many children, but could easily take until three, or even four! Having a self-defined postpartum period feels important because we seem to have a collective agreement that parents with babies need help, but there is a sudden withdrawal of this help when "babies" become "children." For example, most parents accessing perinatal mood support age out of these programs when their baby/babies are twelve months old, or when they return to paid work — which is when they often need it the most!

Gender-Neutral Language: I have centred the language in this book within a queer-inclusive and gender-neutral lexicon. Every book I have read about perinatal mood and anxiety disorders uses the language of mother/mama, pregnant woman, or some other gendered way of speaking about primary parents and people who give birth. I don't do that. I talk about parents in a nongendered way because I love and respect our trans and genderqueer birth and parenting communities, and I know that fathers and non-birth parents also struggle with their mood (I'm sorry that you have been excluded from these discussions). And because I'm a cis, queer, femme parent who is partnered with a genderqueer parent, and our family has personally felt the impact of this exclusion.

However, I do understand that people who identify as women/mothers continue to make up the majority of primary parents and have to navigate some significant gendered parenting gaps, so there are times throughout this book when I specifically refer to feminized experiences of parenting. I make it clear when I'm referencing research that was conducted with people who identify as mothers and similarly when I'm talking about pregnant people who birthed, because I know not all mothers give birth to their children. This is an important aspect of working toward cultivating an anti-oppressive approach to perinatal mood.

Cultural Analysis of "Good" Parenting: There are a lot of different ways to think about the origins of perinatal mood disorders. Some take great comfort in assigning responsibility for our mood disorders to our brains and our bodies. Others want to understand how the dramatic decline in parental support over the last century with the dramatic increase to parental expectations negatively impacts our mood and identity. Whatever narrative you have about why we develop perinatal mood and anxiety disorders is a welcome, important contribution, but please know that a significant focus of this book is to identify the ways in which cultural messages about how to be a "good parent" negatively shape our mood, rather than hyperfocusing on the biology behind mood disorders. Psychiatrists and other medical practitioners know a lot about the biology of perinatal mood and anxiety disorders and how to treat them with medicine, and significant public discourse is already dedicated to those aspects of perinatal mental health.

I'm a family sociologist, clinical social worker, and retired doula who has been in this messy-beautiful world of parenting for over ten years, which means my orientation to parental mood is rooted in structural-social concepts. We have a common understanding that parenting is hard, but quite limited discussion about what it is exactly that *makes* parenting so hard. We talk about the social determinants of children's health, but not the social determinants of parental health. In this book we explore the complicated interconnections of the many influences on parental mood so that we can most effectively address parents' needs. Not just because it's beneficial to children, but also because parents deserve to feel safe, be cared for, and experience pleasure in their parenting. I am proposing a framework for perinatal mood that I hope you pull apart and put back together combined with your own experiences and knowledge. You should feel welcome and encouraged to agree or disagree with the material as you engage with it.

Intersectional Feminism: Finally, as a feminist practitioner, I want to be transparent about my social location, and I strive to be aware of my own biases and privilege and how they shape the ideas outlined in this book. As such, I've attempted to weave in the importance of social location and anti-oppression when discussing perinatal mood. I'm queer, but femme, so I don't have the experience of birthing in a gender-neutral or masculine body. When I had my first child, I was a young single mother who was very poor and experienced a lot of institutional surveillance in the way that poor young single mothers do. While I am sensitive to issues of class and relationship status, I am no longer young, poor, or single and no longer occupy those identities. I'm able-bodied but continue to work hard at my mental health and still struggle to manage intense social anxiety. I'm also white, which has granted me unearned privilege as I have navigated complex social systems throughout the years. I don't ignore racial inequities throughout this book, but I also don't try to speak about experiences I couldn't possibly fully understand, so for that context I link to the work of brilliant Black/Indigenous/People of Colour (BIPOC) parenting researchers and practitioners.

While my goal was to keep this book rooted in intersectional awareness, I know I miss stuff or get it wrong sometimes and that this causes harm to others. It's not okay when this happens and it is okay to call it out if you see it. I do recognize that raising harm awareness is unpaid emotional work, but if you reach out, I commit to hearing you and believing you, and will quiet my fragility to own and address harm I have caused. I'm also not going to speak for all queer parents, parents with mood disorders, young mothers, single mothers, or poor mothers, as I honour the individual uniqueness that is embedded within shared experiences and identity.

MY STORY

Like most of us who gravitate toward helping work, my interest in this area was influenced by my own experience. I had postpartum depression or anxiety (PPD/A) with both of my children. As I mentioned above, during my first postpartum experience I was young and a solo parent and had no idea what was going on. The birth was traumatic, I felt ashamed that I couldn't nurse, and my first-born resisted sleep in a way I didn't know was possible for a baby. Getting hardly any REM sleep, I quickly became so depressed that suicidal fantasies were one of the only things that brought me peace. Without access to the support and information I needed, I assumed that this was just how motherhood was and that I had ruined my life.

It was three years before I realized that I had had depression, which I was only able to name as I had reluctant conversations about having another baby with my partner at the time. I agreed to have another baby, and when I got pregnant I was so focused on watching out for depression I completely missed out on the anxiety creeping into the pregnancy until a small, uncomfortable moment with another parent on the playground made me so sick with social anxiety that I couldn't bear to take my older son to kindergarten. Seeing this parent would give me panic attacks and there were many days when we didn't make it to school. By the time I was four months postpartum, I was flooded with enough intrusive thoughts about sudden infant death syndrome (SIDS) that although my baby slept, I couldn't. Because I was lucky enough to have an amazing family doctor at the time, I received the medical and therapeutic support I needed to find my way back to myself again.

Having future children felt dangerous, and I became obsessed with understanding the decline of my own postpartum mental health. This led me down a path of extensive research on parenting, mood, and the social construction of motherhood that resulted in my obtaining two graduate degrees and building a full-time social work practice. During my M.A. in sociology, I wrote my thesis on the social construction of "good mothering" and "bad mothering" narratives, and during my Master of Social Work (M.S.W.), I expanded on these concepts to write my major research paper about the macro-level cultural influences on postpartum depression and anxiety. In my counselling practice, I work primarily with parents having a tough time with their perinatal mood (including those dealing with reproductive loss and trauma), and this book contains much of what I have learned from these years of research and practise.

I hope this book challenges you, encourages you, and resonates with parts of your experience. I also hope you add to the concepts and ideas where I have left gaps or oversights. What I really want is for all of us to talk openly about perinatal mood and parental mental health and focus on how to get support to every parent out there. My goal is for no parents to fall through the cracks and suffer alone.

PART 1

NAMING

One of the most common questions I hear from parents with a perinatal mood disorder is *"Why do I feel like this?"* We don't know why some parents struggle with their mood in the early years of parenthood and others don't, but it remains a central question among mental health researchers and clinicians. Attempts to answer this question commonly involve two factors — human neurobiology and thinking patterns — but not everyone agrees about the relationship between these factors. As perinatal mental health clinician Karen Kleiman explains, "Some experts believe that the negative thoughts are *symptoms* of depression. Treat the depression, and you will think less negatively. Others say that negative thoughts *cause* the depressive thought process. Learn to reframe the thinking into positive channels and you will begin to feel better, these experts believe."[1]

Although *why* is a worthy question to answer because it opens treatment possibilities, and examining the clinical symptoms of mood disorders gives us an entry point for understanding what is happening, I think it's equally important for parents to be able to *name* what it's like for them to experience depression or anxiety in plain language. Listening to parents' personal experiences and creating the space for them to analyze and interpret their thoughts, feelings, and circumstances allowed me to develop the Perinatal Mood Framework. Over time, the individual stories of parents struggling with their mood started to merge into a collective narrative, not just because they were all expressing similar feelings, but also because they often shared internal and external expectations of what it means to be a "good" parent. The "rules" of parenting had become so narrow and confusing that they were starting to feel unattainable. I call this *the culture of impossible parenting*, and it is having a devastating impact on the mood of new parents. In this first part of the book, we'll explore the framework and impossible-parenting culture in detail, to provide a basis for exploring the most painful parts of this culture — birth, sleep, relationships, and body — in part 2.

QUICK REFERENCE FOR NAMING PMADS

While we're on the topic of naming, I'll point out that Perinatal Mood and Adjustment Disorders (PMADs) is a catch-all term that encompasses mood disorders that occur during and after pregnancy, such as depression, anxiety, post-traumatic stress disorder, obsessive-compulsive disorder, bipolar disorder, mania, and psychosis. This book focuses primarily on the experiences of postpartum depression, postpartum anxiety, and to some extent postpartum post-traumatic stress disorder related to birth and reproductive trauma, so I want to provide a common understanding of what is meant by those terms.

Baby Blues

- **What is it?** Temporary moodiness, weepiness, and overwhelm in the first few weeks after becoming a parent. Impacted by hormonal changes and adjusting to sleep deprivation.
- **How many parents are affected?** Estimated 80 percent.
- **Symptoms:** Mood swings, weepiness, irritability, restlessness, sadness, anxiety, loneliness, grief, feelings of loss or regret.

Postpartum Depression (PPD)

- **What is it?** Clinical depression that develops after becoming a parent.
- **How many parents are affected?** Estimated 12–20 percent.
- **Symptoms:** Sleep changes, forgetfulness, appetite changes, crying spells, negative thinking, hopelessness, loss of interest in life, emotional withdrawal, uncommunicativeness, overwhelm, lower self-confidence.

Postpartum Anxiety (PPA)

- **What is it?** Clinical anxiety that develops after becoming a parent.
- **How many parents are affected?** Estimated 17 percent.
- **Symptoms:** Intrusive thoughts, racing and/or fearful thoughts, heart palpitations, trouble taking deep breaths, insomnia, chest pain, panic attacks, fear of being alone with the baby.
- An estimated 2–3 percent also develop **Postpartum Obsessive-Compulsive Disorder**, which is characterized by obsessive worries about health (own or baby's), excessive concerns with cleanliness or germs, hyper-protectiveness of baby, repetitive/obsessive thoughts.

Postpartum Post-Traumatic Stress Disorder (PP-PTSD)

- **What is it?** Trauma in response to difficult birth or reproductive experience, which could include sexual, emotional, physical, structural, nursing, or loss trauma.
- **How many parents are affected?** Estimated 9–17 percent.
- **Symptoms:** Flashbacks, nightmares, panic attacks, dissociation, hyper/hypoarousal leading to feelings of helplessness or panic.

Here's my concern with defining perinatal mood disorders like this: While the medical definitions of PMADs are important for a clinical diagnosis, definitions like this are hard for parents to interpret for themselves because the experience of early parenthood is intense for just about everyone. I can't count the number of parents who've said to me, when reflecting on their postpartum experiences, "I think I might have had a little bit of PPD." And that's because clinical definitions don't capture the emotional nuances of grief and disappointment (of yourself, baby, partner, or community), confusing identity changes (you may not recognize yourself), and how deeply you want the very best for your baby/babies (Are they okay? Can I give them everything they need?). Even when you don't meet the clinical criteria for a PMAD, you may still be experiencing a lot of strong scared or sad feelings. This is why naming matters — not the labels themselves, but the discussion about what you're dealing with. Regardless of what you call it, you deserve support.

TWO

THE PERINATAL MOOD FRAMEWORK

I looked at my doctor, and my eyes welled up because I was so tired of being in pain. Of sleeping on the couch. Of waking up throughout the night. Of throwing up. Of taking things out on the wrong people. Of not enjoying life. Of not seeing my friends. Of not having the energy to take my baby for a stroll … I still don't really like to say, "I have postpartum depression," because the word depression scares a lot of people. I often just call it "postpartum." Maybe I should say it, though. Maybe it will lessen the stigma a bit.

— Chrissy Teigen

Though life with a baby is generally known for being overwhelming, it can be difficult to understand what is happening *specifically* with the mood and mental health of a new parent. I created the Perinatal Mood Framework to help parents deconstruct the confusing landscape of information that they're bombarded with. I wish I knew why so many new parents struggle with their mood, but what I *have* concluded is that trying to understand perinatal mental health through the lens of thoughts versus biology is far too limiting. My position is that perinatal mood disorders emerge from a complex set of biological, psychological, and social factors.[1] Becoming a parent is a messy, confusing, identity-altering process, accompanied by a shocking amount of adjustments to both gestational and non-gestational parents, including financial, hormonal, neurological, and identity changes, as well as completely new day-to-day routines. And it requires a curious, compassionate response.

THE PERINATAL MOOD FRAMEWORK

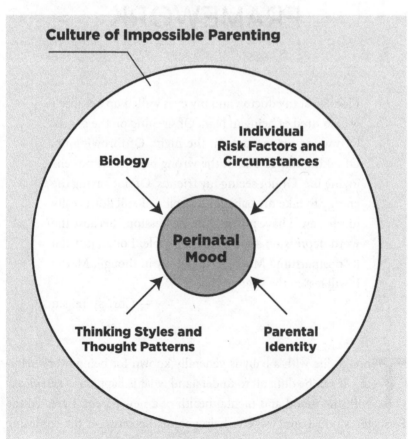

Influence One: Biology

There are many biological influences on perinatal mood, most of which affect parents who carry a pregnancy and give birth. Some of us are probably more susceptible to postpartum depression and anxiety because of our genetic makeup. In fact, a gene study at Johns Hopkins University suggested that there's a link between two genes and PPD, which prompted an international research project (which is still ongoing) to fully understand the role genes play in perinatal mental health. This could lead to the option of prenatal testing for pregnant people who want to know if they're at heightened risk for PMADs.[2]

Hormones also play a role in perinatal mood. According to Dr. Laura Kent-Davidson (ND), estrogen and progesterone levels initially plummet after parents give birth to the placenta, which can contribute to low mood and is likely a factor in "the baby blues." Nursing parents experience additional hormonal changes that can affect mood, as prolactin and oxytocin (a hormone and neurotransmitter that helps you feel loving, calm, and connected) increase and act as a mood protector for parents that enjoy nursing. But you don't need to be a nursing parent to reap the benefits of increased oxytocin, because snuggling your baby/babies, particularly skin to skin, can also cause levels to increase. Thyroid imbalances are also a common problem in the first year after childbirth, and can also increase feelings of depression and anxiety.[3] However, while it's important to have a sense of how birth affects our hormones, I'm wary of chalking up mood changes to hormone variations exclusively. After all, in both depressed and non-depressed birthers, hormone levels readjust in the weeks after birth (although the readjustment is generally not complete until the birther resumes menstruating), nursing parents can get PMADs, and birth hormones don't explain why non-birth parents also struggle with their perinatal mental health. It's important to remember that the hormonal experience of each parent is unique.

Brain chemicals affect postpartum mood. When neurotransmitters such as serotonin, dopamine, norepinephrine, oxytocin, GABA, or melatonin are out of balance, deficient, or not firing effectively, it has a massive impact on our mood — postpartum or otherwise.[4] As I mentioned, snuggling babies can increase oxytocin levels and increase feelings of love and connection, but there are unfortunately many aspects of postpartum life that make it hard for our neurotransmitters to fire effectively. These aspects can affect all parents, regardless of whether you gave birth, and include sleep deprivation, malnutrition, or high stress combined with minimal time for the stress-management habits you used to rely on.[5] To restore the efficacy of some neurotransmitters, doctors can prescribe antidepressants, most commonly serotonin reuptake inhibitors (SSRIs), or potentially mood stabilizers. Research also suggests that gut health and inflammation affects our mental health, making many microbiome researchers excited about the potential of probiotic treatments for depression and anxiety in the future.[6]

Pregnancy, birth, and the postpartum period are hard on our bodies. We need to support our bodies through these many transitions and intentionally address parts that need healing, whether from emotional or physical pain. But biology isn't everything. It's just as important to address our thinking styles and thought patterns.

Influence Two: Thinking Styles and Thought Patterns

Parents who are prone to negative thinking, worrying, perfectionism, rumination, or heightened critical analysis are, unfortunately, prone to postpartum depression and anxiety.[7] And many of us do struggle with these types of thinking patterns because they have a protective function. Negativity bias, anxiety from trying to minimize our exposure to threats, and existential fear of death have always been critical to human survival because they contribute to keeping us safe! It makes sense that these thinking styles and thought patterns increase when we have children, because suddenly we're not only responsible for keeping *ourselves* safe but also for keeping *them* safe. What makes this even more challenging is that most of us tend to overestimate how much control we have over our ability to protect ourselves and our loved ones, which creates an incredibly stressful and confusing thinking process.

For example, many new parents struggle with intrusive thoughts, which are sudden thoughts or images of frightening, tragic, or violent circumstances happening to their baby/babies (or to them or their loved ones). The first time I had an intrusive thought, I was six months pregnant and I tripped near a wide-open 450-degree oven door. I was able to steady myself, but I was flooded with images of falling stomach-first into the hot oven and somehow burning my growing baby. Other common intrusive thoughts include dropping the baby, wounding someone with a knife, drowning, having a car accident, or falling down the stairs. One theory suggests that parents have intrusive thoughts because the part of our brain that is constantly engaged in risk assessment needs to be retrained to understand what is safe to do with a baby. It *is* risky to walk downstairs or use sharp knives. You could fall or cut yourself! And when we were first learning to go downstairs or use knives, we were really careful to minimize the risk, but over time as we gained confidence in our ability to do these activities safely, we stopped paying much attention to how risky they are — we began to do them automatically. When we have a baby, it's suddenly not obvious how safe it is to walk down the stairs holding a baby or how risky it could be to chop vegetables while eight months pregnant, so our internal risk assessor sends us a warning, through terrifying images that get us to pause, slow down, and be careful. When I have clients with intrusive thoughts about falling down the stairs with their baby, I often suggest that they lovingly remind their internal risk assessor that they are capable of walking down the stairs safely and that they will be extra cautious by holding on to the rail and the baby tightly. With repetition and intentionally noticing how many times they walk down the stairs safely, the intrusive thoughts often disappear (or at least become manageable).

Thankfully, there's a lot you can do to challenge thoughts and influence thinking patterns. This is why various forms of talk therapy can help with depression and anxiety (as well as lots of other things). Therapists and counsellors use a variety of strategies to help clients process and cope with thoughts that are negatively impacting their mood. This is *not* the same as making the ridiculous and insensitive statement "Just think more positively and you'll feel better." If parents *could* feel better, they *would* feel better. Challenging negative and anxious thoughts is difficult, and finding the right practitioner with the right therapeutic focus is often the most important part of doing this intense work. Good therapy also supports the healthy functioning of brain circuits in a way that is different from medication, which is why therapy and medication are such a powerful combination for treating PMADs.[8]

Influence Three: Individual Risk Factors and Circumstances

All new parents need to navigate a complex set of individual circumstances, while completely exhausted and very limited on time. Research has also shown that there are a number of particular risk factors or life circumstances connected to PMADs. The list is very long:

- relationship dissatisfaction
- limited support
- stressful life events
- unwanted/unplanned pregnancy
- young/advanced maternal age
- history of intimate partner violence
- difficult infant temperament
- history of thyroid issues
- trouble nursing
- weaning
- birth and reproductive trauma
- challenging pregnancy
- premenstrual dysphoric disorder (PMDD)
- challenges with fertility
- history of addiction
- history of eating disorders
- unhappiness with baby's assigned sex at birth
- financial concerns or unemployment
- solo parenting
- experiences with discrimination

Broadly speaking, anything that a parent considers an added stress, trauma, or barrier to coping belongs on this list, which continues to grow with more research. Knowing the risk factors for PMAD is simultaneously helpful and unhelpful, because there are so many ways in which a parent could be at risk. I have concluded that *every parent* is at risk. Rather than think of risk factors as a warning list, I suggest that parents use it as a guidepost for problem solving and deepening their understanding of their experience. It makes total sense that you would feel anxious if your family was feeling financially strained, or if you are pregnant during a pandemic! Or if you identify that part of what's contributing to your depression/anxiety is a lack of support, you can start creating individual solutions for you and your family.

Influence Four: Parental Identity

All parents go through a process of developing their parenting identity, which can have a dramatic impact on their perinatal mood. You're exploring both your individual parenting identity, meaning how you feel about yourself as a parent, as well as your community parenting identity, meaning how successfully you publicly meet the ever-evolving cultural norms and expectations of parenting. These two aspects are intertwined, yet there is often a discrepancy between our individual parenting identity and our community parenting identity. I've known people who felt like "bad" parents, yet whose community members were constantly trying to convince them that they were "good" parents. I've also known parents who felt like they'd been identified as "bad" parents but who personally felt like they were actually doing a pretty good job!

The interconnection of our individual and community parenting identities is significant. There seems to be a collective agreement that babies and children are innocent blank slates that require a certain style of parenting in order to become successful adults. Many parents measure themselves against the social obligation to raise happy and healthy children, using that to self-assess whether they think of themselves as a "good" or "bad" parent. Propping up this belief are all kinds of systems of social surveillance designed to ensure that parents meet these standards, such as unsolicited parenting advice from friends and family, well-baby checkups, and investigations by child protective services, with marginalized groups of parents encountering unequal levels of surveillance and intervention due to systemic discrimination. Ideally, we would all intentionally develop a positive parenting identity through individual reflection and supportive conversation with our peers and older, more seasoned parents. But unfortunately, through criticism and judgment from ourselves or our community, or through public policing, some of us develop a negative parenting identity.

In the early 2000s, nurse and researcher Linda Clark Amankwaa conducted a study about the experiences of Black mothers in America diagnosed with PPD.[9] She started to notice a pattern in the experiences of the women she was interviewing. These moms weren't delivering their baby one moment and then suddenly depressed the next. They were having children, feeling the weight of mothering, and then slipping into depression at varying speeds. As Amankwaa explored this pattern, a theory about the impact of community mothering identity on an individual mother's mood began to emerge. Amankwaa's theory outlines the process of maternal identity development that mothers navigate as they are figuring out what it means for them to take on the *social role* of mother, and how this process contributes to the onset of PPD. First mothers with PPD experience maternal role strain, then maternal role stress, and finally maternal role collapse.[10] Before we explore these three concepts, I want to clarify that although Amankwaa was specially researching cisgender women with postpartum depression, I apply her theory to primary parents of all genders and I extend it to include postpartum anxiety as well.

Role Stress: "This is harder than I thought."
Take a moment to reflect on where you learned what it means to be a successful parent. Can you even remember the origin of those messages? If you were lucky enough to be raised by people with a parenting style that is generally admired, you would likely start by listing the qualities or behaviours your caregivers demonstrated or the values that they passed on to you. Perhaps your grandma played a significant role

in modelling good parenting to you. Or maybe you learned about good parenting by critiquing the negative experiences of your own childhood and having vowed to do the opposite. We also learn how to parent by observing our friends, extended family, and community members, and we almost always include ideas that we've learned from television, books, professional parenting experts, or any other cultural narrative about what makes someone "good" at it.

Because we spend many years learning about what it means to perform the role of "good parent," when we eventually have children, we already have a sense of what we're supposed to do. For example, if we understand that a good parent is someone who looks after children, teaches them right from wrong, and keeps them alive, then that's what we aim to do!

Amankwaa suggests that mothers who find meeting their internalized expectations of this newfound social role unclear, difficult, or conflicting, or those who encounter emotional and physical resource deficits while attempting to fulfill this role, experience *maternal role stress*.[11] In other words, parents become stressed when the vision they had for themselves doesn't match the reality of their experiences. The challenge is that until we become a parent, we only have hypothetical ideas about what it's going to be like, and our visions don't always align with our lived experiences, which generally leaves us feeling confused and overwhelmed. The good news is that maternal role stress is normal! All parents experience a discrepancy between what they thought parenting was going to feel and look like and what it's actually like.

Role Strain: "I don't think I'm doing a very good job." This emotional reaction — the growing fear that we're not going to be able to do this or that we may have made a mistake by becoming a parent — is what Amankwaa calls *maternal role strain*.[12] Essentially, parents' feelings of failure or guilt for not being able to fulfill their parenting role in the way they had envisioned starts to accumulate, and it can cause them to feel down, overburdened, or withdrawn. Some parents don't fall too far down the role-strain tunnel. They just readjust their expectations and accept their limitations through a lens of self-love or pragmatism or some combination of the two. They may not like every moment of postpartum life and may still feel like they don't know what they're doing, but they're able to focus on the bright and joyful spots and take care of themselves along the way.

Others don't cope with role stress as easily. Not having our parenting expectations met makes us feel like failures or that something is wrong with us. When we internalize this experience, we personalize it and blame ourselves and all our perceived flaws. When we externalize it, we become angry and blame our difficult babies or difficult partners or lack of adequate support (and, as you will read later, these aren't necessarily wrong places to lay the blame). This doesn't mean these parents aren't doing a good job, it just means *they* don't believe they are, and it's causing them distress. If you're having a tough time adjusting emotionally, it's important to get support at this stage, because without it you can find yourself in a full role collapse.

Role Collapse: "I'm a failure."
Maternal role collapse occurs when parents start to feel like they aren't capable of fulfilling the role of parent anymore.[13] Parents experiencing Amankwaa's proposed maternal role collapse will show clinical symptoms of PMADs, and they often feel like they can't cope effectively with the day-to-day demands of life or regulate their emotions.[14] At this stage, parents may no longer be able to care for themselves or their infant(s). Negative thoughts and feelings take over. Anxiety gets trapped in the body and destroys the ability to go to sleep and let go of intrusive thoughts. Some parents feel like they can't control their behaviour, as the negative thoughts, insomnia, and chronic stress escalate the biological and neurological responses in the body.

This is what many parents who have been diagnosed with PPD/A will refer to as a living hell. The speed at which parents arrive here varies. Sometimes it takes just a few days, but often it happens slowly over the course of weeks or months, and even with the onset of returning to paid work or weaning. The severity of the symptoms and the ability to get through the day-to-day also varies widely. But what remains consistent is that parents experiencing role collapse deserve support, and sadly we know that not everyone gets it.

Influence Five: Parenting Culture

While Amankwaa's theory that our inability to enact our envisioned maternal role (which I will refer to as parental role from here on) negatively affects our mental health certainly resonates with many of the parents I work with, Amankwaa's work doesn't spend a lot of time describing exactly *what* the social role of parent looks like or discussing what about it feels so burdensome to so many. But it is critical to analyze the relationship between the culture of parenting and parental mental health, because our socio-economic family systems (meaning how families are shaped by structures such as employment, education, child care, community belonging, or health care) affect every aspect of the Perinatal Mood Framework. The biological aspects of perinatal health are influenced by the social determinants of health, such as food and housing security. Our thought patterns and thinking styles are influenced by our parenting role models and our access to information, such as being able to afford therapy or post-secondary education. The individual risks and circumstances of parents are influenced by our experiences with relational and intergenerational trauma, discrimination, and barriers to resources. And a positive parental identity is influenced by how successful we think we are, and our community thinks we are, at meeting the markers of "good parenting."

Because socio-economic family systems shift cross-culturally and over time, what it means to be a "good parent" is continuously changing, and there have been two social changes that have profoundly affected the Western culture of parenting over the last seventy years. The first was the sharp increase of women into the paid workforce, resulting in the normalization of dual-income families and, at the same time, the cultivation of intensive-mothering culture (more on that below). The second was how the emerging fields of psychiatry and psychology produced a new set of knowledge about parenting practices and child development, leading to the creation of self-proclaimed parenting "experts" and increased parental surveillance to ensure children develop as optimally as possible.

In the 1990s, researcher Sharon Hays coined the term *intensive mothering* to describe the cultural demands of parenting that required mothers' full-time investment and preoccupation. Intensive mothering insists that mothers be continuously available for their children's physical and emotional needs, ideally anticipating these needs before the children even communicate them, and that they invest heavily in their children's intellectual, educational, and social development.[15] It encourages mothers to make parenthood the most important aspect of their identity and assign themselves responsibility for their children's academic, peer, and personal success — with little to no consideration of their own parental mental health, needs, or desires. According to intensive-mothering ideology, there are three core beliefs that underpin what it takes to be a "good mom": (1) parenting requires that time, energy, and financial resources be centred around the needs of the children; (2) parenting decisions need to be informed by research and led by experts; and (3) children require constant attention and nurturing by a biological mother.[16] Although Hays's research is thirty years old, the belief that intensive mothering is best for children remains the prevailing parenting ideology in Western cultures.[17]

Many scholars on motherhood argue that the way intensive mothering has been enacted and performed in family life was through the development of attachment parenting practices, commonly referred to as *attachment parenting (AP)*.[18] There seems to be a lot of confusion about the difference between attachment theory, attachment parenting philosophy, and attachment parenting practices. I want to make those distinctions clear, because while they all inform each other, they can have a significantly different impact on parenting identity and confidence.

Attachment Theory: Popularized by psychoanalyst John Bowlby, attachment theory emerged out of the body of psychological research on the impact of children's early experiences. Bowlby argued that in order to be emotionally healthy, infants needed to attach (or bond) to a primary caregiver, who would become the secure basis for children to understand the world and become the model that forms their child's future relationships.[19] Poor attachment, according to Bowlby, would result in future mental health concerns and behavioural problems for those children. While he agreed that children could form multiple attachments, he also felt that a child's primary attachment should be to their biological mother, and he valued mother-child relationships above all others.[20] So much so that he developed a theory of maternal deprivation, meaning that that if babies' cries or bids for attention are not continuously and quickly responded to by their mothers, they risk losing their connection or failing to secure attachment.[21] According to Bowlby, if mothers are unable to provide this for the first two, and ideally five, years of their child's life, their children could suffer irreversible health and development consequences, ranging from poor behaviour to psychopathy.[22]

Attachment Parenting Philosophy: Attachment theory led to the development of attachment parenting philosophy, which created a framework for parents to raise children. It's made up of eight principles that are said to create secure attachment between infants/young children and their parents:

1. *Prepare for pregnancy, birth, and parenting:* Although AP refers to the language of being "informed," this principle maintains the intensive-mothering belief that parenting must be expert-led and well-researched.
2. *Feed with love and respect:* While nursing is often associated with AP, it is not required. However, non-nursing parents are encouraged to bottle-feed in ways that maximize connection.
3. *Respond with sensitivity:* AP parents are instructed to respond quickly and gently to their children's needs and provide a lot of positive attention, with the argument that this will benefit children neurologically.
4. *Use a nurturing touch:* AP parents are encouraged to touch their children lovingly and with a lot of frequency, especially if kids are sick, injured, or emotionally upset.
5. *Ensure safe sleep, physically and emotionally:* AP refers to responding to infant and child waking in the night as *nighttime parenting,* and encourages parents to respond to their children at night in the same way they would in the day.

6. *Provide consistent and loving care:* AP believes that children have the best outcomes when given consistent nurturing, empathy, and age-appropriate boundaries.

7. *Practise positive discipline:* Parents are encouraged to discipline through non-punitive, teaching strategies and to avoid physical or harsh punishments.

8. *Strive for balance in personal and family life:* Parents are encouraged to do their best to take care of themselves, so that they can be the best parent they can be. Interestingly, AP started out with only the first seven principles, but this eighth principle was added by Dr. William Sears (a popular American pediatrician and one of the most well-known advocates for attachment parenting) after years of hearing stories of maternal burnout and mental distress, likely because the way in which these principles are often turned into parenting practices is incredibly demanding, both physically and emotionally.[23]

Attachment Parenting Practices: Developmental psychologist Alan Sroufe is wary of these principles, and argues that "attachment is not a set of tricks … These [attachment parenting principles] are all fine things, but they're not the essential things. There is no evidence that they are predictive of a secure attachment."[24] So while there isn't an exact prescription for how to live the principles of attachment parenting, often parents will use the "tools" of baby-wearing/child-carrying, on-demand nursing (often extending beyond the first year), co-sleeping, and no-cry sleep strategies. Other lifestyle trends associated with attachment parenting may include committing to full-time parenting, home-schooling, or trying to create a "natural home" (e.g., eating organic, not using plastic), but these are aren't necessary for meeting the eight principles of AP.[25] While it can be tempting to follow a set of clear rules for early parenting because it helps us feel like we are doing it "right," parenting according to this narrow (and exhausting!) script comes at cost. A study of mothers actively engaged in attachment parenting practices finds that while they are adamant that their parenting style is the most natural and biologically informed approach, they also agree that it is intensely physically, financially, and emotionally demanding.[26]

There is an interesting contradiction that emerges from the mothers in this study, because they argue that they parent instinctually, yet they rely on scholarly research and expert knowledge to inform and defend their parenting practices. And while many of the mothers in the study describe mothering as very enjoyable and rewarding, they also describe feeling "utterly shattered" in areas of their life, particularly their sleep and energy.[27] Although many attachment parents describe themselves as operating outside of mainstream parenting, attachment parenting practices are so closely connected to the popular intensive-mothering belief system that it can be hard to distinguish between them.[28] Given that so many mothers with young children engage in paid work, AP creates quite a conflict for parents as they try to figure out how to be fully present for their work and be fully present for their children at the same time. As Hays says, parents are expected to build a career like they don't have children and parent like they don't have a career.[29] Part of how parents sometimes rectify this inner strife is to compensate by spending money on their children (throwing elaborate birthday parties or booking expensive lessons) or by engaging in emotionally absorbing parenting in the evenings and on weekends as a way to "make up" for having to take time away from parenting to go to work.[30]

Attachment Is Only One Part of Parenting

While I agree that attachment to a loving caregiver is important for children, I have some major concerns with the way information about attachment is provided to parents, as well as the prescriptive, labour-intensive way parents, and especially mothers, are instructed to attach to their kids. One concern is with the idea that the eight principles and the tools of attachment parenting are the best way to secure attachment. When we look historically and cross-culturally we find that there's a wide variety of parenting styles and practices that create secure attachment.[31] Some of the earliest research in this area compared the attachment experiences of neglected children with those of well-cared for children whose parents followed 1950s cultural parenting norms, such as bottle-feeding, cry-it-out methods of sleep training, and limiting physical touch with babies out of a fear of "spoiling" them. As expected, there were long-term mental health and developmental concerns with chronically neglected children, but children raised in loving families were deemed to have healthy attachment, even though the behaviour associated with loving parenting was very different from the behaviours we associate with it today.

It also concerns me that attachment is often discussed as though it can be empirically measured, yet much of the early attachment research involved the personal observations of male doctors who had presumably never been the primary caregiver to a child. Attachment theory is, well, *a theory*, and it relies on a lot of assumptions about infant, child, and parent intentions and consequences. Unless the early researchers were using feminist research methods to identify their personal biases and how those might impact their results, it's likely that each doctor's interpretation of secure attachment was heavily influenced by whatever childhood outcomes they personally valued. If so, it means that attachment theory was built on white, gendered, able-bodied, middle- or upper-class, heteronormative nuclear family values that idealize the fantasy of capitalist success. This doesn't leave a lot of room for parents whose ultimate goal for their children isn't how much they can align with dominant cultural norms.

I want to be clear that I don't think attachment theory is useless, but I do think that, like all theories, it needs to be understood within the context in which it was created, so that we can take what we need from it and leave the rest. I'm concerned that the way we talk to parents about attachment makes it feel outcomes-focused, rather than focused on how we anchor ourselves in relationship to our children. I don't think attachment research was ever meant to have parents fearfully questioning whether they are attached to their children or not, and I encourage you to let go of this fear and to instead play with the idea that there is an ebb and flow to closeness in *all* relationships, involving children or not. You generally can't destroy a social bond with one misstep or by going through times of disconnection, nor do you have to enact someone else's idea about how you should bond to your children. For many parents, it's actually quite interesting to identify the unique and nuanced ways in which they build relationships in all aspects of their life.

I find the assumption that developing emotionally healthy and socially successful children requires continuous maternal caregiving deeply problematic, not only because it excludes parental sex and gender diversity, but also because it limits the expectations of other caregivers in the child's life, such as co-parents, friends, family, and hired professionals. It's critical to remember that parental and caregiving relationships are not the only ones that impact children's development. It's common for children to abandon the values and behaviours held dear by their parents (much to our frustration) and instead pick up on social cues from their peers.[32] Each new generation of children also internalizes their particular generation's cultural norms, and rejects any of the norms that feel outdated from their parents' generation. Think about how intensely family values and communication have changed across Baby Boomers, Generation X, and Millennials, and how the iGeneration is being shaped. When I accidently threw something out that should have been recycled, my eleven-year-old called me out by rolling his eyes and sarcastically quipping, "Okay, Boomer. It's not like we're trying to save the planet or anything." And I'm not even a Boomer!

The narrative that "good parents" raise "good children" who turn into "good adults" is too flat and overly simplistic. That's partially because I'm not totally sure what it means to be "good," but also because there are a lot of children who grow up in secure households, with parents that are committed to their development, who still struggle emotionally and socially as an older child, adolescent, or adult — either chronically or for short periods of time.[33] It's normal to have times of personal and relational strife, and, while it is true that early family relationships are important for development, there are many other serious environmental factors that contribute to the children's outcomes, such as poverty, discrimination, or trauma.[34]

Similarly, there are babies/children who are raised in chaotic households with confusing attachment relationships who find strategies to become secure and functional adults.[35] I suspect that this is because personal grit, resilience, and stress management stems from both *internal resources*, such as autonomy, problem solving, and a sense of purpose, as well as *external resources*, such as caring adults who model emotional regulation and set high expectations.[36] These need to be analyzed together in order to theorize about children's outcomes, as most parents of multiple children would acknowledge that every child is born with their own unique attributes that shape their experiences in the world. And as neuroscientists continue to learn more about just how plastic and flexible the brain is, it becomes more difficult to assume that the first few years of life solidify a child's destiny, because humans' ability to learn, grown, and heal is pretty spectacular!

My final critique of attachment parenting and intensive mothering is that there is such a hyperfocus on creating positive experiences for infants and children that the experiences of parents, particularly mothers, is an afterthought. Much of attachment theory prioritizes the mother role above all else and seems to imply that mothers should willingly forfeit their own autonomy in the quest for attachment. Although attachment theory does suggest that attachment requires a bidirectional relationship between mother and baby, I find it often ignores the idea that individual mothers are — and should be — whole people, and pays insufficient attention to how the temperament of babies/children contributes to the parent-child relationship.[37] Sometimes high-needs babies wreak havoc on their parents' nervous systems. Sometimes an infant's night waking creates debilitating sleep debt for its parents. Sometimes parent and child temperaments clash. There are many reasons that parents need distance from their children to tend to their non-parent parts!

Does this mean that it doesn't matter how parents interact with their children? Of course not! Parents and children deserve a parenting relationship that is anchored in love and support.[38] Unfortunately, what it means to feel loved and supported varies widely from person to person, and for some relationships it can feel exceptionally difficult to decode each other's love languages. It's also normal and okay to *not* be consistent, loving, and supportive of your children 100 percent of the time. We cannot continue to hold one parent, usually a mother, responsible for the outcomes of their children when partners, family, friends, and community share in the responsibility. Additionally, the target of raising "happy, healthy, and successful" children is problematic and needs to change (I explore this in detail in chapter nine).

Clearly, there is a lot to consider as we try to wrap our heads around perinatal mood. Biology, thoughts, identity, and parenting culture influence each other, creating an intricate web that spins parents in deeply personal ways that affect their mood. What the Perinatal Mood Framework gives parents is a starting point for unpacking their individual experiences. Parenting is complex. Mood is complex. But working to understand the complexity of perinatal mood matters, because it dramatically affects the support that parents get when they reach out for help.

THREE

IMPOSSIBLE PARENTING

How to be a mum in 2017: Make sure your children's academic, emotional, psychological, mental, spiritual, physical, and social needs are met while being careful not to over stimulate, underestimate, improperly medicate, helicopter, or neglect them in a screen free, processed foods free, plastic free, body positive, socially conscious, egalitarian but also authoritative, nurturing but fostering of independence, gentle but not overly permissive, pesticide-free two-story, multilingual home preferably in a cul-de-sac with a backyard and 1.5 siblings spaced at least two years apart for proper development — also don't forget the coconut oil.

How to be a mum in literally every generation before ours: feed them sometimes. (This is why we're crazy.)

— Bunmi Laditan

Parents are well aware of the problematic nature of today's parenting culture, and they're usually able to identify the overwhelming messages as contradictory and ridiculous. We poke fun at "good parenting" ideals and the judgment and competition that comes with them. The popularity of movies and shows such as *Bad Moms*, *Workin' Moms*, or *The Letdown*, and websites like Scary Mommy, suggests that we understand that we're overdoing it. We can laugh about our fixation with developmental milestones and our competitiveness around things like lunch-box art. Unfortunately, while mocking it might be easy, letting go of the internal expectations to be a perfect parent is a much greater challenge. A 2014 study about the impact of intensive-mothering messages found that while parents can see the inherent problems of setting this gold standard of good parenting, we are actually working harder than ever before to try to achieve it.[1] Parents I work with often express this contradictory feeling of "I know better but I can't seem to do better or feel better."

The rules of parenting are moving targets, and since I first became a mother fifteen years ago, I've watched intensive-mothering expectations morph and become even *more* impossible to achieve. While the goal of a "happy, healthy, and successful" outcome for children is not unique to our era, the number of resources required to achieve it is unprecedented and parents' efforts toward it are more highly scrutinized than ever. Parents in the 1980s might have felt pressure to make sure their children were eating enough vegetables, but now we're expected to give children a comprehensive diet of organic food that's cooked at home, and ideally gluten- and sugar-free as well. We still look to parenting experts, but the amount of information available to us is contradictory and always changing, making it hard for us to know what to trust. And with the rise of the internet and social media, the intimate details of our lives are now witnessed publicly in a way they never were before.

Western parenting culture is now dominated by a parenting philosophy that I call *impossible parenting*. Impossible parenting is rooted in the core concepts of intensive mothering that demand child-centred families, research-based decisions, and continuous responsiveness. But now that is no longer enough, and parents are also expected to obsess over health and risk aversion, hyperfocus their attention on psychological outcomes, and ensure everyone experiences gratitude and joy along the way. And all of it must be demonstrated on social media, because in many ways parenting has become a lifestyle brand that aligns with whatever community subculture you want to belong to, such as attachment parents, free-range parents, tiger parents, or feminist parents. While each community interprets impossible-parenting standards slightly differently, there are six core values that underpin this new culture.

VALUE ONE: THE MORE YOU SACRIFICE, THE MORE YOU LOVE

Sacrifice has long been connected to the concept of parenting, and there *is* a certain amount of personal sacrifice involved. How we spend our time, energy, and financial resources changes dramatically when we have children, particularly in the early years. This is normal. But when groups of parents get together, a competitive edge sometimes creeps into the conversation about how much we have suffered. While I think this is because we want so badly to have our sacrifice acknowledged and validated, it can often show up as a race to the bottom: who's the most tired, who had the worst recovery from birth, who had to soothe a screaming baby for the longest. A close friend of mine who had a relatively smooth birth, whose baby took to nursing easily and was a pretty good sleeper right from the beginning, said that she was reluctant to share her experience with other parents because she felt like it would upset them. She felt as though her contributions about her struggles with parenting were dismissed because in some ways she was suffering less than them.

I experienced a stark example of this myself when I participated in an invasive medical study when my children were very young and I was very poor. My family celebrates Christmas and that year I didn't have enough money to buy the children presents, so when I learned that this study paid $400, I jumped at the opportunity and considered myself lucky to be selected. It involved several steps, but the big day involved lying in a CT scanner with an arterial line into my left wrist so that they could easily draw blood every thirty minutes while I was in the machine. My head was strapped down using a mesh mask, and the research attendant stretched two small holes for my mouth and nose before the mask hardened to lock my head into place. As they slid me into the bore of the machine, which felt like a teeny tiny space, it triggered a claustrophobic response and I started to panic. I should have quit right then, but I was so desperate for the money that I silently suffered through a two-hour-long panic attack. I tried desperately to stop my body from shaking, and I wasn't sure what to do with the tears flowing into my ears and my nose, because the mask was so tight they had nowhere to escape. I was so traumatized that when it was all over I couldn't regulate my heart rate. The staff was worried about letting me leave because of the wound from the arterial blood draw; they threatened to stitch it shut surgically if I didn't calm down. Overall it was an awful experience, and it left me without the use of my wrist for almost a week because I was afraid that if I moved it, I would bleed out (I wouldn't have). When I started to tell people what had happened in the days that followed, I wasn't met with outrage, or support for how I'd felt the need to endure this traumatizing procedure. Instead I was met with praise — *so* much praise — about what a good mother I was to give my children the beautiful Christmas they deserved.

Unfortunately, we do receive subtle (and not-so-subtle) messages that reinforce the idea that the more we sacrifice, the more we demonstrate our love for our children. This is obviously a false connection, and it can lead us to put our physical and mental health in jeopardy. Normalizing parental suffering as an act of love prevents people from getting the mental health support that they need. Telling people that they're better parents if they suffer more can artificially boost their parenting confidence, creating a sick cycle of rewards for (often unnecessary) sacrifice. This sacrifice/love cycle emphasizes the message that good families are child-centred, as opposed to a family-centred philosophy where every family member's needs matter equally.

VALUE TWO: INVEST UP FRONT, BE REWARDED LATER

There's an increasing amount of pressure for parents to "get it right" with children in the early years, with vague hints that there could be devastating consequences if you don't follow the rules of parenting experts. Or not-so-vague hints, as in Bowlby's threats of possible adult delinquency or psychopathy for children who don't manage secure attachment before age five. During my first year of parenting, the Ontario government rolled out a campaign that used the slogan "The Years Before Five Last the Rest of Their Lives," which advocated for attachment parenting practices and early learning strategies as the best way to set your children up for social and academic success later in life. It was probably the most terrifying message that I, a poor, depressed mother with a high-needs baby, could have received. I attended some of the free classes offered, and I was told that what happened in his life during the first five years would create his psychological imprint for lifelong relationships and program the neuropathways in his brain. This left me anxiously flip-flopping between trying to get my baby to watch Baby Einstein videos or stare into my eyes while I fed him, and feeling like there was no point because I had surely already messed him up.

Parents start investing in their children's future during pregnancy, with pregnant parents making diet or lifestyle changes so they will be as healthy as possible for the baby. It continues with birth, as many parents fear that if they don't give birth a certain way they won't give their baby the benefits of the vaginal microbiome, or that they won't be able to nurse if they don't do immediate skin-to-skin. Anxiety continues to grow as new parents try to figure out what to do with their babies' sleeping/ eating/activities/socializing to ensure they are smart/confident/social/ healthy. Although it's common for parents not to immediately bond with their baby, concern that they won't be able to can quickly convince parents that they aren't cut out for this or that their children will never be able to form a healthy relationship.

One of the biggest challenges is that you are expected to parent in multiple timelines. You have to parent the child you have in front of you, with all the day-to-day problem solving that requires your immediate attention (e.g., feed them when they're hungry); you're expected to parent for the child you want (e.g., set boundaries and manage tantrums); and you're also somehow required to parent a child that will turn into an awesome adult (e.g., teach them sound morals). It is really tricky and complex! Not to mention that doing so contradicts the parenting advice about just "being present" or "being in the moment" with our children, a complaint that many parents have brought to my office. They don't feel like they can just relax into moments with their children, because so much of parenting requires you to be multiple steps ahead in the hopes you can make the future easier. You need to leave the park in the next ten minutes so you can make it home in time to give the baby lunch, otherwise they won't go down for their nap on time, which means they won't sleep well at night, which means they will be cranky tomorrow. So much of parenting involves preventive planning, making it difficult, if not impossible, to live in the moment all the time.

A significant influencing factor in the *invest up front* belief is the concept of *status safeguarding*, which Melissa Milkie and Catharine Warner describe as "extensive maternal labor in the service of creating a thriving child who is distinguished as unique and, more fundamentally, over the many long years to adulthood, set to achieve a similar or better place in the world in the social hierarchy compared with his parents."[2] In other words, parents want their children to have similar or better life experiences than they did, and we work hard to ensure this happens. But it's not easy, because status safeguarding demands individual approaches for each child, with unique strategies and interventions to protect their academics, talent, social status, emotions, class, and access to resources.[3]

There has been an intense boom of classes for babies in recent years, including music classes, movement classes, yoga classes, and communication classes such as baby sign language courses for children that don't have hearing or oral communication impairments. One of the goals of baby sign language seems to be to help parents meet their babies' needs even more efficiently, as we have very little tolerance for dissatisfied babies.[4] The idea is that the natural development timeframe for language-based communication is too slow, requiring an early-investment strategy to speed it up.[5] The notion that children need extra classes to develop the skills they need for life continues to grow in popularity. Parenting researcher Linda Rose Ennis argues that it's really a way for working parents to alleviate their guilt by giving them a way to support and entertain their children without being present. Essentially, the activities parents schedule their children into "may be more about providing a transitional space between separation and connection to be with one's child where guilt is appeased, more than a way to educate and prepare one's child for a rich future."[6] Of course, not all parents have access to the same amount of time or financial resources to invest in their children, which can have a negative impact on their parenting identity.

VALUE THREE: DANGER IS ALL AROUND US — STAY VIGILANT

Parenting itself is scary and filled with unknowns, but impossible-parenting culture is laden with fears. Parents are bombarded with messages about all the ways their children might be in physical or emotional danger. Much like the *invest up front* messages, worries about potential threats to the family begin in the fertility process, particularly related to age and pregnancy: every client I've had in their thirties has shared fears about trying to conceive after age thirty-five, even if they have no evidence to suggest that fertility could be a challenge for them. This worry only increases during pregnancy, as pregnant bodies are given a long list of dos and don'ts. Don't consume sushi, unpasteurized diary, sugar, processed meats, coffee, or alcohol, or you could harm your fetus. Do eat organic, watch your calorie intake, and move your body, or you can harm your fetus. This is heightened for people with a history of loss, as fears about staying pregnant can be all-consuming, despite how little control we have over it.

These fears intensify once we meet our children. Concerns about sudden infant death syndrome (SIDS) are what I hear about the most from anxious parents, which I can relate to personally. Fear of SIDS was a significant part of my PPA and insomnia, and I became obsessive about watching my baby breathe, fearing that if I stopped watching him he would stop. But SIDS is not the only thing that overwhelms parents with fear. I've met parents desperately afraid of poor attachment, baby carriers, infant flat head, allergies, car seats — there seems to be no end to what might threaten a tiny infant. Researcher Solveig Brown's study of maternal fear found that mothers are also very afraid of the impact the outside world will have on their children, citing rising fears about screens and social media, good relationships with peers, fitting in at school, abduction, molestation, illness, safety, body image, and healthy habits, along with fears about drinking, sex, and drugs.[7] That's a heavy emotional load for parents to carry! All parents want to give their children happy and care-free childhoods, but many feel a tension about raising children today because it feels less safe than previous generations.[8] While I couldn't even begin to accurately assess the risk of an entire generation of children, it certainly *feels* scary, with more and more of my clients needing to process anxiety related to apocalyptic fears, such as climate change, food and economic security, war, terrorism, police brutality, and oppressive government policies — particularly for racialized, marginalized, and newcomer families. And I've found that these fears are directly correlated to postpartum anxiety. This has certainly been true for fears related to the most recent pandemic.

While these fears are valid, it's also true that marketers leverage parenting fears to sell products by reinforcing messages that children are innocent, priceless, helpless, and constantly in danger.[9] Parental anxiety makes it much easier to sell video monitors, sleep sacks (instead of blankets), or wearable breathing monitors. With the rise of parenting experts and research-based parenting, and more access to trauma stories than ever before, vigilant monitoring of children has dramatically increased, resulting in a significant lack of confidence for many parents who are terrified they won't be able to keep their kids safe.[10]

It's an incredible burden for parents to realize that physical and emotional suffering is not just a theoretical part of the human experience but will be a part of their personal experience and their children's experience. And in a culture that is very uncomfortable with acknowledging death and loss, many of us understandably don't cope well with the unavoidable fact that we, and everyone we know, will someday die. It feels abnormal and extra painful for children to die before their parents, and I very much related to wanting to wrap my children up in bubble wrap and keep them safe from *anything* that might harm them. Yet we will all face death and suffering, even though it's painful, not equally distributed, and often unfair. And while I have a lot of compassion for the depth of anguish a person can experience, it's problematic that impossible-parenting culture has tried to convince parents that suffering can be prevented with enough worry, planning, and safety products, because when the unthinkable does happen, we think it's our fault.

VALUE FOUR: KEEP IT NATURAL

Related to both the *invest up front* belief and the *danger is all around us* warning, but deserving of a category of itself, is the parenting phenomenon of getting back-to-the-land and keeping everything as "natural" as possible. Many parents have concerns about things like toxins and chemicals, with varying degrees of understanding about what these buzzwords actually mean (I'm still not sure I quite grasp it). There's a general fear about the health of our children's bodies, and concerns about the impact of plastics, off-gassing, pesticides, and fragrances abound. As a result, parents are opting more and more for products, particularly clothes, toys, and foods, that feel less processed or mass-produced. Marketers are slapping labels on products with words like *all natural* or *organic*, with pictures of farms and trees and animals to evoke a wholesome feeling of safety. This also inspires fears around the impact of particular foods, such as sugar, food dyes, and even infant formula, on babies and children, and many parents are looking for ways to limit their children's exposure to such things.

How we define what it means to be healthy and what individual practices contribute to this goal are very personal, but the *keep it natural* messaging has two major impacts on parents. This first is how much time it takes to research, source, plan, and prepare health products and practices in a socio-economic system that values fast-paced, productive living. For example, making your own baby food and cleaning products requires an intense amount of work for a generation of parents that is exceptionally time-starved. Parents are afraid their kids aren't getting enough natural movement, which increases the demand for evening and weekend activities in an attempt to manufacture opportunities for children to exercise.[11] There are even hypervigilant and labour-intensive practices such as going diaper-free, which essentially means starting toilet training right from birth, because it's more "natural."[12]

The second impact is that "all natural" products, health providers, and organic foods are very expensive and not all parents are able to access them, making this impossible-parenting value very class-based. The equation of keep it natural = health = good parenting is deeply problematic, because it means wealthy parents get to feel like good, empowered parents, while low-income parents are left feeling guilty or inadequate. Class-based health inequities are exacerbated by inadequate access to resources such as medical care, therapies, medication, and stress-reducing activities.[13]

VALUE FIVE: PRESCRIBED SELF-CARE

This impossible-parenting value of *prescribed self-care* is so significant that I have an entire chapter dedicated to redefining our relationship to self-care. The self-care movement has taken hold in parenting communities, but not very successfully, because parents are burnt out and struggling with their mental health in significant numbers. I suspect that this is because the idea of self-care has become tied to a particular set of resource-heavy behaviours, such as spa visits, nights out, or fitness activities. Having self-care activities prescribed to parents by others completely misses the point: what's required to tend to each person's needs is personal and complicated and constantly changing. Yet impossible parenting uses self-care as a weapon against parents, leaving many of us blaming ourselves if we struggle with our mood, health, or energy and we haven't been engaging in self-care in the ways we think we should.

Prescriptions for self-care often hyperfocus on the *individual* experience of wellness and overlook the importance of the *community* wellness experience in a way that sometimes feels like we need to compete or hoard "care" resources. Telling parents that the path to wellness is individual ignores the socio-economic and structural barriers that make it so incredibly difficult to balance the work of caring for yourself, your family, and your community. Yes, we need to find ways to take care of ourselves effectively, but we can't focus so inwardly that we forget to look out for each other or to set expectations of how we want to be cared for. Later in the book I explore the idea of community care and collective care in a few different ways, but for now know that self-care shouldn't cause distress, be just another thing on your to-do list, or be an isolated experience. But, in many ways, that's what it's become.

VALUE SIX: MAKE EVERY MOMENT MAGICAL

And finally, impossible parenting demands that we *make every moment magical*. This includes documenting the growth and development of our children in carefully curated ways to preserve our memories, to make sure our children know their histories, or to share with those in our community, such as grandparents. Parental performances such as "gender" reveal parties, professional birth photographers, and elaborate cake smashes at one-year-old birthday parties have become extremely popular. These contribute to the idealized vision of parenthood, an aggression-free, attuned, blissful celebration of parent-child relationships.[14] While there are many enjoyable aspects of parenting and celebrating is fun, the fact that we share so many of these happy performances does tend to encourage us to silence any negative feelings toward children or parenting. This, tragically, leaves many parents suppressing or pathologizing their negative thoughts toward their children, rather than interpreting them as a normal, or even necessary, part of parenthood.[15]

Many parents feel pressured to demonstrate how good they are at nurturing their children and following expert parenting advice, and, most importantly, that they spend the majority of their non-paid-work time *enjoying* their children.[16] This isn't necessarily done in competition with other parents, it's more like a way to reinforce our "good" parenting identity. Social media gives us an easy way to do this, providing parents with real-time validation that they're doing a good job, with their friends and family literally "liking" their posts and photos. It's been interesting to watch the impact of social media on parenting unfold. It has provided many avenues of support and community and a platform for parents to share their experiences, while simultaneously inciting feelings of guilt and envy as we see vignettes of the most positive moments of other parents' lives. I suspect that the intentional crafting of an online family presence is mainly about wanting our friends and family to see our children as just as special and important as we do, but there is certainly a level of performance happening too. Seeing everyone else's displays of perfect parenting can create tremendous ambivalence and tension for parents, especially if a lack of resources makes it hard for them to compete.[17]

PARENTAL IDENTITY AND MENTAL HEALTH ARE IMPACTED

If you see yourself in any of these descriptions, that's okay. I am also guilty. As I write this chapter, I am at a yoga retreat trying to fill my self-care prescription. And that's because there's *nothing inherently wrong* with wanting an unmedicated birth or making your own baby food or posting monthly updates of your baby on Instagram with a chalkboard announcement of their developmental milestones. The problem is when we value the tenets of impossible parenting to the point that they become our personal litmus test for whether we're "good parents." Impossible-parenting values are also a problem when it comes to gendered differences in parenting; people who identify as moms and primary parents are held to higher standards than people who identify as fathers or support parents.

Impossible-parenting culture has a significant impact on our mood, behaviour, and identity and can produce negative mental health outcomes.[18] The suggestion that there are "good" parents and "bad" parents provokes all kinds of anxiety. Everyone wants good parents. Everyone wants to *be* a good parent. Parents live with a constant fear that not being a good parent could lead to a variety of social, physical, or psychological damage to their children, the most innocent people in our communities. Yet the social, physical, and psychological toll of trying to be a "good parent" is often overlooked. In fact, spending *more* time with your children and giving *more* of yourself to parenthood is often toted as the solution; Bowlby advocated for minimal separation between mothers and babies in the first five years to protect attachment.[19] But maybe the desire to be alone, untouched, and unbothered by the needs of others is normal, and the resentment we sometimes feel toward children is simply a nudge that our needs have gone unattended for too long. Perhaps it's actually the suppression and pathologizing of negative feelings that are the problem, rather than the feelings themselves.

Authors Susan J. Douglas and Meredith Michaels suggest that "motherhood has become a psychological police state."[20] When we break down impossible-parenting values one by one, it's no wonder so many parents say that kids are "all joy and no fun," as they bring us deep emotional connection while taking the adult fun out of our life, albeit temporarily.[21] Not only do parents need to hit the behavioural and economic markers of "good parenting," they also have to like it. The result is that parents are working harder than ever to figure out how to build a career and take care of themselves, their partners, and their community while always prioritizing their children's needs. And it's really hard — impossible, actually — to do all of these at the same time. Research on the impact of current parenting messages indicates that parents swept up in all this ideological rhetoric said they feel they're "so stressed," "going crazy," "losing their minds," "depressed," and "hav[ing] trouble in their social relationships."[22] My clients with diagnosed mood and anxiety disorders use very similar language.

How is the culture of impossible parenting contributing to low perinatal mood? Returning to Amankwaa's theory of role collapse, how we interpret what it means to be a "good parent" is critical to our parental identity, which is in turn critical to our postpartum mood.[23] Having an idealized vision of parenting that's based on such perfectionist values creates an impossible challenge, because parents can never meet the standards. They have to choose between feeling like a failure yet working themselves to exhaustion to perform good parenting publicly and try not to get caught, or rejecting these standards and risk being deemed a "bad parent." And it isn't difficult to be publicly scrutinized for your parenting choices (just ask anyone who has ever asked an online parenting group for advice about sleep training) because people rarely realize that the rules about how to be a "good parent" are socially and economically constructed. While overt impossible-parenting messages might make for a funny TV show about how mom groups judge each other, the extent of the damage these messages do remains invisible. While we laugh at the standards, we simultaneously hold ourselves to them and are held to them by our communities.

Judging parents as "good" or "bad" has implications beyond poor parental confidence or internalized shame. There are public consequences if you don't perform "good parenting" appropriately because of parental surveillance, or what I call *parental policing*, whereby community members and experts monitor parents to make sure they're doing a good enough job. If they aren't, they get in trouble, which could mean anything from awkward conversations with daycare providers to interactions with child protective services. Of course, not all parents are under surveillance in the same way. Marginalized parents are most at risk for parental policing, which means that those who feel the most pressure to perform "good parenting" often have the most hurdles to do so. It's not surprising that, young parents, low-income parents, newcomer parents, refugee parents, and BIPOC parents have increased rates of PMADs.[24]

IMPLICATIONS FOR MARGINALIZED PARENTS

I didn't get support for my PMAD the first time. Partially because I didn't fully understand what was happening to me, and partially because it didn't feel like it was safe to talk about my mood given the landscape of surveillance I had to navigate. Young and single and unemployed, I felt an intense need to perform "happy parenting" in front of others, especially helping professionals, because I had this looming fear that if anyone knew how I was really feeling, they would take my baby away. When I was interacting with medical or social services, I felt like I was constantly bombarded with subtle messages, such as when an ER triage nurse asked where my "baby daddy" was when I came in with a sick baby, or not-so-subtle messages, like when I was asked, as I left the hospital after giving birth, if I had somewhere safe to live (something I was not asked with my second child, when I clearly had a partner). It didn't feel as though they were checking on my well-being. It felt like they wanted to make sure I was up to the task of parenting.

One of the consequences of leaving the values of impossible-parenting culture unchallenged, as I've said, is that not all parents have the same access to resources to meet these expectations.[25] Impossible-parenting values presume that families are coupled, white, middle-class, cisgender, heterosexual, able-bodied, English-speaking, economically independent, with citizenship, which creates barriers for huge subsets of the population through no fault of their own.[26] It creates "an institutional form of discrimination against single, poor, and minority mothers that seeks to 'other' and shame women who cannot and/or will not mother in this way," which I argue applies to all parents and not just those identified as mothers.[27] Not to mention the fact that the messages of how to be "good" at parenting are contradictory and confusing.[28] How does a single parent provide enough financial resources and be child-centred at the same time? Do they put a young infant in daycare, or take a hit to their income and stay home? It feels cruel to hold parents to impossible-parenting standards that are out of reach. It's the culture of impossible parenting that needs to be called out as a problem, not a parent's ability or inability to perform "good parenting."

There's a community agreement embedded in our culture to protect children from "bad parenting." The intention of the agreement is to ensure that children are not raised in neglectful or abusive households, but what it means to be abused or neglected is sometimes subjective, which creates tension for parents who want to reach out for mental health support, as they risk being labelled unfit, which can result in unwanted, unsupportive, and harmful state intervention.[29] For a parent in the PMAD community, it can be terrifying to hear stories of parents who seek help, only to have their doctor call child protective services because they have misunderstood what it means for a parent to have an intrusive thought about drowning a baby. (Intrusive thoughts are just thoughts, terrifying and distressing thoughts. They aren't desires or soon-to-be actions.) The hum of surveillance and analysis of parenting behaviour is particularly high for low-income and BIPOC parents; they often express feelings of being *extra* policed.[30] For example, I once provided doula support for a Canadian newcomer who had learned English as a second language. It was suggested at her four-week well-baby visit that her child required an X-ray because of possible shoulder distortion. The parent was hesitant to subject her newborn to radiation, so she followed up with the delivering doctor who assured her that her baby was healthy. When this parent turned down the referral to radiology, police arrived at her door a few hours later because her pediatrician had reported that she "misunderstood" the importance of the X-ray and was putting the infant in danger. Although the baby was deemed healthy and not in any danger, child protective services opted to keep her file open "in case she needed support," despite her insistence that having an open case file felt intrusive and that if she needed additional support she was fully capable of sourcing it herself.

The culture of impossible parenting is hurting families. Children just don't need their parents to follow such a narrow script.[31] While it may feel overwhelming to think about the work it will take to change this problematic ideology, it's incredibly important work. Through the rest of this book, I propose how we can change parenting culture for the better, to ensure that all family members — you, your partners, your children, your extended families — have permission to be imperfect, embracing all the messy and difficult emotions that coincide with imperfect humanness. In later chapters, we will delve into ways that we can ease the internal expectations of good parenting, but first let's explore the four areas of parenting that feel the most difficult: birth, sleep, relationships, and bodies.

PART 2

HURTING

The culture of impossible parenting shapes our experience of parenting before we ever become parents. A lot of expectations and assumptions are placed on us, by others or by ourselves. This section, called "Hurting," explores four significant pain points for parents: (1) birth, including how we become pregnant, how we stay pregnant, and trauma associated with birthing; (2) sleep, or the lack thereof, which can feel torturous during the postpartum years and often creates feelings of desperation; (3) relationships, which often feel strained and pushed to the limits as frustration grows about sharing the work of parenting; and (4) bodies, including physical suffering related to the size of our bodies and distress surrounding infant feeding.

I think a lot of the pain we feel in the early parenting years stems from facing the limits of our control and trying to navigate the contradictory messages from impossible-parenting culture. Unmet internal or external expectations are common reasons people feel depressed or anxious. This next section explores how the culture of impossible parenting shapes our desires and tries to convince us that we have more control than we actually do.

FOUR

BIRTH

Before I address the impact of the culture of impossible parenting on birth, I want to touch on the politics of choice about even becoming a parent. All people, but especially those who identify as women, are warned that if they don't have children they might miss out on their life purpose or never feel completely fulfilled.[1] That's a pretty significant threat! In a culture where childrearing remains the norm, negativity or ambiguity about having children is often regarded as risky behaviour. And once you decide to parent, any negative or ambivalent feelings about parenting can be read as personal flaws or weaknesses. You can find yourself trapped in a climate of coerced positivity, fuelled by the fear of being outed as an unwilling, incapable, or just plain bad parent. These feelings of "am I doing this the right way?" can begin the day you find out you're expecting. They can also begin long before conception.

Western family culture is deeply informed by the concept of *pronatalism*, which is the idea that parenthood and raising children should be the central focus of every person's adult life.[2] This belief system includes assumptions such as *the purpose of marriage is to raise children* and *becoming a parent is a necessary stage in the journey to adulthood*.[3] While all genders receive the message that parenthood provides the greatest source of meaning and contentment, pronatalism impacts women in a distinct way because it convinces them that a woman's destiny is to become a mother, and that it is ciswomen's "biological" instinct to want children.

When I first learned about Laurie Sanci's work coaching women who did not have children, it had never occurred to me to question where my desire to have children came from. She explains that pronatalist ideas pervade every aspect of our lives. At school, sex-ed classes focus on when is the best time to have children, not whether or not to have them. At work, flexibility is often offered to parents because of their need for work/life balance, but less so to people without kids because it's presumed that they don't have lives that require balancing. Many new young couples are asked when they're going to have kids, and feel pressured by their parents to produce grandchildren. "Pronatalism accounts for the relentless speculation in the tabloids as to whether or not Jennifer Aniston is pregnant, with the idea that until she becomes a mother, she hasn't really made it," says Sanci. "The media we consume is mostly absent of female characters who are not mothers or of childless couples, but when they do appear, they are portrayed as sad, desperate, or suspect in some way."

There is, of course, nothing wrong with the desire to have children. The problem with pronatalism is that it makes parenthood mandatory for everyone and creates a stigma around not having kids. The desire *not* to have children becomes abnormal and unnatural. As Sanci says, "It makes women who don't have them seem worthy of pity or scorn. It makes men who don't have them seem immature. It makes marriages without kids seem pointless. And it creates a divide between those who have kids and those who don't." Have you ever noticed how different it sounds to refer to non-parents as child-*less* versus child-*free*? Pronatalism can lead people to believe that if they don't have children, a life of joy, meaning, and purpose just isn't possible; if they don't have kids, they'll miss out on the only experience that can really truly provide those things. Essentially, while parenting is incredibly demanding, becoming a parent also comes with of social privilege.

On the flip side, Sanci explains, pronatalism also seems to deem some people more "socially acceptable" for parenting than others. Financially independent, partnered, straight, cisgender, married, and able-bodied people are expected and pressured to become parents, while low-income, young, old, queer, or people with (dis)abilities[4] are often questioned about their ability to succeed at it and their pregnancies are seen as immoral, selfish, or unwise.

Of course, there's a lot of diversity among people who do not have children. Sanci points out that there are those who have made a conscious choice not to have children and who might use the term *child-free* to describe themselves. Others wanted to have children, but encountered barriers to doing so, such as infertility, not finding a partner in time, or not having the financial resources to be a single parent. These people, who are affected by circumstance, might be more likely to refer to themselves as *child-less*.

IMPOSSIBLE FERTILITY

There is arguably no process where the limits of our control are more evident than in fertility. While I understand the biology of conception, the ability to become and stay pregnant still feels very mysterious to me. An estimated 16 percent of people who want to become parents will go through hell to try to carry a pregnancy.[5] Even with our ability to create all the necessary biological conditions, through cycle monitoring, hormone dosing, or embryo implanting, fertility feels like a bizarre game of luck or chance. Some people with known fertility concerns, such as polycystic ovaries, fibroids, endometriosis, or partners with low/inactive sperm, are able to get and stay pregnant easily, while others with no known concerns do not. Just as strangely, some people conceive easily for their first pregnancies, but then struggle to conceive again (often referred to as secondary infertility). The messages about fertility seem to target women and centre largely around age, with many people under thirty not expecting to struggle, while those over thirty-five get to enjoy medical terms like "old eggs," "high risk," and my favourite, "geriatric pregnancy."

The emotional experience of infertility is intense, and the fertility process can easily take over your life. Not only because of all the tracking, scheduled sex, or early morning medical appointments, but also because of the emotional roller coaster of the repeated cycle of "I hope this is the month!" followed by the devastating disappointment of an unsuccessful try or a loss. The lack of control over fertility and the desperate frustration it can cause is escalated by our culture that is so deeply uncomfortable with suffering and loss.

Not surprisingly, depressed and anxious feelings are a normal part of fertility struggles. And then there's the jealousy! When you're trying to conceive it feels like everyone you know is getting pregnant and having babies, which can create significant internal tension — should you go to your friend's baby shower and feel heartbreaking envy, or avoid it and feel like a bad friend? There's so much that is unfair about infertility and it's common to feel rage or a sense of undeservedness.

The fertility experiences of queer couples generally feels different than that of cis-bodied heterosexual couples, because for most of us there is no ability to have a spontaneous pregnancy at home. Some queer couples have access to both a uterus and sperm between them, such as transgender speaker, activist, and birth parent Trystan Reese and his partner, Biff Chaplow, or some use a known donor and attempt nonclinical pregnancy through penetration or at-home insemination. But I suspect that the majority of queer couples become pregnant through fertility clinics. For queer families trying to conceive, there isn't necessarily a conception challenge to overcome, but rather an access-to-sperm-or-egg challenge. This presents its own set of inequities, because families where one or more of the intended parents has a uterus are significantly advantaged over those that do not, and many cis-bodied, gay male couples feel as though becoming parents will be an uphill battle.

Fertility treatments are also very classed. Intrauterine insemination (IUI, a procedure to put sperm in a uterus) is more affordable that in vitro fertilization (IVF, which involves several procedures, including egg extraction, fertilization and embryo development, and then implantation), and even in regions that provide funding for IVF cycles, intended parents still face many additional costs, such as pharmaceutical drugs, biological materials, or genetic testing. IVF usually requires time off work for cycle monitoring and insemination, and it's harder to maintain privacy when you have to explain why you're coming in late or taking days off. And while all fertility treatment is expensive, surrogacy can be prohibitively expensive, especially since our confusing legal system has not caught up with reproductive technology. And adoption is challenging in its own way.

Even when parents become pregnant through fertility treatments, miscarriages or nonviable pregnancies are common. I don't feel that there's enough support for pregnant parents seeking termination for a nonviable pregnancy that they desperately wish was viable, or who are carrying multiples and choose to selectively terminate. These can be very lonely, isolating experiences. There is so much potential for heartbreak for those who want to become parents. Reproductive rights remain deeply political, and access to various privileges determines who has the right to, who is enabled to, and who is encouraged to become a parent.

A BRIEF HISTORY OF BIRTHING PRACTICES

When families are successful in becoming and staying pregnant, the next major event they need to prepare for is the birth. Fantasizing and planning for birth is a rite of passage for all soon-to-be parents, including those who are pregnant and those waiting for a surrogate or adoptive birth. Contemporary birthing practices are the result of evolutions in medical technologies and health care practices, both of which are deeply informed by the politics of class, sex, and gender. To capture the last 130 years of birth history in Western culture, I interviewed Bianca Sprague, a doula with over fifteen years' experience and owner of the doula training school bebo mia. She explained to me that historically most births were not deemed to be medical events requiring interventions, and they were often attended by community midwives or birth attendants. This all changed in the early 1900s when the rise of private medicine quickly led to 50 percent of births being attended to by doctors for a fee, with the other half being attended to by midwives. In 1920, American obstetrician Dr. Joseph DeLee argued that if obstetrics (then a novel and evolving field) was ever to be regarded as a medical specialty, births would require the routine use of analgesics, episiotomy, and forceps. This shifted our perception of birth; it went from a common experience to a medical event that required continuous monitoring and interventions. While birth always has an element of risk to it, it was rebranded as a dangerous experience that could only be facilitated safely with the help of Western medicine. This had a significant impact on birthing practices, and by the 1940s hospital births outnumbered home deliveries in most communities.

Birthing practices now vary widely depending on where you live, with the majority of North American births occurring in hospitals. And medical procedures to support safe birth, such as epidurals or surgery, can come with hefty price tags. This has less of an impact on birthers with government-funded health care or full coverage through private insurance, but it puts low-income and underinsured parents in a difficult situation. Some of my midwife friends (who support birthers in Ontario whether or not they have insurance) have shared with me some chilling stories of uninsured, newcomer birthers in Canada who are refused epidurals by hospital anesthesiologists until they pay hundreds of dollars cash, only to have to pay again if there's a shift change and a new anesthesiologist comes on shift. While I have some deep critiques of the documentary *The Business of Being Born*, it did highlight stories of significant mistreatment of birthers in America, common among them the overreliance on C-sections and an overall attempt to streamline the process, which should be deeply personal and unique to each situation. Some stories about birther mistreatment by medical practitioners seem stranger than fiction, such as the 2019 public scandal out of North York General Hospital where Dr. Paul Shuen used induction medication to bring on labour in his pregnant patients without their knowledge or consent, in an effort to attend as many births as possible and maximize his revenue.[6] Even more bizarrely, he was met with only minor professional and legal consequences.[7]

I don't mean to demonize obstetrics. I understand that birth is complex and unpredictable. I personally experienced this and had a dangerous and traumatic birth with my first child. The experience was so intense the doctor on call offered my mother a sedative because she was so afraid of losing me or her grandchild. Although I found ways to exercise control over my body and my choices in the birth space, which was important to me, I have significant love and respect for the obstetrician who safely delivered my child. Instead, I share this history to contextualize the problematic experiences some parents have at birth, although Western medicine is not the only source of tension in the birth space.

Natural Birth Industry

The natural birth industry emerged in the 1950s as a response to mounting fears about losing choice and agency in birth, and confusion about the level of risk associated with uncomplicated births. Sprague explains that one of the founders in this area was Dr. Fernand Lamaze, a French obstetrician who promoted childbirth as an active, natural, and empowering event. He advocated for holistic, non-medical pain management techniques such as breath, visualization, and targeted body relaxation techniques. His work was so influential that by the 1960s there was a renewed interest in unmedicated childbirth, soon to be dubbed "natural" childbirth, resulting in an increase in medically unattended births or births assisted by non-legal midwives. In the early 1990s the demand for legal support for home birth led to the licensing of midwives in many states and provinces. Although the regulation of midwives and their scope of practice varies widely across jurisdictions, today midwives are, more often than not, legally able to provide medical care for those who want to give birth at home or the hospital. An entire industry of products, services, and courses designed to support unmedicated birth exploded, amplified by the *keep it natural* belief from the culture of impossible parenting. Books, childbirth preparation classes, hypnobirthing recordings, pregnancy yoga, portable TENS machines, birth tub rentals — there seems to be an endless number of things you can buy to try to have a "more natural" birth. A set of parents has also emerged who call themselves "free birthers," defined as opting out of the obstetrical and midwifery systems entirely to give birth unassisted, generally because of strong libertarian or religious values, but also because they have felt traumatized by the medical system.

Although there is no universal definition of "natural" birth, many parents I know define it as vaginal, without epidural or induction, and possibly at home — with as little medical intervention as possible. And while birthers can refuse medical interventions, the challenge is that birthers who are committed to having maximum control and minimal interventions at their birth still expect a healthy physical outcome for themselves and their baby/babies. Unfortunately, that isn't always possible, which has always been true for birth. Natalie Grynpas, a perinatal social worker who has worked with many free-birth parents to help them to fully explore the cost of their choices, suggests that some clients are so committed to birthing outside of the medical system that they are willing to risk death (their own or their child's). Although they certainly don't wish for it, they are able to accept it as a possible outcome. For some, this could be because of religious beliefs that the outcome of the birth is God's will, while for others the thought of a negative outcome is less traumatic than the thought of losing control or freedom in the birth space.

An accurate assessment of potential risks associated with pregnancy and birth is difficult to come by. Even the most seasoned physicians or midwives can only speak in generalities and likelihoods. But we do know that not all parents have the same level of risk; racial disparities put Black and Indigenous birthers at a disproportionate risk of birth complications, including death.

Many discussions about risk associated with pregnancy and birth seem to be designed to either terrify parents about all that can go wrong or convince them that everything will be fine as long they keep away from medical interventions. Fear is what initially convinced parents to have babies *in* hospitals, yet some feel that the natural birth community uses fear to motivate parents to *avoid* hospitals, or at least medical procedures, during birth. The result is that it can feel difficult for some parents to find trustworthy information about safe birthing practices about their specific pregnancy. If the goal of the medicalization of birth was to increase parental and infant health and safety, and if the goal of the natural birth movement was to normalize birth and give people agency and choice in their experience, it doesn't feel like anyone is winning. Instead we've told parents to pick a side. Sadly, when taken to extremes, both sides of this debate can feel unsupportive for birthers.

The Rise of Doula Care and Informed Choice

Interest in the emotional experience of birth has been getting a lot of attention over the last ten years. Though *healthy mom, healthy baby* has long been cited by medical practitioners as the ultimate birthing outcome, this idea of what constitutes a "healthy" birther is evolving to include not only physical health, but mental and emotional health as well. In 2018 the World Health Organization (WHO) published a commitment to patient-centred care in its report *WHO Recommendations: Intrapartum Care for a Positive Childbirth Experience*, which

> recognizes a "positive childbirth experience" as a significant end point for all women undergoing labour. It defines a positive childbirth experience as one that fulfils or exceeds a woman's prior personal and sociocultural beliefs and expectations, including giving birth to a healthy baby in a clinically and psychologically safe environment with continuity of practical and emotional support from a birth companion(s) and kind, technically competent clinical staff. It is based on the premise that most women want a physiological labour and birth, and to have a sense of personal achievement and control through involvement in decision-making, even when medical interventions are needed or wanted.[8]

In order to try to protect the comfort and emotional support of birthers, many parents turned to birth doulas, who provide informational, emotional, and physical support to families during pregnancy and birth. This role on a birth team is not a new concept, as historically there were often female birth attendants whose job was primarily to care for the birther. What is new is that birth support service providers are now professionally trained, certified, and becoming a fast-growing, and often expensive, component of the birth industry. One of the strategies many doulas and other pregnancy support workers use is to help their clients make *informed choices* by helping them interpret information about their health, pregnancy, and birth options. The goal of informed choice is to clearly outline the risks and benefits of all testing and intervention options, and importantly, respect whatever decision(s) birthers make. While this is a worthy goal, it can be hard to truly achieve. For one thing, according to Grynpas, there isn't really such a thing as informed choice, because it's impossible to fully understand the outcomes of each choice ahead of time or how you will feel about them. For example, a client committed to vaginal delivery over surgical birth may know that vaginal birth comes with increased risk of pelvic-floor damage, but it's very hard to fully grasp what it might be like to live with chronic fecal incontinence.

Another challenge to empowering birthers to make informed choices is that medical professionals can be held liable for choices that are made during a birth, so they have a vested interest in the outcome. There's an incredible amount of pressure on medical professionals to always have the right answer and to never make mistakes, which is understandable because birth can be a matter of life and death. Liability aside, they also want good outcomes for their clients! I have worked with many medical professionals who feel incredible tension between their desire to support their client's choices and their fear for the client's well-being. Feeling torn in this way can be terrifying and can cause vicarious trauma for midwives, nurses, and doctors. There's also legal confusion about whose life takes priority: the birther or the baby? And who gets to make that choice? The medical staff? The birther? The partner? This becomes even more confusing in the case of surrogacy births, where there are two families' interests on the line.

A third difficulty with informed choice is that a birther's choices may not always be practised or even allowed where they give birth. There's a difference between *evidenced-based care* and *practice-based care*. Although we'd like to expect that medical practices will evolve to stay up to date with research and recommendations, there's often a significant lag between what *research suggests (evidence-based care)* and *this is how we have always done it here (practice-based care)*. A good example of this is antibiotic eye drops that are administered to babies after birth. Ophthalmia neonatorum is an infection commonly found in babies born to parents with active sexually transmitted infections (STIs), and it can cause vision defects. Before we had heightened public awareness about STIs such as chlamydia or gonorrhea, before condoms were readily available and popular, and when soldiers were returning home from war having contracted STIs through sexual encounters while away and unknowingly infecting their spouses, some babies born vaginally would contract ophthalmia neonatorum.[9] In response, recommendations and laws were enacted to give antibiotic eye drops to *all* newborn babies. These measures did reduce vision problems in at-risk babies, but today we treat STIs during pregnancy, so the need for antibiotic drops is much smaller. There are some minor risks to giving antibiotic eye drops to all babies, so the current evidence lends itself to the recommendation of only giving eye drops to babies that have a high risk or that show signs of infection. However, in places where antibacterial eye drops remain the law and hospital practice, parents can face investigation by child protective services for refusing to allow medical staff to administer the drops, even though it is no longer recommended by numerous medical associations — so even the most well-informed birther may not be able to choose when it comes to eye drops.[10]

BIRTH AND REPRODUCTIVE TRAUMA

Unfortunately, the result of all this confusion, unmet expectations, and lack of support is a substantial amount of birth trauma. It's so common that about a third of all birthers report feeling traumatized by the process.[11] I'm not going to give detailed horror stories here, but I will write plainly about common traumatic experiences, so this section may be difficult or triggering for some. Please take care of yourself accordingly.

Birth and reproductive trauma are not the same as PPD/A, but I do put them in the broad PMAD bucket that I usually refer to as postpartum post-traumatic stress disorder (PP-TSD). Trauma affects the brain and body differently from PPD/A, and although you could have both, each requires different treatment and support. I don't think birth trauma gets treated with the same levels of care and awareness that other forms of trauma receive, such as sexual or physical violence, relational or child-hood trauma, or war and natural disaster trauma. Many of my clients share this sentiment, saying that unless they've experienced physical or loss trauma (described below) they feel confused about where to go for help. The "healthy baby and healthy parent" mantra makes non-physical PP-TSD invisible. There's a sense that if everyone is okay, you should just be grateful; go home and enjoy your baby and forget about it. And yet we would never tell a hurricane survivor to just be grateful that they made it out alive and to enjoy the nice weather now that it's over.

Birth trauma is also minimized because medical staff are familiar with crisis and comfortable with surgery while many of us are not. I don't be-lieve that the majority of medical staff mean to be dismissive about our birth experiences, but I do think they can tend to miss what the experi-ence is like for the patient because they're so focused on the medical re-sponse to the situation rather than the emotional. Some birth profession-als may act overly calm in an attempt to reassure anxious patients that they have everything under control, which can be annoying to clients who want to have their feelings validated. Also, birth professionals are concerned about complaints or liability, so they might try to frame what happened as small and commonplace to avoid repercussions.

Birth trauma is also unusual because we don't usually expect to go through a trauma multiple times! But any birther who wants to car-ry future children is faced with a difficult decision, knowing that they could be triggered or that they could suffer a new trauma. Depending on what happened at their first birth, they may have limited options for subsequent ones; for example, it can be difficult for someone who's had two surgical births to find a practitioner who's willing to support a home delivery, or the opposite, someone who wants to have a surgical birth can feel pressured into a VBAC (vaginal birth after Caesarian). I've heard many clients say that they desperately want to have more kids but aren't sure they can "go through that again."

Of course, it isn't always what happens during the birth itself that's traumatic. Sometimes it's what happens immediately after the birth or in the weeks just prior or just after. This is why I refer to it as birth *and* reproductive trauma. Over the years, I have seen reproductive trauma show up in a few different ways, and given my sudden uptick in birth trauma client work directly related to the pandemic, I suspect there will be a new category of "pandemic trauma."

Sexual Trauma: People who have a history of sexual violence are particularly vulnerable to trauma during birth. Giving birth is an incredibly vulnerable experience, but it's especially so when your body has been violated in the past. It's not very often that we are asked to undress and have our genitals displayed and touched by multiple strangers. That alone can be retriggering for a sexual-violence survivor, even if they are deeply respected during the birth. Many sexual-violence survivors say that during their assault they experienced a loss of control over their body, that it was robbed from them, and so they're anxious about losing control over their body and their choices during their birth. When a birther gets an epidural for pain management, parts of their body are numbed, and surgical birth usually involves having a curtain placed between the birther and the surgical staff. While this makes sense — the curtain protects them from having to watch surgery being performed on their body — it can feel like a total loss of agency to have limited sensation and no visuals but to feel tugging and pulling in their abdomen. It's also true that sometimes during birth, consent is violated. During my doula years, I saw situations in which birthers said, "No, stop — that hurts!" during cervical checks but the medical staff kept going, saying, "Just one more second — I'm almost done!" To be clear, this is never okay, but it can be especially traumatic for a sexual trauma survivor.

Physical Trauma: Physical trauma occurs when birthers experience unmanaged pain or suffering in their body during the birth, or when they or their baby/babies become unsafe or come close to death. This can happen if an epidural doesn't work, or if a birther becomes violently ill for the duration of the birth. Physical trauma can also stem from an emergency, such as low fluid, (postpartum) pre-eclampsia, placenta or heart rate issues, a micro-preemie baby, or a baby that's born lifeless. Trauma also commonly occurs when a birther gets into a crisis and needs to be suddenly fully anesthetized for a surgical birth, as it is a very confusing experience to go to sleep pregnant and wake up with the baby having been removed.

Surviving the birth is only one aspect of it; physical healing is another. There are times when there are long-term physical consequences of giving birth, such as severe tearing, wounds that don't heal or that get infected, prolapses, emergency uterus removal, or babies that develop unexpected (dis)abilities related to events during the birth or shortly after it. Physical trauma can affect the ability to bond with or care for a new baby, leaving many birthers turning to friends and family for support they were not expecting to need.

Emotional Trauma: With my clients, this most commonly occurs with people who have experienced a loss of control over their bodies or their choices, such as a consent violation, an extremely rapid birth, an unplanned surgical birth, an assisted delivery, or being given an episiotomy without discussion. It can also stem from an emergency transfer to the hospital when a home or birth-centre birth becomes too risky. Sometimes birthers feel emotionally traumatized by feeling disrespected or not listened to by their birth team, or by having a partner who doesn't make it in time or is not adequately able to support them during the birth.

Trauma can often be avoided in birthers who have to deviate substantially from their ideal birth if they are given enough time to understand the risks and opt to change course, rather than being *told* what is going to happen next. They might feel disappointed, but still be able to process the experience. But unfortunately this doesn't always happen; emotional trauma is often overlooked as long as everyone is considered physically healthy.

Structural Trauma: This occurs when clients feel oppressed or excluded in the birth space based on an aspect of their identity that has been historically (and continues to be) marginalized. Many people who identify with a marginalized group have personal and intergenerational histories of structural trauma and microaggressions, and the birth space can quickly become unsafe or re-trigger them. For example, when I was a doula, one of my Black clients was accused of lying about her drug use during pregnancy (she didn't use any) by a white nurse who couldn't believe that someone who lived in "that part of the city" wasn't using drugs. In another case, an Indigenous birther, who was also a doula, was forced to have a conversation with child protective services before she was "allowed" to leave the hospital with her baby because she disclosed that she'd used some prescribed THC during pregnancy to manage pain. I've heard many parents with both invisible or visible (dis)abilities needing to prove their parenting competence to medical staff before taking their baby home. Trans and genderqueer parents run the risk of not having pronouns respected and birthers with large bodies often describe body shaming during the birth process. When these aggressions happen, it puts birthers in the very difficult situation of having to choose between the emotional labour of calling out staff members and risking comprised care, and the emotional labour of staying silent and feeling uncomfortable during an experience where trust and safety are critical.

Nursing Trauma: Nursing a baby can be really hard. Parents who expect to nurse but run into barriers often describe the experience as traumatic. It can be frightening to have your baby/babies lose weight rapidly, get very dehydrated, or grow so hungry that they cry a lot. Parents often describe the early days of nursing as traumatic when it involves nipple mutilation, pain from clogged ducts and mastitis, tongue-tie releases, round-the-clock pumping, and tube, finger, or cup feeding. This is often escalated by worry for their baby, internalized feelings of failure, externalized pressure to nurse, and general confusion about where to get accurate information because there's so much contradictory advice out there. And even parents who eventually manage to nurse exclusively can continue to be traumatized from those initial challenges.

Loss Trauma: Failed fertility transfer, miscarriage, chemical pregnancy, ectopic pregnancy, stillbirth, or death shortly after birth are often recognized as traumatic and grief-filled experiences, because they are devastating, painful, unfair experiences by their nature. But there are aspects of loss that can escalate these already-traumatized feelings. The first is that inexperienced staff are sometimes so uncomfortable giving the news that they avoid using the words "Your baby has died" and use softer, confusing language such as "I can't find the heartbeat," leaving parents to try to figure out what's happening on their own. Second-trimester loss in the case of a missed miscarriage can be particularly painful because parents may not be offered a birth and death certificate, so they can't bury or legally name their baby, which can feel invalidating or leave parents feeling like their experience was minimized or erased. And if a baby dies after being released from the hospital, there is generally a police investigation, which escalates the trauma.

Pregnant people who choose to terminate a pregnancy can also experience loss trauma. This is especially true for wanted pregnancies that aren't viable, but also sometimes for unwanted pregnancies, because the decision to terminate an unwanted pregnancy is not always easy. Often there's a gap between the decision and the procedure itself, which can be particularly painful for birthers who are carrying a dead fetus. Generally, those seeking termination are not allowed to take a support person into the room with them, so they're expected to cope on their own or with the support of an unknown medical professional. Every client that I've supported as they make choices about termination has been afraid that they'll encounter protesters showing misleading and intentionally traumatic visuals in an effort to shame and disturb them, or that they'll be refused by medical staff at the hospital.

Who Gets to Define Trauma?

One of the issues with birth and reproductive trauma is that there's some confusion about who gets to name and define it as trauma. In my years as a doula, I noticed that everyone interprets the birth through their own lens. The birth parent might have one narrative, which is different from mine or the midwife's, which could be different again from their partner's, with only *some people* who attended the birth feeling traumatized by the experience. It's not uncommon for those with birth or reproductive trauma to struggle with flashbacks or intrusive thoughts, to ruminate or think obsessively about the birth, to avoid anything that could remind them of the birth, to have panic attacks, to have trouble sleeping, to disassociate, or to find themselves stuck in a hyper- or hypo-aroused state. Birth and reproductive trauma can be debilitating, which is why it's so important to find support and why it's important that we seek to understand the experience of birthers who feel traumatized before we seek to diagnose.

While psychological research in this area suggests that birthers should have the right to define their birth as traumatic or not, not everyone who self-describes a traumatic birth will meet clinical criteria of PTSD according to the *Diagnostic and Statistical Manual of Mental Disorders (DSM)*.[12] As Grynpas suggests, the challenge is that the word *trauma* is used both colloquially ("I was traumatized by watching that scary movie!") and clinically, which some refer to as a brain injury or nervous system injury, and often people who talk about their traumatic birth experience colloquially are trying to express the extent of their grief and disappointment with what happened at their birth. But some people feel as though their experience is invalidated by only focusing on the clinical definition, and this can even prevent them from accessing funded care.

THE BIRTH HOUSE

There are several types of therapy that are designed to help you process traumatic memories and events, such as sensory motor therapy, brain spotting, eye movement desensitization and reprocessing (EMDR), or expressive arts therapy. These therapies require that you work with a therapist trained in that specific area, but there's one tool I can share with you that I use with clients to help begin processing their birth stories, called the Birth House. If it's too triggering for you think about your birth, I suggest finding a trauma-aware specialist in your area and skip the Birth House exercise.

If you can tolerate writing about your birth, then the Birth House can be quite valuable. That's true even for people who didn't have a traumatic birth, because giving birth is intense, and I personally believe that all birth stories need to be processed. You can use this tool to help you process the birth itself or even other events related to reproduction. You also don't need to be the birther in order to use it.

Start by drawing a picture of a house. Add as much detail as you like, but I'd like you to sketch in a few rooms in particular. You can see an example on page 73.

First, draw the outside of the house. Allow this to represent what other people would say about your birth, and write down what their words might be. What happened? Who was there? What was the order of events?

Now label the living room in the house. The living room is generally the room that we have guests in, just like you may have had guests at your birth. You likely have feelings about the roles that each of those guests played, including partners, medical staff, doulas, family, or friends. Jot down the role that each person played and how you felt about them. You might feel grateful, disappointed, or angry, or a combination of many feelings. Make a note of anything that you wish you could say to each person.

Next, label a bedroom in the upstairs part of the house. Your bedroom is a private place where not many guests are allowed. It is your place of refuge, reflection, and intimacy. Spend some time writing about how *you* feel about the birth, and any beliefs you have about yourself as a result. These could be positive, negative, or neutral. The goal isn't to change your inner narrative, but to reflect on the impact the birth has had on you.

Identify a basement next. The basement is a common place where we dump things we don't need or things that we don't want to clutter up our house. Often basements can be creepy and uncomfortable. What part of your birth do you not want to think about or want others to know about? What do you wish you could pack up and never talk about again? Or what parts are so scary that they're hard to remember? Write about these in the basement.

The Birth House

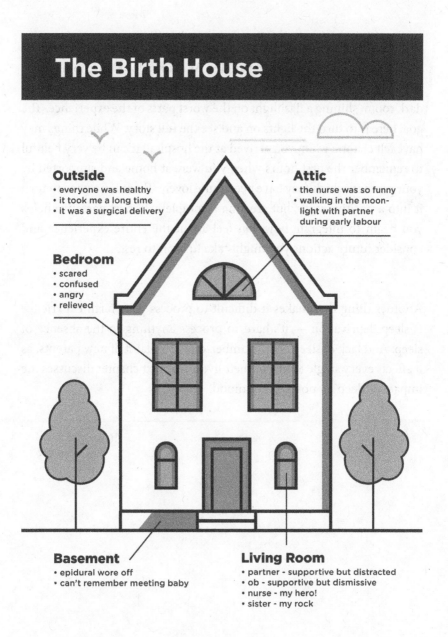

Outside
- everyone was healthy
- it took me a long time
- it was a surgical delivery

Attic
- the nurse was so funny
- walking in the moonlight with partner during early labour

Bedroom
- scared
- confused
- angry
- relieved

Basement
- epidural wore off
- can't remember meeting baby

Living Room
- partner - supportive but distracted
- ob - supportive but dismissive
- nurse - my hero!
- sister - my rock

Finally, label the attic. Attics are the place where we store the things that are important, and that we want to protect. It's also the place where light tends to sneak in through cracks. What parts of the birth do you hold dear? What do you remember fondly? Put those in the attic.

I use the Birth House exercise with my clients to help them see their birth from a variety of different angles. As counsellor Kim Thomas says, when we retell a traumatic birth story, it can feel as though we are in a dark room, shining a flashlight on the worst parts of the experience. The goal here is to turn the lights on and see the full story. While things may have felt chaotic when you arrived at the hospital, it can be very helpful to remember the first hours when you were at home and supported by your partner, which may have been quite lovely. There is no need to turn it into a positive story, but creating a complete, honest narrative helps you begin to integrate how you feel about the entire experience and consider future actions you might take to lay it to rest.

Another thing that makes it difficult to process your birth experience is sleep deprivation — it's hard to process anything in the absence of sleep. And lack of sleep is the number-one complaint of new parents, as it affects every single aspect of their lives. The next chapter discusses the impact of sleep on postpartum mood.

FIVE

SLEEP

In the second month you are, in the words of surviving
parents, "over the hump."

— Dr. William Sears

I laughed out loud the first time I read the quotation above. Navigating
infant sleep may be one of the most challenging tasks new parents
face, and rarely is a resolution found by the second month. Getting
babies to fall asleep and stay asleep while also trying to get enough
sleep yourself can feel like an impossible balance, and everyone has an
opinion about it. Too often, exhausted parents are told that this time of
broken sleep will be relatively short-lived or to "sleep when the baby
sleeps." These generic responses are not helpful, and they diminish the
impact that sleep deprivation can have on parents' moods. Without a
proper analysis of just how much sleep everyone is getting, parents have
no idea if what they are experiencing is sustainable or survivable. While
it's normal for new parents to complain about being tired, we should
never make assumptions about what that means for them or how much
sleep they are actually getting. There's a big difference between getting

up for two twenty-minute intervals to feed a baby each night for the first six months, and having your sleep interrupted every hour or two for eighteen months with an average of four hours of sleep a night.

While the impossible-parenting value of *the more you sacrifice, the more you love* minimizes the impact of sleep deprivation, the statistics about parental sleep don't paint a very healthy picture. It takes parents an average of four to six years to recover from postpartum sleep deprivation, and mothers, particularly nursing mothers, have the most significant sleep debts.[1] This has negative impacts on parental health, because we need to sleep! While most of us can cope with a few rough nights here and there, chronic sleep deprivation has been linked to emotional volatility, lower immunity, heart disease, blood sugar dysregulation, and hormone imbalances.[2] Sleep deprivation also increases our level of daily risk, due to forgetfulness or accidents.[3] One mother, who was so tired that she fell asleep holding her baby and dropped them, luckily with no injuries, invented the Joeyband to help prevent such incidents. Postpartum sleep disruption can also have devastating consequences on mental health and can intensify depressed and anxious feelings, as well as make it harder to manage stress and overwhelm.[4] What's even more scary is that severe sleep deprivation is linked to postpartum psychosis[5] and mania,[6] which is why many postpartum sleep experts refer to severe insomnia/sleep debt in the first months postpartum as a *sleep emergency*.

THERE ARE A LOT OF BARRIERS TO POSTPARTUM SLEEPING

Part of why finding solutions to postpartum sleep is so challenging is that that each family's experience is unique and inconsistent. Some babies just start sleeping ten hours a night from the very first few weeks, some don't nap well but sleep through the night, some have no predictable schedule whatsoever, and some wake up every forty-five minutes around the clock and can't be set down. Your baby will probably do something entirely different. Extra-exhausted parents often describe feelings of helplessness and desperation; those I talk to have usually tried many interventions without much success. Some are too tired to even attempt to research solutions — they're just trying to get through each day and each night, and they describe living in a state of limbo or "just waiting" for the sleep to improve. Parents' own issues related to falling and staying asleep can contribute to the challenge; if you had trouble sleeping before kids, you may very well continue to struggle postpartum even if you're physically exhausted.

Each family has its own set of systems and beliefs regarding sleep patterns, such as where people sleep, what time is considered bedtime and wake-up time, or what their wind-down routines look like. These systems can be a support or a barrier for parental sleep. For example, some couples decide to protect the sleep of one parent, commonly the one who works outside the house, and agree that that parent will sleep in a quiet part of the house while the other does all the night parenting. Clearly that sets one parent up for all the advantages of adequate rest and the other up for fatigue. Some families decide to share a bed together with their children, especially if they're nursing, so they can respond to a hungry baby in a matter of seconds and fall back asleep right away. But not every parent sleeps well with a baby in the bed; wiggly babies can make it hard to fall into a deep sleep. In families where one parent is nursing their baby exclusively, that parent often feels as though they can't share the night-parenting work — the baby needs them specifically and they can't go all night without feeding without becoming engorged with milk. Families are often unaware that there are other sleeping arrangement options available to them other than the one they've fallen into.

Taking naps as parents can also be a challenge! Parents may have visitors that they feel like they need to entertain, they may have older children that need to be taken to school or tended to, or they may need to go to paid work during the day, hugely limiting anyone who might otherwise try to get some sleep during the day.

And some parents struggle to get to sleep or stay asleep even if their baby/babies are sleeping, for all kinds of reasons. Often this starts during pregnancy, with night waking and trips to the bathroom causing parents to feel exhausted before they even give birth. Parents are advised to try to get as much sleep as possible immediately after giving birth, but many of us know how difficult that is to do. It's common to have some insomnia in the first few days of parenting, because you're so excited to be with your new baby, because you're amped up from all the adrenalin from the birth, or because of pain during the recovery from the birth. For some, this insomnia continues because of anxiety, frustration with partners, difficulty soothing their nervous systems after being woken up, or intrusive thoughts about harm coming to their baby/babies. My obsession with SIDS after my second child's birth left me struggling with serious insomnia for several months; I would spend most of the night compulsively checking on him to make sure he was breathing.

WHY ARE SOME BABIES BETTER AT SLEEPING THAN OTHERS?

The other barrier to postpartum sleep is that you have no idea what kind of relationship to sleep your baby/babies will have. Like adults, some babies just have an easier time falling and staying asleep than others. To learn more about why this happens, I spoke with Stephanie Kishimoto, an attachment-based infant and child sleep educator who owns a company called Sleep Parenting; our interview informs much of this part of the book. She suggested that there are many reasons why a baby might struggle with sleep, and that if parents are suffering from exhaustion, it's worthwhile to explore the underlying issues because they each require different strategies.

The first reason for disrupted sleep is simply age-appropriate waking. Before twelve months of age, most babies need to wake in the night because of varying biological and neurological factors. It's a way of ensuring babies are safe overnight and continue to thrive — they often need to eat. Before six months they just aren't wired for regulated sleep patterns yet because the sleep centres in their brains are just developing. Parents will likely start to see the emergence of a regular sleep pattern during the day around the six-month mark (such as three naps, of predictable length and at predictable times of day), but overnight sleep patterns may be less predictable. Under six months, there's a significant variability in how long babies will sleep, because very young babies have a very underdeveloped ability to regulate themselves, meaning they need a caregiver to help co-regulate, to bring them from a state of dysregulation ("things are not okay") to a state of regulation ("things are okay"). They are seldom able to independently fall asleep with any kind of consistency, which is why Kishimoto doesn't suggest sleep coaching or following a strict sleep schedule before this age. Instead, she offers parents education about what is normal, tools to cope with exhaustion, and support strategies for implementing healthy sleep hygiene, such as tuning in to your baby/babies' personal sleep cues.

After six months babies are usually better able to self-regulate and understand object permanence, meaning that they understand that their parents haven't disappeared forever when they leave the room. At this point parents can start implementing sleep schedules and routines more effectively, although this will look different from one family to the next depending on many factors contributing to the family dynamic. Another reason some babies have trouble sleeping is linked to their personality, as babies that are very alert and curious about their surroundings may resist sleep because they don't want to miss out on anything. "It's essentially baby FOMO," says Kishimoto, laughing. She suggests that these babies usually have at least one parent who admits to having trouble unwinding at the end of the day. These alert babies are typically the ones that reach their milestones super early and have trouble sleeping because of all of their rapid-fire neuroactivity. Meeting milestones is one of the reasons babies' sleep habits can regress, meaning they have a sharp and temporary decline in falling or staying asleep, owing to what many refer to as developmental leaps. There isn't much to do about developmental leaps except wait them out, and thankfully they tend to be short-lived.

It's also possible that babies aren't sleeping well because their parents rely on a lot of sleep associations (sometimes called sleep crutches) to get them to sleep, such as rocking them, holding them, or feeding them. Sleep associations, such as brushing your teeth, putting your pyjamas on, and reading in bed, are normal for all of us at every age and an important part of sleep hygiene. Although using sleep crutches with babies sometimes gets a bad rep, there is nothing wrong or bad about using associations to help your little ones sleep, and they can be very helpful while you're learning how to get your baby to sleep. Almost all parents use them in the first few months of parenting. But there is a limit to how supportive sleep associations can be for babies. If, past six months, they are still waking more than four times a night and need help to get back to sleep, it can create very fragmented sleep for both parents and baby. These babies usually need support and opportunities to develop the skills necessary to fall asleep independently.

Finally, it can be important to rule out health issues that can contribute to poor infant sleep. Babies can have underlying medical issues such as reflux, tongue or lip ties, or breathing issues, such as asthma or sleep apnea, and these issues often require medical support to resolve. Also, babies who aren't getting enough to eat during the day often do need to eat frequently at night, so it can be helpful for parents to focus on increasing daytime calories so that they can eventually wean their baby/babies from night-feeding. In the first year of life, sleep and feeding are incredibly intertwined.

THE HISTORY OF SLEEP POLITICS

Sleep is a hot topic for new parents — everyone talks about it and everyone seems to have an opinion about it. Like many aspects of parenting culture, how we manage and understand family sleep has gone through many changes over the last century. Kishimoto shared with me that family sleep was dramatically different before the invention of the light bulb in the late 1800s. Without artificial lights and the blue light from screens, such as cellphones or computers, which interfere with the release of melatonin, the hormone that allows us to feel sleepy, human sleep patterns were less disrupted. The result is that most of us today feel less sleepy in the evening and go to bed later than our historical counterparts, and some of us struggle to fall and stay asleep. That's why one of the first tips of healthy sleep hygiene is to eliminate the use of screens in the evening. But many people find this challenging, because we rely on television or social media to help us relax at the end of the day. It's one of parents' most popular sleep associations! There is some evidence that before the 1900s families didn't aim for eight hours of uninterrupted sleep in a row, and instead had three chunks of sleep throughout the day and evening. Historical records from some African and South American tribes and some parts of pre-industrial Europe suggest that in many communities sleep looked more like this: there would be a first sleep in the early evening (sometime from sunset to the middle of the night); followed by a middle of the night waking where people would pray, read, or rest by candlelight for an hour or two; followed by another period of sleep before they finally rose with the sun in the morning. Then they would have a nap in the early afternoon, which work environments were organized around — farmers coming in from the fields to lunch and a nap, or businesses shutting down for a period midday. Many parents didn't have access to child care but did have to work throughout the day, so baby-wearing was common, which allowed babies to fall in and out of sleep as they wanted to instead of trying to establish napping schedules. In many communities it was (and still is!) common for families to sleep in one bed, often referred to as *the family bed*. Although the family bed may not always support good sleep for all parents, babies and children often do sleep better when they have company.

Most family systems and structures have changed significantly from the 1800s and now the cultural norm is to use artificial light, screens, cribs, and children's beds, and to aim for eight hours of uninterrupted sleep a night. Long work hours, chronic stress, and very little time to rest have created a culture where fatigue and sleep debts are common, so it's understandable that new parents are looking for solutions, and that interest in family sleep has led to the creation of infant and child sleep experts. Kishimoto explains that at first those claiming to be parenting experts were mostly male doctors, such as Dr. John B. Watson, who suggested in the 1920s that appropriate psychological care of babies and children involved maximizing independence and minimizing physical contact. Watson suggested that babies and children were prone to manipulating parents to get attention. He advised limiting intimacy such as kissing, hugging, and holding, and he warned against too much "mother love." This philosophy influenced the development of sleep training, starting with the extinction sleep method in the 1950s, which was widely promoted by Dr. Marc Weissbluth. The extinction method advises parents to put their babies in cribs at a reasonable hour, firmly say goodnight, and then not return until morning. Obviously, this usually involved a lot of crying, which is why this strategy has been dubbed the *cry-it-out* method. Many variations of the extinction method have evolved, such as gradual extinction (also known as the "Ferber" method), where parents leave the room for short intervals (such as five to ten minutes) and then return to their baby, settle them, and then leave again; or the "camp out" or "gradual shuffle" methods where parents stay in the room next to the crib, possibly moving slowly away from it, while limiting interactions with their baby.

In the 1980s, Dr. William Sears achieved popularity with parents who were uncomfortable leaving their baby to cry by introducing attachment parenting sleep practices and coining the term *nighttime parenting*. Sears suggested that it was natural for babies not to sleep for long stretches and to want to sleep with their parents, and he advised parents to accept infant and child night waking and to respond quickly to their children regardless of the time of day. From this, many *no-cry* sleep strategies were developed.

Like most aspects of parenting, the politics of sleep at any given time are deeply informed by other popular infant and child behavioural politics. Since the rising interest in child psychology in the 1900s, there has been a sharp rise in research about infant sleep. Kishimoto explains that while some of the studies on infant sleep were conducted in sleep labs with the goal of better understanding infant and child sleep cycles or sleep apnea, much of the research was based on subjective parent questionnaires. This work led to theories about wake windows, suggesting that there is an optimal amount of time for a child to be awake before we should attempt to put them down for a nap or for the night. Some neurological development and stress researchers advocate against extinction methods because there is evidence that levels of cortisol and other stress hormones increase in the short term when babies are left to cry, and they believe this can have a long-term negative impact on them. But long-term studies have found this to be untrue, and the picture is even further complicated by research that suggests that *not* letting children learn to self-soothe can have negative long-term impacts on sleep and emotional regulation.[7] The result of all this has been an intense political divide about what is best for children, which often overlooks the issue of parental exhaustion and creates confusing messages about what parents are supposed to do.

GETTING PROFESSIONAL HELP WITH INFANT AND CHILD SLEEP

Some parents turn to their pediatrician or doctor for sleep solutions, but Kishimoto suggests that many parents are unsatisfied with the answers they receive because poor infant sleep usually stems from behavioural, not medical, concerns. To fill the gap, a new industry of sleep consultants has emerged, but the decision to use sleep-coaching strategies to help your children sleep is a deeply personal one, and it's not always possible financially. If you do decide to work with a sleep consultant, finding the right one for you can be challenging. There are many different ideological and political frameworks for sleep coaching, and consultants have varying degrees of training. I find most parents want something in between the behaviourist approach (Watson, Weissbluth, and Ferber) that assumes all infant sleep behaviour can be conditioned, and the "just accept it" approach that assumes parent sleep isn't important — and both are overly simplistic and ignore the cost of each strategy on both parent and child. This is why the developmentalist approach, based on Dr. Gordon Neufeld's work, is gaining in popularity in the sleep-coaching world. This approach assumes that all children have the potential to develop into good sleepers, but it requires parents to get curious about their baby/babies' sleep barrier, adjust the environment, and allow opportunities for growth. Under this model, sleep training is more like *sleep experimenting* and requires lots of observation, practice, flexibility, and often discomfort and mistakes.

One consistent requirement of sleep consulting is to reassure parents about the process, because the politics of infant sleep has created a lot of fear about permanently damaging children. Kishimoto says that parents often feel differently about hearing their baby cry during the day than during the night. If a baby cries for ten minutes in the car, while it's distressing for the parents, it doesn't usually lead to fears about permanently damaging the baby. Yet parents often feel anxious that they'll cause harm if they allow a baby to cry in its crib for ten minutes at night. Kishimoto encourages all parents not to measure their ability to be a "good parent" by how much their baby/babies cry, especially parents with high-needs or difficult-to-soothe babies, because we have such limited control over the crying.

Exploring sleep solutions with your baby/babies is hard, and it's often highly emotional work. Many parents feel anxious during this process, maybe because there's some crying or because they don't see results right away. Some parents do make great progress, but then feel isolated and housebound because they're afraid that leaving the house will tamper with the sleep schedule they've worked so hard to implement. And, of course, if parents are struggling with their own insomnia, helping their baby sleep longer is only part of the solution. Parents' biological need for sleep and their sleep debt must be considered when talking about infant sleep. It's very challenging to feel connected and enjoy moments with your baby when you're exhausted or resentful of their sleep resistance — you deserve a sleep solution that works for the whole family. No parent seeks out sleep consulting or tries out complex sleep programs if they're coping well with sleep disruption; they do it because they're desperate.

MAKING DECISIONS ABOUT INFANT SLEEP

Obviously, because every baby's relationship to sleep is unique, not all parents will feel that sleep intervention is required, even if they themselves are exhausted. It isn't really within my scope to recommend particular parenting practices; sometimes parents ask me what to do, and I always avoid a direct answer. That's partially because I know it's important to first understand what the sleep issue is, as Kishimoto suggests, but mostly because I think that the right strategies are the ones that parents think are best for them, which differs from family to family. Instead I help parents understand how the culture of impossible parenting might be affecting their thoughts or ideas about infant sleep. The idea that the choices we make about our children's sleep could affect them for the rest of their lives is directly linked to the *invest up front* value from the culture of impossible parenting, and it generates incredible pressure. Parents need to make decisions about sleep training with imperfect data, but really, that's true for all parenting decisions.[8]

My approach to assisting clients with sleep-related concerns is to help parents get clear about their personal parenting values and support them in creating family-centred systems that respect these values. These processes are outlined in chapters eleven and twelve. Ideally I want parents to factor their own well-being into their approach. Sleep can be such a big issue that it *becomes* the primary, pivotal issue related to life as a parent, and it often needs to be conceived and then re-conceived. This can be very disorienting for parents who thought they had clear ideas about infant sleep before they met their baby/babies. Many parents who once said, "I'd never let my baby cry" or "I will never let the baby sleep in our bed" soon find themselves willing to try anything to get more sleep.

I encourage you to make guilt-free decisions about managing your baby/babies' sleep in whatever way works for you. No matter what you decide, you may experience criticism, with others claiming that their position is supported by research, but when it comes to infant sleep, you can find evidence to support whatever position you want to take. What's generally accepted is that if your sleep debt is high and you're struggling with your mood, it will be very challenging to improve your mood without finding a way to get more sleep.

COPING WITH EXHAUSTION

Many parents I've worked with who have been diagnosed with PPA say that the turning point for their anxiety was getting adequate sleep, and for parents who are recovering from a recent traumatic event, such as a traumatic birth, sleep is *extra* important, because it's so critical to nervous system regulation. In fact, some trauma therapists believe that if people can get enough sleep (and support) after a traumatic event, it can make the difference between neurologically processing the event or not, meaning sleep can protect against clinical symptoms of PTSD. In these cases, often finding someone else, such as a partner, grandparent, or night nanny, to take on the majority of night parenting (even temporarily) is most effective. Naps are often suggested for sleepy parents, but many people, including myself, can lie down and try to sleep in the day, but their bodies just won't do it. In such cases, I often suggest that parents continue to protect their time to lie down somewhere quiet and away from the children, and focus on at least getting some rest.

Having enough energy to look after your kids twenty-four hours a day is a complex problem that requires a nuanced and compassionate approach. How can you protect yourself when sleep feels out of control? I encourage tired parents to think about their energy very strategically. I've learned a lot about energy management from my favourite reality television show, *Naked and Afraid.* The premise of the show is for two people to survive for three weeks alone in the wilderness, naked (and presumably afraid), by finding food and water, making fire, and building a shelter. People on the show are literally starving and severely sleep deprived, and the impact of not being able to access adequate energy becomes startling obvious, as hopelessness, fear, anger, and trouble with emotional regulation sets in quickly. Those who make it to the end of three weeks are those who are very strategic about how they use their energy, often doing minimal daily activity; those who work as hard as they do when they're well-fed and rested always deplete themselves to an unrecoverable state and need to leave the challenge early. Exhausted parents can learn a lot about energy conservation from *Naked and Afraid,* such as the importance of dividing tasks with your partner, slowing down and doing the bare minimum, lying down as much as possible, and eating to maximize energy. While only you know what foods are energizing for your body, and this will be different for everyone, I'm a big fan of easy-to-make carbohydrates, such as smoothies or toast, because carbs are our bodies' main source of energy.

Sleep deprivation is not cute or funny or something to be taken lightly. We cannot ignore the needs of parents, or worse, dismiss their experiences with quips like "It won't last forever." Many parents describe feeling tortured and obsessed about when they will sleep again. Often, the first person we turn to when we want to get more sleep is our partner (if we have one). Unfortunately, as the next chapter will discuss, negotiating high-stakes parent work, like deciding who's going to do night duty, is hard for a lot of couples.

SIX

RELATIONSHIPS

Marriage is mostly just sending each other memes while your kids destroy the house around you.
— James Breakwell

There are few things that will test a romantic relationship as significantly as having a baby, because, contrary to the messages of impossible parenting, babies can be incredibly destabilizing to relationships. Supporting another person takes a significant amount of emotional work under ideal circumstances, but a postpartum mood disorder, a high-needs baby, or a traumatic birth (or any combination of the three) can make it feel impossible. That's why I suspect that in many families *both* parents struggle with a postpartum mood disorder, though non-gestational parents rarely get help for it because of the assumption that only birth parents are at risk for PMADs. Even if neither partner has a mood disorder, I almost always hear some variation of the same five complaints from clients. The first — "We are so tired!" — is covered extensively in the previous chapter. The extreme fatigue of postpartum life creates a clunky ebb and flow of support between couples as they try to balance their own needs, the baby/babies' needs, and the needs of their partner. The next most popular complaints are "When did we become roommates?," "They don't understand how hard I'm working," "Where did the intimacy go?," and "We never used to fight this much." This chapter is dedicated to exploring these complaints one by one, starting with "When did we become roommates?"

ROOMMATES

Postpartum life can leave parents feeling like roommates instead of lovers or even friends. Pre-kids, couples generally get into a groove and a routine that guides how much time they spend together, how much rest and downtime they each get, and how they split up the work it takes to run a home. Even if their systems aren't perfect or are a source of conflict, they are at least predictable.

Babies and young children disrupt that. They don't care that their parents like to get busy on Sunday mornings or snuggle in bed watching the ten o'clock news every night. They communicate their immediate needs on an unpredictable schedule. It can take months or even years for parents to find enough time and energy to protect the non-parental parts of their relationship.

Every time a new child joins the family, couples go through this adjustment process all over again, and each time it's a little bit harder to come back together because multiple young children often demand a divide-and-conquer approach in which a couple splits up the household work and child care to save time. It sounds something like this: "You bathe the kids and I'll get dinner started and we'll meet back in half an hour." This approach is often effective for getting things done, but it can feel lonely.

The work required to raise children to adulthood is outrageously time-consuming — it's often estimated as the equivalent of two and a half full-time jobs — and it uses a complex range of skills. Think about how far-reaching parent work is. At any moment parents are doing some or more of the following things:

- **Chores:** This is all the physical work that needs to be done over and over again. Feed the baby at 3:00 a.m. Get groceries. Do the laundry. Clean the bathroom. Repeat.
- **Emotional support:** This means figuring out how to help kids develop emotionally, including soothing babies when they're upset, and helping older children build resiliency, like helping them recover from not making a team. It can be fun, like throwing the child a special birthday party. It also includes all the worrying and stressing that parents do about their children.
- **Moral development:** No parent wants to raise a jerk, and that means teaching kids what's okay and what's not okay through setting boundaries and holding children accountable. This is frustrating work; it often means saying "We don't hit people!" a hundred times before a lesson sinks in. It can also be heartbreaking, as you watch their confused reactions when you try to explain social justice concepts such as racism, sexism, or homophobia.
- **Teaching life skills:** Parenting requires a lot of teaching to help kids eventually survive in the world on their own. Potty training. How to clean up. How to read. Often this can involve spending a fortune on special classes and activities, not to mention all the transportation required.
- **Social skills instruction:** This is the process of helping kids build and maintain relationships, by showing them how to resolve conflict, how to make friends, and how to live harmoniously with others. It's trying to demonstrate the constant negotiation between setting clear boundaries with others and putting your own needs second for the sake of the larger group.
- **Administration:** Parenting demands a lot of scheduling and organization, as well as remembering bizarre things, like how much money other families spent on birthday gifts at your child's birthday party so you can spend a similar amount when it's their child's turn. It also includes copious amounts of research like reviewing car-seat safety ratings, assessing daycares, and reading books about the culture of impossible parenting. Managing the family calendar and to-do list could easily be a full-time job, and it often is for at-home parents.

Obviously, the contents of each bucket vary from family to family and can dramatically increase in particular areas when there are family members with (dis)abilities or chronic health issues. And different ages and stages demand more time, energy, and resources than others. I think it's normal that some parents like some types of work more than others, which means that some stages will have you feeling like a rock star while others make you feel incompetent. For example, when I was on maternity leave with two young kids at home, doing chores on repeat made me cry every day and drink wine every night, but I'm finding the moral development work of raising my teenager challenging and fascinating.

How the work is shared in the family can have a giant impact on the quality of the relationship, which brings me to the third most common complaint I hear from couples: "They don't understand how hard I'm working."

SHARING THE LOAD

How parenting and household work is shared in two-parent households has been in a state of flux in Western culture for many years now, and how family systems are organized and how work is distributed impacts every member of the family, outlining expectations and determining how much leisure time everybody has. The suggestion for many parents with PMADs is to get more help so that they can focus on their mental health and prioritize sleep, and most often they turn to their partners for support, with varying degrees of success. The support they get depends quite a bit on the family model they follow. Here, I share some of the history of family models, with the caveat that, of course, not all families/parental partnerships have advanced through these models uniformly.

After the industrial revolution, many heterosexual couples operated under an *absent dad and busy homemaker model* that had a clear gender divide between "blue jobs" (make money) and "pink jobs" (look after the house and kids). Everyone understood their role in this relationship model, even if it was unfair to share the work that way. Some couples still organize themselves in this way, or would like to, but the rising cost of living can make it very prohibitive to have one parent at home full time for prolonged periods. Nowadays it's common that families operating from this model will have one parent doing the paid work and the other primarily responsible for organizing the household and child care work, but with the working parent still participating in some housework and prioritizing building relationships with their children.

With the onset of the women's movement and the rapid rise of women engaging in paid work, expectations of male contribution to housework and childrearing started to climb. Here we see a shift in many families to an *angry mom and confused dad model*. As suggested by much of the historical literature from second-wave feminism, such as Judy Syfers's iconic 1970s essay "Why I Want a Wife," some mothers were pretty angry about their husbands' resistance to contributing more around the house and their lack of ability to do so successfully. Here you might have seen women frantically trying to cook a week's worth of dinners on the weekend because she didn't trust her husband to adequately feed himself and the children while she was at work, or a bumbling sitcom dad who had us laughing about how bad he was at changing diapers.

We still sometimes see variations of the *angry mom and confused dad model* at play today, but as men gained more confidence as parents and same-sex parents gained visibility and legal recognition, we saw the rise of the *captain parent and sidekick parent model*. This has one parent, usually the gestational parent, being the leader of the family systems and the keeper of all the family knowledge and the other parent becoming the sidekick who needs to be asked to participate in family life and is often given detailed instructions for how to help with specific tasks. For example, the sidekick parent may have agreed to take the baby to its six-month doctor checkup, but the captain parent would have set up the appointment in advance (knowing it takes three weeks' notice to get a morning appointment), packed the diaper bag with extra clothes and snacks, researched parking options, written a list of questions that came up since the last appointment, and pre-purchased infant Tylenol in case the baby didn't feel well after getting its shots.

The challenge with this model is that much of the work of the captain parent is invisible, and it's rarely acknowledged that their parenting workload is significantly more intense than that of the sidekick parent. In their book *The Second Shift*, Arlie Hochschild and Anne Machung give us some insight into this and outline the different types of work that are required to run a household with children.[1] The first, *paid work*, is easily understood as work; we have an entire cultural understanding that paid work requires time and energy resources. They call domestic work, such as chores and childminding, *reproductive work*, because it's the work that doesn't feel done for very long, and doesn't have work hours that you can clock in and out of. You might do the breakfast dishes, but when lunch comes around you have to do it all over again. We've made strides in seeing reproductive work as real work that requires time and energy, and many couples are trying to share that load, especially if they both work full time. But all the thinking, remembering, and noticing that is required to keep the family systems flowing, called *emotional work* or *the mental load*, is still not well understood to be a drain on time and energy and often goes unseen and invalidated.

The research on this topic is not particularly inspiring. Even in the most progressive and feminist heterosexual relationships it's estimated that women still carry 65 percent of the family work in the household, even when both parents do paid work full time.[2] A recent sleep research study discovered that women with children sleep less than child-free women, with only 48 percent of mothers under forty-five years old reporting getting at least seven hours of sleep, compared to about 70 percent of child-free women.[3] But interestingly the study found no correlation between fathers and child-free men.[4] Although the research primarily focuses on heterosexual couples, the problems with the *captain parent and sidekick parent model* shows up in queer relationships as well. I have seen this at play with many queer clients that I work with, but I also find that queer couples can more quickly reorganize themselves to a shared parenting model, because in the absence (or heightened awareness) of stereotypical sex and gender family roles, many queer couples are familiar with negotiating domestic work.

And this unfair sharing of the load leads to a lot of fighting, mistrust, and anger in relationships. Captain parents live in a state of chronic disappointment with their partner and desperately want their workload to be shared or at least validated. Sidekick parents often accuse their partners of being inflexible, controlling, or bossy and are confused about why their captain partner gets frustrated when they have to ask them to help.

Part of the task of the current generation of new parents is to find a way out of the captain/sidekick model into a *shared parenting model*, where they are truly co-parenting. When parent work is equitably shared, each partner knows what is expected and doesn't need instruction or accountability conversations. A *shared parenting model* incorporates four principles:

1. Each parent gets to be the captain of some household and parenting tasks, but not all the household and parenting tasks. Sharing the load doesn't mean every task needs to be done by both people; it doesn't always require two people to throw a load of laundry in. Instead, the goal is to negotiate what each parent is going to be primarily responsible for. For example, one parent might be the captain of dinners while the other is the captain of laundry. This would mean that the captain of dinners would put the grocery list together, make sure all the ingredients were in the house when needed, and assign cooking duties as needed. And they would have the energy for this because they never needed to think about getting laundry done. Instead, their partner would gather up all the dirty laundry and ensure it was washed, dried, and put away within a reasonable timeline.

2. There's an equitable ratio of captain to sidekick responsibilities. The exact breakdown of how the load is split doesn't matter as much as a feeling between the two partners that the load has been fairly negotiated. I often ask couples to write down each of the tasks and thinking work they do for each bucket of parent work — chores, emotional support, moral development, teaching life skills, social skills instruction, administration — on individual Post-it Notes (this often requires a lot of Post-its). Once all this information has been collected and reflected upon, I put all the Post-it Notes into one large pile and invite the couple to begin the

slow process of negotiating each task one by one to decide how it should get done and who will be the captain of it.

3.   There's an attempt to allow each parent to be the captain for the household and parenting tasks that fall within their unique strengths/availability. For example, if one parent wants to nurse the baby exclusively and full time, it doesn't make sense that the other parent would share in that responsibility. In our house my partner, Janna, loves planning family vacations. They get excited by the research, it brings them great joy to find activities that they think the kids will love, they love to brag about airline deals, and are a master at organizing complex itinerary information into simple-to-understand excel spreadsheets. I feel overwhelmed by the options on Airbnb, so we very quickly realized that it made sense for Janna to oversee vacation planning. And while I haven't done a load of laundry in seven years because I was given feedback early on in the relationship that not doing a separate load for white clothes is "utterly ridiculous," Janna comes home from work most nights to dinner ready for them, because I work from home and have more time for cooking. It's totally okay to be fully in charge of a task if it feels fair and logical.

4.   There is expressed gratitude for what each parent contributes. Because so much of household and parent work is culturally invisible, it's critical that each parent recognize it as work and appreciate how they and their children benefit from the work that their partner does. Don't assume your partner knows you are thankful for all that they do — find ways to communicate it! You can tell them, offer them an extra sleep-in, or rub their tired feet at the end of the day — whatever resonates for them. And do it regularly.

While embracing a shared parenting model will not eliminate PMADs, I do think it functions as a protective factor that reduces its impact, because having enough help is a key aspect of postpartum resiliency. It also serves as a way to resist the impossible-parenting culture value *the more you sacrifice, the more you love*, because it reduces the perceived need for parental sacrifice.

Solo Parenting and Co-Parenting

Of course, shared parenting models privilege two-parent families, and not all parents are romantically partnered, with almost 13 percent of households in Canada led by solo female parents.[5] Financial security is commonly a struggle for single-parent families, with 54 percent of low-income parents represented by single mothers, compared to 24 percent by single-dad families and 12 percent by two-parent households.[6] But that doesn't mean solo parents aren't sharing some of the parenting load with others. Single parents by choice often rely on their family, friends, and others in their communities, as well as professionals like doulas and nannies, to help spread the load around. The importance of solo parents leveraging their relationships — romantic or otherwise — for support seems obvious. It's not reasonable to expect one person to care for an infant (and possibly other children) non-stop *and* run a household alone, and not having enough support is a huge risk factor for PMADs. Yet when it comes to parents that *are* partnered, we often assume that having a partner is enough, which is completely inaccurate. There's a new term that's developed to describe what it's like to raise children with someone who refuses to participate with the family work in an equitable way: *married single parent*. Many single parents hate the term, however, because it trivializes the emotional weight of carrying the parental load on your own, and overlooks the fact that two-income families benefit from additional financial resources.

Sharing some of the work with others does not reduce the level of responsibility or decision-making stress that a solo parent has. I had negotiated a lot of help from my parents when I had my first child on my own, but I still always carried the weight of knowing that I was the bottom line and that support was never guaranteed, because stuff like illness can change your plans at the last minute. So, while they may find ways to take breaks, single parents are never truly off-duty, which can make them feel very trapped.

Co-parenting with an involved ex-partner, on the other hand, is a very different experience from single parenting without the involvement of a secondary parent. While it involves a certain loss of autonomous decision-making authority, which can be infuriating and feel burdensome, it also comes with forced sharing of parent work. In my previous marriage, the household was organized under the *captain parent and sidekick parent model* (much to my frustration). It wasn't until we separated and I had regular time off from parenting that I realized how much energy I'd been expending to be the captain and how much it could negatively affect my mood. After the split, I was able to stop multitasking housework with childminding (most of the time), and I realized how glorious it was to cook dinner without being screamed at by a hungry toddler. On the days when I didn't have the children at my house, I was able to get on top of housework, get a full night of sleep, start exercising again, and even develop a social life. And while there are many painful parts of divorce and co-parenting with someone you may not always like very much, more and more I am seeing exhausted, burnt-out captain parents come back to life after having even one night a week to restore themselves while their children are cared for by their ex. As another divorced and co-parenting friend said, "Part-time parenting is the best. I miss my kids when they're gone so I'm ready to play with them when they come home; we spend way more quality time together." Of course, couples don't need to separate in order to share the work more equitably. Changing unfair dynamics can happen through a combination of intentional self-reflection, recognition of privilege, and experimentation with new ways of being in a relationship together.

Families who are co-parenting with more than two parents are able to share the load even more. Some people choose to parent with each other without the romantic relationship part through all kinds of creative arrangements, sometimes even living together. Like all co-parenting relationships, this can be difficult to negotiate, but when it works well, it works really well, either because part-time parenting was set up and negotiated from the beginning or because cohabitation has built-in perks.

Re-partnering after a divorce or breakup comes with its own mood challenges. Not only because it can add friction to the co-parenting relationship and put stress on the family, but also because it's hard for someone to join a family system that's already been established. There is a lot to negotiate regarding the parenting work. Does the step-parent want to take on discipline, make family appointments, and teach life skills to the kids? If so, are the kid/kids young enough to make that a smooth transition? (It's much easier to step into a parenting role with a one-year-old than it is with a sixteen-year-old.) What if both parents have children? What if the two sets of children don't get along? There can be many obstacles to overcome.

When Janna and I moved in together we read the only book on lesbian step-parenting that exists, which suggested it can take up to seven years for a blended family to feel solidified.[7] Figuring out how to live together with kids is tough, and many new couples opt to have more children together, forcing them to do the simultaneous emotional work of managing the blending of families and negotiating life with a newborn, with all of the pressures that can put on a relationship.

One of my favourite exercises for parents who find themselves bickering about complex family dynamics is to take a bird's-eye view of the argument and decide together what the overarching unresolved issue is. For example, if a couple is fighting about perceived unfair discipline between stepchildren and biological children, I say to them, "If we imagine that *you* [pointing to one half of the couple] are not the problem here and that *you* [pointing to the other half of the couple] are also not the problem here, then what *is* the problem that is illuminated by this argument? Let's name it so that we can let the problem be the problem, rather than trying to make a person the problem." In this case, the problem the couple is trying to solve is ensuring consistent and fair discipline for all the children in the house. I would then write *Problem to be solved: Ensuring consistent and fair discipline for all the children in the house* on a piece of paper, place the paper in front of the couple, and ask them to work as a team to resolve the issue before them.

SEX AND INTIMACY FEEL NON-EXISTENT

After unfair division of labour, the next complaint I hear the most from new parents is "Where did the intimacy go?," i.e., that sex and intimacy feel almost non-existent. While it's important to distinguish between sex and intimacy, because it's possible to have one without the other, often when I ask clients if they miss sex or intimacy they say, "I don't know but I think both. I miss the sex and then the cuddling afterward."

It's not surprising that sex would slow down or be put on pause during the postpartum period because of many of the reasons mentioned throughout this chapter. Several research studies show that new heterosexual parents have less sex than they used to in the first year after childbirth.[8] The (limited) research about sexual intimacy for lesbian parents is pretty bleak, suggesting almost no new parents have sex a few times a month in the early years of parenting.[9]

There are other reasons that sexual play may be limited during the postpartum period. The most obvious is that if a parent has given birth, their genitals are off limits for a few weeks to a few months while they recover (whether they gave birth surgically or vaginally). If there was any kind of birth injury, couples can expect that time to be extended. A traumatic birth can also have a psychological impact that can leave both parents feeling uninterested in sex. Even if there wasn't an injury, it's common for there to be pain when couples start experimenting with sexual intercourse — it's one of the biggest reasons that people who give birth seek out pelvic-floor physiotherapy. And, of course, if one partner is on an SSRI medication for a PMAD, reduced sexual desire is a common side effect.

Even without physical barriers to sexual touch, parents of infants often express feeling "touched out," particularly if they're nursing. Snuggling a baby all day raises oxytocin levels, which is the same feel-good hormonal hit we get when we're intimate with our partners. Many full-time parents don't crave touch from their partners because their oxytocin needs are already being met by their children, but that can be emotionally painful or feel like rejection for their partners. Nursing parents often describe feeling like they're sharing their bodies with their babies and don't feel interested in also sharing their bodies with their partners; they're craving some sense of body autonomy.

Tynan Rhea, a Toronto-based sex and relationship therapist, says that a disparity in desire is the number-one reason that brings postpartum parents to their practice, and they note that sometimes issues of desire discrepancies exist in the relationship before having children and are heightened due to postpartum stress. They often start with clients by explaining the science of desire and debunking the myth that sex is spontaneous for everyone. Rhea shared that most (not all, of course) men experience spontaneous arousal, while most (again, not all) women experience responsive arousal, which requires more time and explicit effort. Couples always have to work at prioritizing sex and intimacy, and all the barriers discussed in this chapter make it challenging for new parents to do that, even if it's an essential component of their relationship.

If there are any feelings of pressure to engage in more sexual intimacy, Rhea candidly asks both parents if they have the physical and emotional energy to invest in sexual play right now. If one parent says no, they encourage the couple to take the type of sexual play they are uninterested in off the table for a period of time, to let the pressure subside and focus on other areas of intimacy in their relationship. For some people, having their partner talk them into having sex is part of what they need to arouse their responsive sexual desire and is helpful for getting in the mood, says Rhea. Sex that happens after one partner has been worn down, however, is not the type of sex that nourishes the relationship; it can be experienced as coercion and assault. The best way to know which scenario applies to you and your partner is to talk about it with each other and reflect on what kind of things feel enticing versus pressuring.

If both parents do want to increase sexual intimacy, Rhea suggests consistently scheduling time to be alone, connect, and allow for the possibility of sex without promising that it will happen. Rhea also suggests making a "no talking about the kids" rule during this alone time so that parents can re-explore the non-parenting parts of themselves together and develop a new kind of relationship intimacy.

HOW ARE PARENTS SUPPOSED TO PROTECT THEIR RELATIONSHIP?

The final complaint I hear a lot of is "We never used to fight this much," which isn't surprising given the exhaustion, overwhelming and inequitable workloads, and lack of intimacy that often come with new parenthood. As a colleague of mine says, "No couple with kids under three is having that much fun." Many couples are also surprised to learn only after they become parents that they have differing ideas and values about how to raise kids. For example, more than once couples have come to me for mediation because one wants to sleep train their baby and the other is adamantly opposed to it.

Excluding verbally, physically, and emotionally abusive relationships, there is nothing weird or abnormal about fighting or having disagreements as a couple. All couples do it! I suggest that couples worry less about how often they are bickering, which may be more than normal in the early years of parenting, and instead focus more on identifying their personal fight cycle, making sure they're fighting fairly, and getting good at conflict resolution.

The danger of having a lot of disagreements during the postpartum years is that it can change the way couples see each other. Relationship researchers Julie and John Gottman suggest that couples first gain some awareness about how many positive, neutral, or negative interactions they have with each other in a day or week, to gauge the quality of their relationship. If couples are having more positive and neutral interactions, they tend to think pretty highly of their partners, and they interpret grumpy moments as situational and lean in to support them. For example, if their partner is snippy one morning because they were up for hours in the night with the baby, they may choose to ignore sassy comments and offer them coffee and a nap.

However, if a couple has more negative interactions, a negative lens tends to develop for interpreting each other's behaviour; everything their partner does becomes evidence for the idea that their partner is a jerk. Even neutral interactions can be read as an attack. A simple text of "Do you need anything from the store?" could cause a rage reaction from a parent who's exhausted from doing all the remembering work for the family.

If couples have slipped into a negative-lens space, often the solution begins with bolstering positive interactions by purposefully seeking them out, even if it means holding back frustration at times. Usually positive responses are met with more positive responses, which will not repair a fracture in the relationship alone, but will make it easier for the couple to have difficult discussions moving forward, because it shifts the focus of the discussion to problem solving rather than on trying to prove why each other is wrong.

Throughout part 3 of the book, I provide more tools and activities for couples who are struggling to connect or get along after becoming parents. If your relationship feels hard right now, you are not alone. And if it's negatively impacting your mood, you are also not alone in that. Wanting help with romantic relationships is one of the most common reasons people seek therapy. There are many aspects of the culture of impossible parenting that also make co-parenting with a partner feel impossible. Thankfully, most couples make it through to the other side with sleep, time, and sometimes professional support.

SEVEN

BODIES

I say I love myself, and they're like "Oh my gosh she is
so brave. She's so political." For what? All I said is that
I love myself, bitch!

— Lizzo

I'm a dieter in recovery. I have likely tried every iteration of diet and
exercise you can imagine. Vegan and yoga. Paleo and CrossFit. Low
fat and running. My weight has gone up and down so many times I've
lost count, as I've cycled through gaining and losing the same pounds
over and over again. Like many children of the eighties, I was born into
a family that modelled a fear of fat combined with compulsive cardio
exercise. While I wasn't a stranger to dieting as a child, my obsession
grew into a seriously disordered state after a substantial weight gain
with my first pregnancy, followed by a depression related weight gain
during my PPD/A recovery after my second child. I forced myself to

lose the weight through what now seem like extreme measures, all under the guise of "just trying to get healthy."

This all came to an abrupt end a few years ago, when I entered into what I now refer to as *The Great Gallbladder Fiasco*, and I had to face the truth that I had been lying to myself about the diets. They weren't about getting healthy; they were about trying to control my body. This realization came after I paid a substantial amount of money to have blood testing done to find me the "right" diet — I lost weight quickly on an extremely low fat, low calorie diet that only had me eating about ten different types of foods. Then I went on a vacation to Mexico and found myself binge eating all the fatty, delicious foods I had been missing, resulting in the first of two excruciating gallbladder attacks. I later learned that eating very little fat for an extended amount of time and then eating very high-fat meals is one of the worst things you can do to your gallbladder. And I paid for it.

The next four months were hell. I started having multiple gallbladder attacks a week. For the lucky among you who have never experienced such an attack, it feels like your ribs are being squeezed through a vice grip, and you fear you'll suffocate because it's so painful to breathe. These attacks would almost always happen at night, and they'd keep me up until 3:00 or 4:00 a.m., my only relief coming from lying in the bathtub with the shower raining down on me until I ran out of hot water. I became very depressed from the exhaustion and unmanaged pain, and I wasn't scheduled for gallbladder-removal surgery for another three months. The attacks increased in frequency and length, until one morning, after an attack had lasted for over twenty-four hours, Janna put their foot down and insisted we go to the emergency department. It turned out I was in such an extreme condition that my gallbladder was removed a few hours later with emergency surgery.

I had some pain relief for about a week, but unfortunately the gallbladder attacks then started up again, which was incredibly confusing. For about three weeks after surgery I went back to the emergency room several times when the pain became unmanageable. While the medical staff at my local hospital didn't appreciate my jokes about having a "ghost gallbladder," they also didn't take me seriously — they treated me like a prescription narcotic seeker until I was suicidal from poor pain management and my eyes and skin had turned completely yellow from jaundice. When medical staff finally heeded my final desperate plea for further investigation, they found that my report had been misread and that a gallstone had been left in my bile duct, causing a major blockage. I was hospitalized for a week while medical staff debated the best course of action. It was the sickest I have ever been in my life and my liver took months to heal.

THE QUEST FOR ULTIMATE HEALTH

As I worked through the trauma of this experience in therapy, I started to grapple with the idea that dieting had almost killed me. And I just couldn't do it anymore. Through the painful work of rebuilding my sense of self after leaving the cult of diet culture, I started to see all the twisted ways in which it has permeated impossible-parenting culture. This is why I have decided to include a chapter that addresses the healthism (the prioritizing of personal health goals above all) and general body obsessiveness that permeates perinatal life. Healthism and diet culture slyly shape our narratives about parents' and children's health by leveraging our general anxiety about what we eat, how much we eat, and how we should move our bodies, and by tailoring it specifically to childrearing. I say slyly because it's easy to forget that claims about health being the ultimate goal are often, consciously or not, marketed attempts at forcing us into particular behaviours.

Victoria Millious, healthism expert, suggests that healthism is deeply embedded in all aspects of Western culture. She says that it works to convince us that we are personally responsible for our health outcomes, as determined by our individual lifestyle choices and behaviour, and minimizes the impact of social determinants of health such as poverty and access to health care. According to Millious, healthism has linked optimal health with mortality, creating the belief that pursuing health is moral, while ignoring or neglecting health is immoral. And once we have children, we are not only morally responsible for pursuing our own health outcomes, but also theirs. The *keep it natural* and *invest up front* values of impossible-parenting culture show up with expectations about pregnancy weight gain, postpartum weight loss, and nursing newborns. How we feed ourselves and our children is very political.

Femme bodies are pressured to be slim and conventionally beautiful, which is billed as attractive to the male gaze. This remains consistent throughout pregnancy and the early postpartum period. Our maternal goddess culture presents pregnancy, birth, and nursing as the ultimate womanly experience, much to the exclusion of trans birth parents and mothers that did not give birth. But when it comes to reproduction, there's a new set of health rules for anyone thinking about getting pregnant, focused on creating a body that's as safe and welcoming to a growing human life as possible. There are entire sections of bookstores dedicated to what to eat for optimal fertility. The Centers for Disease Control and Prevention basically suggests that all potential birthers keep their bodies at peak form, with weight guidelines[1] and sobriety recommendations "just in case" you get pregnant.[2]

Once pregnant, birthers lose agency over their bodies as they become vessels for growing a fetus (or two or more). Birthers navigate restrictions on certain foods, such as sushi, unpasteurized cheese, or shellfish, with allowable foods highly scrutinized to make sure they are "healthy" enough to sustain a growing fetus. Messages about how much food you should eat while pregnant are confusing, too. You aren't supposed to diet while you're pregnant, but you also aren't supposed to gain too much weight either; there's often a recommendation to only increase calories by three hundred a day. Alternatively, pregnant people with hyperemesis gravidarum (severe morning sickness lasting throughout most or all of the pregnancy) are given strict instructions to find ways to get and keep food in their bodies. Thankfully there are pregnancy-care providers with an awareness of disordered eating who are dedicated to changing the way weight is discussed with patients during pregnancy. Midwife Brittany-Lyne Carriere says, "I don't regularly weigh my pregnant clients because I know it can be triggering. It also does not offer me a lot of insight to their wellbeing. Weight isn't a good indicator of a healthy pregnancy. I rather discuss their relationship with food and movement if *they* are concerned about weight in pregnancy. The only time it feels medically relevant for me to weigh someone is for genetic screening, and at term, in the event the client needs general anesthesia."

Once that baby is born? Time to lose that baby weight! There seem to be endless marketing messages and programs encouraging birthers to get rid of any evidence that their bodies have grown and birthed a baby, such as baby bootcamp classes, diets designed to help birthers lose weight without impacting their nursing supply, and anything Instagrammed by a postpartum Kardashian. Simultaneously, diets for weight loss alone have fallen out of fashion and have been replaced with diets disguised as "lifestyle" changes to improve health. Gone (largely) are the days of people experimenting with quick weight-loss strategies like the grapefruit diet. Instead of focusing on caloric restrictions, all the new fad diets look at restricting food groups for purposes such as blood sugar maintenance (keto), gut healing (paleo), or detoxing (juicing). As a client of mine once said, "I don't feel like such a shitty feminist if I tell myself I'm eating for health instead of eating to lose weight. But who am I kidding? I'm in it for the pre-pregnancy jeans."

When we look past our fear of fat, there are common reasons that some parents might gain weight postpartum. Not sleeping and higher levels of stress often lead to cravings for carbohydrates and calories, because our bodies need the energy and serotonin boost that comes from simple carbs.[3] Many exhausted parents talk wistfully about getting to the end of their very busy days of caregiving and wanting to plop down on the couch with chips or cookies, or whatever they find delicious, as a way to relax before bed. Often clients will tell me that they feel guilty about this, but I encourage them to see it as a pretty innocent, easy way to soothe themselves at the end of the day. There are, of course, lots of positive health goals, such as reducing pain, increasing energy, or managing chronic illness, that food or exercise can help with. But advocates of the *Health at Every Size (HAES)* philosophy argue that the vague advice of "lose weight and you'll be healthier" is far too often unhelpful and untrue, and that high-quality medical care should be able to treat ailments in anyone, regardless of their body size. We need to detach from the myth that skinny = healthy; critical illnesses such as heart disease or cancer can strike anybody.

Yet, regardless of whether parents call it a diet or a healthy-eating lifestyle, attempts to lose weight through diet control have dismal success rates, with only 3–5 percent having any long-lasting results. Many parents find themselves pulled into the binge-restrict diet cycle. I first learned about this diet cycle through an online course taught by body-image coach Summer Innanen. She explained that we are most vulnerable to new diets when we're seeking more control or excitement in our lives. So it's no wonder postpartum parents are at risk, given the combination of new-parent overwhelm, adjusting to body changes, and the reproductive nature of infant care; all of these can make the dopamine hit that comes with starting a new diet very appealing. We feel good that we're taking control and find ourselves feeling better about ourselves and our circumstances just by *planning* to go on a diet. Yet once we start the diet, it's only a matter of time until we feel deprived, break the diet rules, and find ourselves eating the restricted foods that we'd tried to ban. A "screw it" mentality emerges, convincing us we should eat all the foods now because we won't be able to have them when we start dieting again. Then we feel guilty and out of control so we commit to starting a new diet, which cues up the dopamine hit again and the cycle begins all over again. This binge-restrict cycle can lead to serious disordered eating patterns and weight gain for some people, which we then read through a fat-phobic lens that tells us large bodies are a result of laziness or a lack of self-control. It's not, and it actually doesn't matter why your body is the size it is, because you're allowed to live your life in a large (or small or medium) body. As activist Virgie Tovar says, "You have the right to remain fat."

BODY POSITIVITY

There has been an interesting twist to diet culture with the rise of the body positivity movement, which says that everyone should have a positive body image, regardless of their shape, size, or ability. As a Lizzo-loving chubby parent, I am 100 percent on board with the idea that all bodies deserve love and celebration, but I also know that feeling this way consistently about *my* body is harder than I want it to be. There seems to be a paradoxical flaw to the body positivity movement, which is that it can feel like a burden to love your body unconditionally; undoing all that internalized cultural worship of thinness takes a lot of emotional work.

It's okay if it takes time to adjust to the changes to your body after giving birth, and it's okay to grieve the old relationship you had with your body, but parents who believe in body positivity often feel like it's a betrayal of their politics to talk about this tension. Many parents I work with, particularly birth parents, say that while they agree in theory that they should love their body at every size, they struggle to access the self-compassion and self-acceptance that would make it possible. The result is an almost inevitable sense of failure. Failure in the sense that their bodies don't align with how the dominant culture suggests they should look, but also failure because they feel guilty that they care so much about it! While today most of us have seen body-positive marketing campaigns that use photographs of sagging breasts and squishy tummies in an attempt to destigmatize post-birth bodies, and we celebrate full-bellied "dad bods," there is often a painful cognitive dissonance when your body politics and your self-image don't align. It's a very similar tension that parents face when trying to reject the culture of impossible parenting. We can see how flawed it is and *want* to reject it, but there are social costs to that rejection. Our emotional response can vary widely; some days we feel empowered and other days we feel deflated.

It's often too big a transition to go from dissatisfaction with your body to a joyful celebration of your body. That's why I often draw from the tools I learned from Innanen and encourage clients to strive for body neutrality before reaching for positivity. That means different things to different people, but it often involves working to create a personal narrative in which you give yourself permission to be fat (or whatever your dissatisfaction is) and accept your body as it is without trying to change it. It also involves a clear transition from eating to manage your weight to a fun exploration of what foods feel good in your body, how much food feels good in your body, and learning how you like to move your body. You might learn, for example, that you feel energized by starting your day with a veggie-dense smoothie, that you like going for walks but only if you've had at least six hours of sleep, and that eating marshmallows straight from the bag after the kids go to bed makes you feel cozy and ready to rest. Exploring eating and movement like this removes weight loss as a goal and focuses instead on tuning in to the internal workings of your unique body. The pathway to building a loving and trusting relationship with your body is similar to a mental health journey; it's often long, with confusing ebbs and flows, and it involves a lot of experimentation. But following a diet will never lead to long-term body love and acceptance.

If you're on board with the anti-diet movement but are struggling to accept the size of your body because of difficult emotions, try using the *emotions mapping* technique. Emotions mapping is a mindfulness strategy that invites you to sit with difficult emotions and gently observe them, instead of trying to change them into an emotion that you think you should feel. When you feel yourself getting triggered and catch yourself engaging in negative self-talk toward your body, hit pause and ask yourself "What emotion am I feeling right now?" Try to name the emotion with as much detail as possible, so dig a little deeper than words like *sad*, *mad*, or *anxious*. Also, fat is not an emotion. If you think you're "feeling fat," you're using it as an adjective. Ask yourself what it means to "feel fat." Often it's more powerful if you can say "I feel disgusting" or "I feel worthless." Once you've named what you're feeling, see if you can "map" the emotion's location in your body by locating where the physical sensation of the feeling shows up in your body, such as your belly, your chest, or your throat. And once you've found where the feeling lives, literally and figuratively give the emotion more space by breathing into the sensation while saying to yourself "I'm allowed to feel [for example, disgusting]. It's a normal human emotion. I accept that this feeling is here and I'm going to give it all the space and love it needs right now." It's amazing how quickly you can move through difficult feelings when you stop resisting or distracting yourself from them by naming them and giving them room.

Learning compassion for our bodies is really hard for most of us (sometimes so hard that it's worthwhile to talk to a professional about it), but I promise you aren't alone with it. It can be extra hard when we feel like our bodies have failed us during fertility or at our births, or when we're figuring out if or how to nurse our babies; it's one of the most challenging and political aspects of postpartum bodies.

NURSING

As I write about the impact of nursing culture on parents' mental health, I feel nervous about how this section will be received by parents on such a divisive issue. My goal is not to perpetuate the divide between human milk and formula. Instead, I argue that feeding a baby is really intense and we need to have more emotional freedom in figuring out how we're going to do it. While there's no debate that nursing is an excellent choice for feeding babies, nursing is a complex physiological feat and can cause new parents a significant amount of distress.

The perceived pressure to nurse that many parents describe stems from an important feminist movement that aimed to destigmatize breastfeeding and provide legal protection for nursing parents, many of whom *still* face nursing discrimination such as being told to cover up while feeding in public or asked to do it in a public toilet. Like many parenting ideas and practices, the popularity of nursing has trended up and down. In the 1930s, when modern formula started to become available, parents were encouraged by peers and medical professionals *not* to nurse and to feed their babies with formula instead.[4] As a result, nursing fell out of fashion and came to be seen as archaic and even disgusting, until pro-breastfeeding health groups starting cropping up in the mid-1950s with the goal of changing this narrative by highlighting the benefits of nursing.[5] This was a difficult cultural change and policy battle that involved significant amounts of advocacy work, but it ultimately led to a normalization of nursing, as well as many protective laws, such as the right to feed in public spaces in many parts of Canada and the United States. One of the strategies used to popularize nursing was the Breast-Is-Best campaign in the 1960s that focused on the health advantages of human milk over formula.[6] One of the goals of the campaign was to increase the number of parents who attempted to nurse, and it was quite successful — the rates of parents attempting nursing at birth shifted from 25 percent in the 1970s to the current rates (as of 2012) of almost 90 percent.[7] It should be noted, however, that the percentage of parents nursing at six months postpartum drops to 26 percent.[8]

Although nursing advocates have dropped the language of Breast-Is-Best, the campaign's legacy has been significant. Unfortunately, the strategy to rebrand nursing as "best" has had a negative impact on the mental health of many new parents. It contributes to nursing trauma, as discussed in chapter four, where parents hope to exclusively nurse their baby/babies but run into significant barriers, and yet they feel so much externalized and internalized pressure to nurse that it starts to erode their parenting confidence and their sense of self. Exclusive nursing can be a difficult thing to establish even in the best of circumstances, and when there are issues such as low milk production, trouble latching, or chronic blocked ducts, feeding your baby can become all-consuming. I have worked with many new parents who describe hellish conditions — mastitis so severe that they need to be hospitalized, nipples that become torn apart due to latch issues, and feeding cycles that leave parents no time for rest.

Here's how one parent described the impact that nursing had on her:

> I was told to try and feed the baby for twenty minutes on each breast. But the baby kept falling asleep and my milk didn't flow very fast, so I had to attach a small tube to my breast and pour pumped milk into it, which was impossible to do alone so I always needed to have someone with me when I was feeding the baby. It was messy and frustrating, and each feed took about over an hour. After I was done, I couldn't rest because then I needed to pump each breast for twenty minutes to stimulate more milk production. I hardly got any milk when pumping, and I would obsess about it, but the lactation consultant kept telling me to trust my body and that how much I pumped wasn't a reflection of how much I had. Once I was done pumping, I had to

clean and sterilize everything, and by the time that was done it was time to feed the baby again because I was supposed to feed him every two to three hours. This went on for weeks. I was so exhausted that all I can remember from the first month of my baby's life is crying and feeling like a failure. We spent almost $3,000 on lactation-consultant fees, herbs and medications, a tongue-tie release procedure, and all the pumping supplies and equipment. Although he did eventually latch, I never was able to breastfeed him exclusively and had to buy formula and bottles anyway. It was one of the worst experiences of my life and every time I would nurse him it *hurt*. But I couldn't stop because I felt like I was supposed to breastfeed, and I'd worked so hard to get here. We wanted two kids, but I don't think we will have a second because I can't go through that again. The strange thing is that if I had another baby I probably would try and breastfeed them because I would want to see if I could do it right this time.

I have heard this story in many different iterations from parents over the years. These parents wanted to nurse because they thought it was best, and though they knew it could be difficult, they didn't (or couldn't) realize just how challenging it could be. The story goes like this: (1) pre-commit to nursing in pregnancy, (2) face unexpected barriers with nursing, (3) invest a substantial amount of time and money and energy into nursing, and (4) feel emotionally depleted or scarred from the experience. What makes it confusing to support parents who reach out for help with nursing is that their responses when being given the suggestion to stop vary widely. I either hear "when my doctor/midwife/lactation consultant/doula reminded me that I could stop if I didn't want to do it anymore, I was finally able to give myself permission to stop and I'm so grateful to them," *or* "when my doctor/midwife/lactation consultant/doula reminded me that I could stop if I didn't want to do it anymore, I felt completely unsupported, but I persevered in spite of them until we figured it out." When a parent is in the depths of nursing challenges, it's hard to predict whether they'll want to be encouraged to keep going or nudged to change course. But what is consistent is that the negative feelings or critical self-beliefs that emerge from this process can remain for years — sometimes into the children's teen years or adulthood — regardless of whether the parents were successful in meeting their nursing goals or not.

Growing concerns about the increased nursing pressure, shame, and even self-hate felt by parents who struggle to nurse (or don't want to) led activists, parents, and some health professionals to support a new campaign in 2016 called Fed-Is-Best. The idea is to encourage parents to make decisions about how they feed their babies that make sense for them and their circumstances, rather than trying to nurse at all costs. Backlash against this campaign by some nursing advocates has led to yet another new and trending campaign called Informed-Is-Best, which argues that parents are more likely to attempt and less likely to quit nursing if they have access to enough information or support, which the campaign aims to provide them. Responses to this newest campaign have been varied. It's true that some parents, particularly low-income parents, don't always have access to good information or support around nursing, and this is a concerning social issue.[9] But it's also true, as highlighted by the parent quoted earlier, that extensive support and information may still not be enough to make exclusive nursing easy or possible.

I fear that the impact of the Informed-Is-Best campaign will be continued parental shame, as it assumes that all new parents *should* nurse exclusively, and if they don't it's because they didn't know better or work hard enough. I'm also not convinced that information and support should be the core issues of nursing politics, because such an approach continues to centre on exclusive nursing as *the best way* and not simply *one way* to feed your baby/babies. My response to clients who feel judged by any of the nursing campaigns is to create their own internal mantra along the lines of Choice-Is-Best, meaning they get to make whatever choice they want about how to feed their baby/babies according to their own individual desires and circumstances, without the external commentary.

The push to privilege human milk is so intense that formula is sometimes demonized, erasing the fact that formula is, in many ways, a miracle. My father grew up in an impoverished community in rural Ontario, and he had twin sisters he never met because they died from failure to thrive, in large part because they didn't have access to formula. Nursing wasn't working for my grandma, and formula was not readily available in the community where they lived, so although she attempted to make her own formula by using a community recipe and also tried sending the babies to a wet nurse, they weren't able to recover from the difficult feeding start. My grandmother carried the grief of that loss through the rest of her life. She often talked about her deep pain of not being able to help the twins, yet stories like hers are common throughout history. Nursing advocates often suggest that nursing is natural because "women have done it for thousands of years," overlooking the fact that nursing has always been complicated and that many babies who weren't able to get adequate nutrition through exclusive nursing didn't survive. While new parents have historically nursed, there have also always been parents who struggled to nurse and found creative ways to feed their babies, such as wet nursing or (often disastrous) attempts at making homemade formula with ingredients such as cow's milk, cream, water, and honey.[10]

While formula may be a miracle, formula companies are not. There are very strict marketing rules that formula companies are expected to comply with, such as not idealizing formula or discouraging nursing, and providing consumers with accurate information about the quality of the product, but it's questionable how compliant companies are. Nestlé, in particular, was accused of engaging in deeply unethical — and deadly — marketing practices in the 1970s by knowingly targeting their formula products to parents in low-income communities that did not have easy access to the necessary resources to safely prepare it. Safe formula use requires access to clean water, bottle sterilization equipment, and refrigeration. It also requires that parents be readily able to afford to continuously keep buying formula, which is very expensive, which was not the case for the families Nestlé was marketing to. In regions of the world that lacked clean-water infrastructure, Nestlé's marketing implied that formula was both easier and superior to human milk, so as you would expect, many parents made the switch and gave up nursing. The result was that many parents prepared formula in unsanitary ways, such as with water that wasn't clean and boiled for infant safety, in part because for many families the only sanitation and preparation instructions provided were written in languages they didn't speak. Poorer parents would sometimes ration formula portions, leading to malnutrition. Children's lives were lost because of Nestlé's marketing strategy and profit-seeking agenda, which is a completely different motivation for formula use than the personal choice of a parent.

While a boycott of Nestlé products in Canada and the United States, as well as changes to formula marketing, have attempted to halt the dangerous marketing strategies, donated sample products from formula companies to vulnerable families continues to be a problem. Formula companies send free samples to families with new babies in hospitals, as well as to individuals' homes. I remember being confused about how so many formula companies knew I'd had a baby; I got four different samples in the mail after my first child was born! This happens both domestically and internationally. Lactation consultant and naturopathic doctor Dr. Laura Kent-Davidson, who works on global strategies to ensure the safe and nutritious feeding of babies all over the world, explains that this is a significant problem in refugee communities, as formula donations arrive when there's a concern that babies could be in need. While there's nothing inherently wrong with sending food for infants, Kent-Davidson says the problem is that nursing parents are given formula without an assessment of whether they want or need it. Often they will switch to formula and nurse their child less, which leads to their milk supply dropping or full weaning. This can have serious consequences on infant health because of concerns about safe feeding, but also because the donations of formula are short-lived. Far too often, these parents switch to formula when it's free only to very soon have to pay out-of-pocket, and they're not given any support to re-lactate if they can't afford ongoing formula. Kent-Davidson explains that the Emergency Nutrition Network organized an interagency publication of a comprehensive document called *The Operational Guidance on Infant Feeding in Emergencies*, which outlines the safest and most ethical practices that should be followed in times of crisis, but not all organizations or even governments are following it (or are aware of it).

The Case for Normalizing Feeding Diversity

Many parents who choose to bottle-feed feel like they need to justify their choice every time they feed their baby in front of new people, even when there is pumped milk in the bottle. One bottle-feeding friend said that every time she went to a parent group and pulled out a bottle, she would try to pre-emptively avoid judgment from others by explaining herself; she had a rehearsed speech that outlined all of the ways in which she'd desperately tried to nurse but it hadn't worked out. She said that she only heard outright verbal judgment or unsolicited advice once or twice and that most people she told were very supportive and empathetic about what she had gone through. But "I just needed them to know I tried," she said, "so they would know that I'm a good mom and that I did my best."

It feels as though our current cultural discourse about nursing is that every parent should at least try it, and it's okay(ish) if they can't, but they have to earn their way out of nursing by trying everything possible before giving up. You can't just opt not to nurse — you have to have a good reason in order to avoid pressure from others, and even from yourself. There is very little room for parents to be indifferent to feeding their baby or to choose formula without attempting nursing. It's accepted in cases of adopted children, children born via surrogacy, or prior medical conditions that interfere with nursing. Yet even in these cases, there is often pressure to induce lactation or to source donated human milk, which is often a difficult, time-consuming, and expensive venture.

There's a lot of focus on the benefits of human milk for babies and nursing parents, but the accuracy of this information is sometimes troubling. Claims that have been used by pro-nursing campaigns have suggested that while being exclusively nursed, babies have fewer colds, infections, allergies, and intestinal issues, as well as lower rates of SIDS and necrotizing enterocolitis (NEC), and that the long-term benefits include lower risk for diabetes, juvenile arthritis, childhood cancer, meningitis, pneumonia, urinary tract infections, and Crohn's disease, as well as higher IQ.[11] As for the nursing parents, proposed benefits while nursing include free birth control, weight loss, healthy bonding, reduced stress and depression, increased friendships (presumably from hanging out with other nursing parents), and the long-term benefits cited include things like lower risk for cancer and osteoporosis.[12] Unfortunately, there just isn't the evidence to support all of these claims. In her book *Cribsheet*, Dr. Emily Oster pulls apart the significant research studies on human milk and formula to help parents differentiate between high-quality research (e.g., those that factor in things like parental wealth) on the subject versus low quality research (e.g., those that suggest correlation is causation).[13] She argues that some of the most well-respected research on nursing, stemming from twin studies, does find some benefits to human milk over formula, but they aren't nearly as impressive as what is commonly claimed. Exclusively nursed babies have fewer allergic rashes, intestinal disorders, and risk of NEC *while they are being exclusively nursed*, and parents who nurse do have a lower risk of breast cancer.[14] So is breast actually best? It does have some very specific benefits, but you can let go of your worry that if you give your babies formula they will have a lower IQ. And do remember that formula and/or bottle-feeding *also* has some very specific benefits, because it allows parents to actively monitor how much food their baby/babies are getting and to share feeding responsibilities with others, allowing for more rest for primary parents and more bonding for co-parents.

The politics of feeding babies are confusing and divisive, but so too can be the experience of nursing itself. Many clients have told me that nursing eroded their bodily autonomy, which is why I am such a big fan of infant feeding strategies that do not place the burden solely on the birth parent. Sharing the responsibility of feeding a baby provides both body freedom and freedom of movement. I have worked with many exclusively nursing clients who were so anxious about causing nipple confusion that they hesitated to introduce a bottle during their first few weeks (or months) of nursing, only to find that when they finally wanted to use a bottle, their baby wouldn't drink from it. This can cause incredible frustration and feelings of being trapped as parents realize that they can only be away from their baby for an hour or two at a time and they are constantly on-call overnight. Although I see this show up commonly toward the end of parental leave, when exclusively nursing parents are in a panic about how their baby will drink milk without them and are desperately experimenting with bottles, cups, and straws, I also see this panic show up in the first few weeks postpartum, as nursing parents come face to face with the reality that overnight help is so limited. This sets up an impossible task for nursing parents, as they are told to protect their sleep *and* to feed their baby on demand. Their chunks of sleep might amount to three or four consecutive hours, and that's if they're lucky. If they're not, their sleep might only come in thirty-minute sprints. That kind of disrupted sleep is devastating for someone's mood and can create a sleep emergency whereby parents are so sleep-deprived that they start to feel suicidal or lose touch with reality.

I have witnessed lots of birthers, many of whom have campaigned for reproductive rights to birth control and safe and legal termination, struggle to give themselves permission to maintain body autonomy when it comes to nursing. The quest for equity in reproduction must include feeding diversity and recognize the negative emotional impact of privileging exclusive nursing above all. There are so many ways to feed a baby — feeding milk directly from the body, formula feeding, pumping and bottle-feeding, using donated milk, or any combination that works for you and your family. In some queer families that have more than one parent who can lactate, non-birth parents also have the option of inducing lactation to share the work of producing milk. Instead of asking "How can I exclusively nurse my baby/babies?" I encourage parents to approach the question from a feeding diversity framework, which instead asks "What *ways* of feeding best respect the physical and emotional needs of every member of this family?"

Extended Food Pressure

The politics of feeding children continues beyond infancy, with many parents struggling with the introduction of solids. It can be baffling to realize the small number of calories and nutrients older babies and toddlers need compared to the energy that they put out. I remember watching my fifteen-month-old child run around wildly at the park, despite the fact that he was on day three of only consuming milk and a few bites of pear, and wondering how on earth he could have enough energy to cause such chaos on so little food. The worry that older babies are eating enough is compounded by the abundance of divergent advice about the best way to introduce solids. Do you try baby-led weaning? Make your own baby food? Buy organic baby food from the store? The pressure to get the introduction of solid foods "right" and establish healthy food practices is a clear demonstration of the *invest up front* value of impossible-parenting culture. Parents are somehow expected to master the art of ensuring their children eat lots of fruits and veggies and not too much sugar or processed food, but simultaneously not create food stress that could encourage disordered eating.

Many parents find this an impossible task, but parents of severely picky eaters or of children with eating (dis)abilities or food restrictions feel this even more intensely. One client told me that the only thing her nineteen-month-old will eat is chicken nuggets and apples, and she has received so much unsolicited advice that she dreads eating with friends or extended family. "Of course I have tried offering other foods! Yes, I have tried not offering chicken nuggets. I have tried it all! But I can't shove food down his throat." Having a child with an anaphylactic allergy can have devastating consequences on parental mental health, related to the trauma of watching your child have an allergic reaction and feeling hypervigilant about keeping them safe. Anaphylactic allergies bring parents face to face with the reminder that they cannot fully control the health and safety of their children. Sending children with allergies to daycare, or even going out into public spaces such as play centres or restaurants, can be terrifying, despite the efforts to make most child centres nut-free.

What is the cost of all of this pressure and confusion? It hurts. It hurts our parenting self-confidence. It hurts our mental health. It's hurts our bodies. In the last few chapters, I've outlined the many ways in which the current culture of parenting can feel impossible, but the good news is that we are not damned to this pain. Whether you noticed this pain related to fertility and birth, sleep, relationships, nursing, or your body, there are ways to heal or at least manage the hurt in ways that feel more supported. And they will be shared in part 3, Healing.

PART 3

HEALING

When I first started proposing this book idea, the parents I spoke with would invariably respond by agreeing with all the ways that parenting felt impossible, and then quickly follow that up with "So what do I do about it?!" If you're feeling a little lost in how much of this feels wrong, fear not! The final section of this book is filled with strategies to make the impossible possible again. In these next chapters, I discuss strategies for cultivating resistance to these external pressures, and I outline a variety of coping tools to help you fill your mental health tool box with solutions that help you get through your personal day-to-day challenges.

I'm aware that naming all the ways in which parenting has become impossible can bring up a lot of contradictory emotions. At times, it feels validating, because it gives us a language to talk about what's happening in the subtext of our parenting lives, and it can feel good to know that your personal story is part of a larger collective one. Other times, it feels overwhelming and hopeless. My intention with the Hurting section is not to create a doomsday feeling. I include it because it feels critical to highlight all the ways in which the socio-political culture of parenting impacts our mental health before we can create personalized healing plans. In their book *Burnout*, Emily and Amelia Nagoski remind readers to always keep in mind who the "true enemy" is (this term will be familiar to fans of *The Hunger Games*); they name the true enemy as the *patriarchy*.[1] I agree, but I'm more inclined to use Elisabeth Schüssler Fiorenza's term the *kyriarchy*, from the Greek *kyrios*, meaning lord or master (without the strictly male or paternal aspect inherent in *patriarchy*). The term is used as a non-gender-based descriptor of systems of power, and I prefer it because it incorporates the many different structures that affect us, including race, gender, class, religion, age, and sexual orientation. All of these create inequitable levels of privilege and power, and they all overlap and intersect. Our individual experiences with perinatal mental health are not created in a vacuum!

I'll get off my sociological soapbox and save this subject for my academic papers, but what I hope you take away from this is that the pain you feel in parenting *must* be understood from a cultural perspective and not just an individual one. There's a reason you feel parent guilt when you haven't done anything wrong. There's a reason you're so anxious for your kids to meet particular outcomes. There's a reason you feel like you can't do it all. And the reason isn't that you're a personal failure — it's that impossible-parenting culture is failing *us*. And the further we are from access to power and privilege, the more acutely we feel this pain. I ask that you hold on to that thought while you create a pathway to caring for yourself — and your family — differently.

EIGHT

RECOVERY

We are all recovering from something.

— Dawn Nickel

It's easy to feel lost and overwhelmed when you've been struggling with your mood, and the demands of having a baby/babies can make it extra challenging to know what to do about it. It can be very helpful to create a Perinatal Mood Recovery Plan, which is a tool for parents to identify detailed action items that have the potential to help them feel better. This chapter offers a broad overview of topics and strategies to consider when building your personalized plan, which ideally you would create or share with your mental health team. In the chapters that follow I provide very specific exercises to support you through the day-to-day challenges of parenting when you're struggling with your emotional health.

POSTPARTUM RESILIENCY

There is a lot to be hopeful for when creating a Perinatal Mood Recovery Plan, because as we continue to learn more about the individual, collective, and biological experience of perinatal mood, we are also learning more about what can protect parents from developing PMADs, or at least minimize their impact. When we acknowledge that many aspects of the postpartum period feel tough as hell, it creates the space for a culture of *postpartum resiliency* to emerge. I define postpartum resiliency as the ability to cope with and endure any obstacles or challenges that emerge during the postpartum experience, while simultaneously embracing and integrating the joyful and positive moments into one's parenting experience. One of my favourite papers on this topic was written by Stephanie Knaak, who conducted a qualitative research study to explore what factors contribute to a positive postpartum experience.[1] I've used her work to identify six pillars that parents can focus on to help develop postpartum resiliency. Together, these pillars form a powerful framework to anchor yourself in, helping parents break through the good-parent/bad-parent dichotomy.

Pillar One — Adequate Self-Care: Parents who purposefully protect guilt-free and unapologetic self-care time have an easier time with postpartum adjustment. How each parent does this is unique, rooted in the activities and boundaries that are important to them, rather than in the culture of impossible parenting's prescriptive style of self-care. While there's more on the switch from self-care to what I call self-parenting in chapter eleven, I want to highlight the importance of feeling entitled to self-care. You, and all parents, deserve to have your care needs met, even though it is often hard to know what care we need to give ourselves, what we need from others, and what we have to give. Parenting is only *one* aspect of your identity. In order to be fully human, parents have to support multiple aspects of their identities.

Pillar Two — Having Enough Help: Help with parenting means different things to different people, but generally it refers to having support with: the day-to-day tasks of caring for a baby/babies, such as comforting and feeding; keeping a household running, such as making meals and completing chores; and emotional help, such as providing stimulating conversation and the space to complain. These needs change day to day and often require a team of friends, family, and paid workers (if it's an option) to be met with relative ease. While it's not surprising that new parents need help, there are two important things to consider, in order for help to feel supportive and not simply another burden. The first is that just like self-care, parents who don't feel guilty about asking for help but instead see it as a healthy part of parenting have smoother postpartum experiences.[2] The second is that parents must feel a sense of control over what kind of help they ask for and who they receive it from.

Postpartum practices such as "doing-the-month" or a "lay-in" are non-Western systems of support designed to maximize rest and recovery in the first month of parenting. How they are practised varies from region to region, but generally these practices include live-in and hands-on help, as well as a nourishing diet, for birthers in the first thirty to forty days postpartum. This practice has been romanticized and appropriated by some Western parenting experts and suggested as well-meaning advice in an effort to increase the amount of support for postpartum parents. However, there are many challenges that Western families face when trying to organize live-in care because most of us don't have the socio-economic systems in place to facilitate it easily. It puts the burden of organizing care onto new parents, and it assumes they have family members who are available for an entire month or that they have enough financial resources to hire a full-time doula or live-in nanny. The global research on the experience of "doing-the month" suggests that parents only find these practices helpful if they have positive relationships with their live-in caregivers and have a personal desire for this kind of support.[3] If parents feel forced to participate in this process or have tense relationships with in-laws or family members, this kind of help is, understandably, a hindrance to their postpartum mood.[4]

I think what's important to remember about the concept of having enough help is that the early postpartum period is a vulnerable time for parents and they need to be accommodated by their community. The sleep deprivation, stress of newborn care, and physical recovery for those who gave birth requires more resources than can be provided by one or two people. Often that support needs to be explicitly negotiated, and community members should never assume that they know what you need (or don't need). I'm also aware that the pandemic has halted brilliantly negotiated support plans because of limitations in people coming to your home.

Pillar Three — Feeling Understood: Having a collection of people who validate our feelings, offer solidarity, and can provide feedback to the many parenting questions — such as "Is this normal!?" — is critical to breaking through the feelings of loneliness and isolation that come with being a new parent. Interestingly, I've found that close friends with kids may or may not be the people who help us feel understood. The people we like to work or party with may not share our parenting philosophies, and this isn't necessarily unusual or problematic, but it is sometimes surprising. Our parenting ideology and practices often shape our parenting identity, which has led to an increase of parenting subcultures, such as attachment parents, tiger parents, dolphin parents, free-range parents, or unicorn parents. Seeking inclusion in a defined parenting group such as these isn't necessary and sometimes leads to feelings of inferiority or superiority, but generally parents who find a parenting group or groups that are a good fit, either online or in person, see them as invaluable for their mental health. I know parenting subcultures can be a loaded topic and I promise to return to this in chapter twelve, but the reason I keep coming back to this concept of community/ collective care is that when parents are able to find a supportive community, it is incredibly protective to their mental health.

Pillar Four — Stress Management: While we can't control external sources of stress in our lives, parents who use stress-management techniques and practice surrendering to circumstances and events that are out of their control find the adjustment to parenting easier. Life can throw some very difficult situations our way during the postpartum period, including preterm babies, traumatic births, job loss, or death of loved ones, and we need to feel as though we have enough internal resources and coping skills to navigate the storm. This doesn't mean we don't feel stress or anxiety when things go awry. It just means we are able to self-soothe, ground ourselves, and feel hopeful that we will survive each difficult circumstance. Even without additional life stressors, handling the competing demands and responsibilities of parenthood is stressful enough and we deserve support in managing our personal set of stressors. Building up your internal resources and bolstering stress-management strategies is something that a skilled therapist can really help with.

Pillar Five — Feeling Ready for the Baby: Getting enough rest before the baby/babies arrive and feeling confident that you know enough to successfully care for them can make a big difference to your mood in the early postpartum days. Parents of preterm babies often struggle with not feeling ready, as do parents with older children who feel like time has passed too quickly and they aren't adequately prepared — they might have unassembled baby furniture or piles of baby laundry to wash and put away. While parents can't control when they meet their baby/babies for the first time, I think it's ideal when pregnant parents feel so prepared and sick of being pregnant that they get bored and wake up every morning hoping that today is the day they go into labour. These parents get a protective mood benefit from this frustrating experience.

Pillar Six — Having Realistic Expectations: As I've suggested, every new parent experiences a discrepancy between what they think life with a newborn(s) will be like and the reality. The smaller the gap, the easier the transition to the new reality, so I often encourage soon-to-be parents to identify and become familiar with the vision they have for their birth and postpartum life. Once they have a sense of what they're expecting, I encourage them to find a variety of birth and postpartum stories that both reflect and don't reflect their vision. The goal is not to induce anxiety or burst their idealized vision, nor is it to reinforce naive optimism, but instead it's to foster a non-outcomes-focused vision where they can both feel hopeful and know that they can cope, regardless of how birth and postpartum unfold. It's also important to acknowledge that we are all trying to figure out how to parent in the culture of impossible parenting, and it's worth questioning and evaluating where our idealized visions of parenting come from.

Developing a sense of resiliency is helpful for all parents, but this is not a foolproof prevention strategy for bypassing a PMAD, because perinatal mood is complex and influenced by a variety of factors outside of our control. The six pillars of postpartum resiliency offer an interesting starting place to think about what goals we have for ourselves and how we might build a bridge toward those goals.

CULTIVATING A PERINATAL MOOD RECOVERY PLAN

To build a template for your Perinatal Mood Recovery Plan, it's helpful to revisit the Perinatal Mood Framework from chapter two. You can create a personalized plan at any time, whether you have been diagnosed with a PMAD or you suspect you might have a PMAD. You can even create one if you are feeling emotionally healthy but are concerned about what becoming a parent will do to your mood, in which case you can simply change the name to Perinatal Mood Protection Plan.

Any plan that you create will need to be adaptable as you learn more about what works and what doesn't. I encourage you to imagine that you're conducting a mood experiment wherein you are both the test subject and the scientist. Scientists never expect to get any experiment right the first time. They understand that each failed attempt provides them new information and brings them closer to understanding what will lead to success. The same is also true when we are trying to determine which strategies will help us manage our mood. As you read through these sections, take note of which tools resonate with you and get you excited, and which ones feel annoying or silly. Try out lots of tools and exercises and don't be afraid to adapt them as you build your Mood-Managing Tool Box, which is an intentional list of actions you can take when you're feeling emotionally charged or ungrounded. Once you have what you need, you can simply leave the rest, knowing you can return to the unused tools at any time if things shift. This is not dissimilar to experimenting with parenting strategies, such as figuring out how to soothe a crying baby or manage a tantrum. Often our parenting tricks work for a time, but soon our kids develop and outgrow them. We are constantly sent back to the drawing board to tweak old strategies and gather new ones.

Please note that the self-support strategies listed here are for those who have the emotional bandwidth to engage in experimenting. Psychosis, mania, or suicidal planning are medical emergencies that require immediate intervention.

Biological Influences

Biological support is a big, broad category that will mean different things to different people. I always suggest that perinatal clients who are having a tough time with their mood start by talking to their family doctor (if they haven't already), and my favourite doctors are the ones that order lab tests to rule out factors that can contribute to low or anxious mood, such as thyroid malfunction. I believe that medicinal support can be an important part of PMAD recovery, but I also respect that the term *medicine* is often associated with allopathic medicine (conventional medicine, provided by someone with an MD), and I know that it's not the only type of medicine that parents use. It's important that we interpret concepts such as health and wellness using an anti-oppressive, intersectional, and cross-cultural perspective, remembering that there are many different approaches to healing the human body. Whatever medicinal system(s) you use, such as allopathic, Chinese, naturopathic, Ayurvedic, or Indigenous, I encourage you to find a qualified doctor that you trust, and ideally someone who specializes in perinatal health.

CHALLENGE PROBLEMATIC THOUGHT PATTERNS AND NARRATIVES

If there is one thing I wish I could give every new parent, it's a therapist that they trust and feel connected to. If it's possible for you to work with a therapist one on one, start by looking for someone who has a deep understanding of perinatal mood. You don't need to have a clinical diagnosis of a PMAD to benefit from talking to a therapist; there is value in processing the experience of becoming a parent and all the identity changes that come with it. I wouldn't get too worried about what approach to therapy your therapist uses; the most significant predictor of therapeutic success is arguably the alliance you feel to your therapist.[5] Being respected and deeply listened to, and having your feelings validated by someone with whom you have a solid rapport, is critical to doing work that by nature requires you to be vulnerable.

When starting with new clients with PPD/A, I often limit a deep exploration of their own childhood and instead concentrate on understanding their current experience, with a forward-looking approach that focuses on developing coping tools, processing emotions, and setting up a family system that maximizes support for their needs while respecting their access to resources. I start here because some parents find that fixating on the ways in which their own parent(s) failed them increases their anxious worries that they will permanently damage their children/babies. Analysis of our past is important work, but it's a big request to make of someone who might only be sleeping for three hours at a time and can't even pee alone.

If you're looking to work through birth or reproductive trauma, you will want to ensure that your therapist has been trained in a trauma-specific modality such as eye movement desensitization and reprocessing (EMDR), brain spotting, or sensory motor therapy. If you are able, shop around for a therapist until you find the right fit. If finances are a concern, don't be afraid to ask if they offer any sliding-scale spots, meaning the session fee is reduced to make it more affordable. They may not, but some therapists do and may not advertise it.

Group therapy can also be very supportive for PPD/A and is usually more affordable or even free. Ask your family doctor for a referral to any hospital programs that are offered, and check out community organizations that run postpartum groups. The not-for-profit I run, Postpartum Support Toronto (PPSTO), offers free online skill-building courses for new parents, run by local counsellors, on topics such as dialectical behaviour therapy (DBT) for postpartum, cultivating self-compassion, expressive arts tools, and overcoming parenting guilt.

Regardless of where you find therapeutic support, it's worthwhile to find a place where you can dump out all the things that have been rattling in your head, have someone help you process your feelings, and figure out what to do with the dark thoughts.

REDUCE RISK FACTORS AND SOLVE SOLVABLE PROBLEMS

Ideally, we would reduce our exposure to some of the risk factors that are associated with PMADs, such as opting not to move or renovate our homes during pregnancy or early postpartum, but many of the risk factors are not within our control. Often I ask clients to make a list of all of the problems they are currently facing, and together we identify which aspects of these problems are solvable or time-limited, such as "My partner is going away for work for a week and I don't know how I'll cope," and which ones needs to be endured for an undetermined amount of time, such as "My partner works evenings, the baby cries non-stop from 4:00 p.m. to 7:00 p.m., and I feel like I can't cope." For the unsolvables, I suggest adopting an *endurance-based mindset*, meaning that you recognize the limits of your control and prepare to endure what feels difficult. Accepting the challenging parts of postpartum life doesn't mean you like them or that you don't get to feel sad or angry about your circumstances, it just frees up emotional space by laying down your resistance to what you can't control. I know that this is easier said than done, which is why many of the tools outlined in the chapters to come are designed to help you cultivate an endurance-based mindset.

RESIST THE CULTURE OF IMPOSSIBLE PARENTING

Parenting culture continuously shifts and adapts, and it's time for the culture of impossible parenting to come to an end because of the negative impact it has on families, whether or not a parent develops a PMAD. I encourage you to find ways to resist it as we clumsily move toward a new culture of parenting. While I am not totally sure I know what that will look like yet, nor do I suggest that I have the solution, I dream of a culture of postpartum resiliency that is rooted in compassion, curiosity, inclusion, and anti-oppressive cultural humility. I hope that the concepts in this book inspire increased public discussion about how to deconstruct the culture of impossible parenting and build a culture of support-focused parenting.

There are many ways to resist the culture of impossible parenting on an individual level. It may be as simple as talking openly about it and challenging its messages when you see them come up in the media, in your personal relationships, or with other parents. Often it involves challenging the problematic messages you have internalized and finding new ways to talk to ourselves. I suggest four strategies to cultivate internal resistance:

1. Soften into the energy of *self-permission* and allow your feelings, honour your desires, and accept the difficult circumstances outside of your control, which can help guard against the values of *danger is all around us* and *keep it natural*.

2. Adopt a *family-centred parenting* approach to organizing family systems and decision-making, as opposed to a child-centred approach, as a way to reconceptualize the values of *invest up front* and *make every moment magical*.

3. Shift from the value of *prescriptive self-care* to *self-parenting* to bring more awareness and responsiveness to your needs and wants in creative ways.

4. Think through how to *be less alone*, by communicating your needs and gently seeking new community members, to help you resist the value of *the more you sacrifice, the more you love*.

Recovering from a PMAD is an amazing feat, but I also want to gently note that when you come out the other side, you may be filled with grief about what it robbed from you. I didn't even realize how much I had missed out on until my friends started having their own babies, and I realized what joy some postpartum families experience. It made me sad and jealous to watch other parents seem to navigate it all so gracefully — so much so that I desperately wanted another baby with my partner, Janna. I had sworn I would never have another baby, but all of a sudden, I felt the strong need for a do-over. As I painfully came to the realization that it wasn't going to happen for us, I realized that grief from experiences that we long for but will never have is a particularly tricky type of grief to process, because there is no anchor or name for it. The challenge with grief is that there isn't much to do about it other than learn how to hold it. I can tell you that it helps to find meaning in the experience. For me, that meaning came from supporting others through perinatal mood hell, which I think is common for many of us who survived a PMAD, but it doesn't have to be that. You might focus on how much you learned about yourself or how you and your partner are now really clear about what it looks like to effectively support each other. You don't need to be grateful and you certainly don't need to try to make it positive — because it *wasn't* — but it can help to integrate the experience in a reflective way.

NINE

SELF-PERMISSION

Pleasure is the point. Feeling good is not frivolous, it's freedom.

— Adrienne Maree Brown

I want to talk about internal permission, meaning what we think is okay for us to do or not do. Our relationship to what feels allowable changes significantly when we have children. Many of us have fully stepped into our adult freedom by the time we become parents and have long let go of needing a hall pass to go to the washroom or hoping our parents will let us stay out past our curfew. While adult freedom certainly comes with adult responsibilities, such as showing up to work so we can pay our bills on time, catering to our individual needs and whims can be deeply satisfying. I think many parents feel unsettled when they realize that their freedom has been restricted by the needs of young children. Parents who nurse exclusively often talk about the tricky dance of getting out of the house but always needing to be home within two hours to feed the baby. There are memes about mastering the art of using the toilet one-handed because you're also holding a baby. For me, that unsettled feeling began the day I realized that if I wanted to walk to the store by myself, a task that would take ten minutes alone or thirty minutes with the baby, someone would have to grant me permission by agreeing to take him. As a result of constantly working to meet the needs of our children, much of early parenting is dominated by restriction and making our own needs smaller.

Parents are bombarded with messages that tell them that if they don't take care of themselves first, they can't take care of their children; you may be familiar with warning messages such as "You can't drink from an empty cup." Yet I have known many parents who care beautifully for the needs of their children, but who can't seem to access the resources to take care of themselves the way they want to. There just isn't enough time. Or energy. Or emotional space. The culture of impossible parenting belief that *the more you sacrifice, the more you love* is extra confusing alongside the *prescriptive self-care* value that demands we take care of ourselves first. There seems to be a subtle suggestion that the reason to take care of ourselves is not for our own benefit or because we are a person with our own feelings and needs that need to be tended to, but instead it's so that we don't compromise our ability to take care of our children properly. Inevitably this leads to frustration, as self-care becomes another to-do on our daily chore list. This process creates a deep sense of self-denial, as parents get skilled at going without for the sake of their children. It's this self-denial that we need to address.

RADICAL SELF-PERMISSION

Cultivating a deep sense of *radical self-permission* is a critical part of healthy parental mental wellness. The concept of radical self-permission is rooted in the work of radical self-compassion or radical self-acceptance developed by authors Tara Brach, Kristin Neff, and Kelly McGonigal, in which they suggest that we cultivate an attitude of "allowing what is" without trying to change it, being kind to the parts of ourselves we like the least, and laying down resistance to difficult circumstances out of our control. My own take on this concept has emerged through watching my clients who have been living in a prolonged state of self-denial start to come alive again as they begin reconnecting with a deep sense of what they need to feel fully human. How is this approach to self-care different? Radical self-permission does ask parents to identify their personal needs, but it's equally about cultivating a *sense of entitlement to feel desire*. So much of the conversation about parental needs in the postpartum period is wrapped up in meeting their biological needs, such as sleeping, eating, or showering, with the unspoken expectation that pleasure and desire (outside of taking pleasure in your role as a parent) should be denied and replaced with joyful self-sacrifice. So many of the messages new parents receive ask them to embrace self-denial, which disconnects them from important parts of their identity, such as their sexual self, their fun self, or their productive self. Remembering internal desire allows parents to stay connected to those parts, even if they can't fulfill their desire in that moment. There's nothing unusual about not being able to fulfill your desires at any given moment, and most of us have strategies that both honour and delay them. For example, we might feel like sleeping in instead of going to work, but we usually get up and go to work while simultaneously acknowledging that we're tired; we allow ourselves to want sleep and we look forward to sleeping in on the weekend.

Radical self-permission is a re-exploration of what we desire. It asks parents to (a) *know* what they desire, (b) *name* what they desire, and (c) *allow* their desire. It's a subversive act against the culture of impossible parenting! So how do you cultivate it?

I start by asking parents to give themselves permission to *know* what they desire. Often they will respond with "I know what I want! I want more sleep!," which is true, but I gently remind them that they need more sleep because they're operating with a sleep deficit, which is different from knowing what they desire. I ask them to shut their eyes, ground into their bodies, connect with their breath, and ask their body, "What am I truly desiring right now?" Then we wait and notice what sensations emerge, and try to locate where feelings like desire, joy, and pleasure live within their body, which is interestingly almost always in the chest/heart. I like to use this as an entry point to explore the experience of knowing when your body is communicating with an enthusiastic *yes* or a clear *no*. Often, we can find ourselves saying *yes* or *no* to things that we don't actually want, because we haven't slowed down enough to check in with our authentic desires. When we say yes out of a sense of obligation, it can quickly turn into resentment and a sense of feeling trapped. For example, if you say *yes* to a large birthday party for your one-year-old because you feel like your family expects that from you and all your other new-parent friends have done it, it's likely that you'll feel overwhelmed by the planning, grumpy about how your guests behave, and regretful of the expense. But if you say *yes* to a large birthday party for your one-year-old because you've been desiring more community connection, celebration, and fun, it's much more likely that you'll see the event as worth the resources you poured into it.

This exercise can be frustrating and confusing for some people. It can be difficult to distinguish between what our rational brain is telling us we want and what our intuitive bodies tell us we want. Often when we give our bodies a question to explore, our brains will pipe up first with a list of demands — "I want a full-time housekeeper" or "I want to go on vacation by myself" or "I want to go back to work." This is normal and okay! I ask clients to notice those thoughts and identity them as just the jumping-off place of what they desire, and I invite them to hold off on exploring those thoughts and see if their body is signalling a different or deeper desire. Once we have a sense of what both the body and the brain want, we can make meaning from the messages. I ask clients to give themselves permission to *name* what they desire. Usually the result is much more clearly defined. It often sounds like "I want to feel intellectually stimulated," "I am really desiring a sense of confidence about my parenting decisions," or "I am craving connection in my relationship," which opens up much more space for solutions.

Knowing what we want and clearly *naming* it brings a range of emotional responses with it. Sometimes these responses feel positive, creating excitement or motivation. But often it feels scary or self-indulgent to want what we want and devastating to realize that we can't have it right now. That's why it's important to give yourself permission to *allow* for what you desire and not to squash or deny it. Even if you can't have it. Even if you wish you didn't want it. I once had a client realize during this exercise that she deeply wanted autonomy over her body and didn't like nursing her child. She had worked really hard to establish breastfeeding and had no intention of quitting because of how much she had invested and because of the social pressures associated with nursing. She also felt guilty because she felt like a good mother would want to breastfeed. I encouraged her to experiment with radical self-permission and allow for her desire to wean without feeling the pressure to do anything with that information. Just knowing was enough for right then. Giving yourself permission to have your desires doesn't necessarily require you to like them or even take action, it just means that you stop resisting what *is*. This parent did continue to nurse exclusively for a few more months, but with lessened internal resistance to it, and she threw a celebratory party when her child was fully weaned.

Those of us with older children can often relate to what it feels like to lay down our resistance. We yield when our children have talked us into something, like going to the park or getting a chocolate bar at the grocery store, by pestering us until we say yes. We may not like what they're asking, but we sigh and respond with "fine," because it's easier to simply allow the minor transgression than continue to fight. My partner, Janna, successfully used this strategy to convince me to buy a minivan, which I resisted for many years because it symbolized the final nail in the coffin of my youth. They just kept casually mentioning "when we get the minivan," every time we talked about getting a new car, until I eventually gave in. We are now the proud owners of a bright red minivan and Janna is thrilled. While there is nothing more frustrating than rocking a baby to sleep and hoping to get a break, only to have them wake up and need to be rocked back down again, if we can accept that a nap isn't coming in the timeline we hoped for, while still honouring our desire for a break, it can reduce the internal tension and frustration in the moment.

When clients are struggling with the concept of laying down resistance, I often use labour contractions as a comparison. Although clearly not all parents labour with contractions, any parent who took a prenatal class learned to work *with* contractions, rather than tensing up and trying to stop them, because they are unavoidable and fighting them makes them more uncomfortable. Prenatal teachers teach parents how to relax into contractions and use a support team to bring as much comfort to the hurts-like-hell experience as possible. Similarly, if you find yourself wanting things that you wish you didn't, see what it's like to give yourself permission to own your wants and desires and give them a little more space. You may find it's easier that way.

Permission to Separate Tasks

Whenever I ask parents what they want for their children, they always give me some variation of the same three answers:

"I want them to be happy."
"I want them to be healthy."
"I want them to be successful."

Unfortunately, these are three impossible assignments for any parent. Think about how hard it is to make ourselves happy, let alone figuring out how to do that for someone else. It's not reasonable to expect people to be happy all the time, and how to build a happy life is a personal journey that you don't get to control. The idea that we can control the outcome of our health is also a misconception, as anyone who has had an accident or who lives with a chronic illness would testify. And success is not only relative, but it also requires that we take risks and face failures in order to build resilience. No one is straightforwardly or continuously successful. Social worker Natalie Grynpas says she reminds clients that they can't protect their children from having a human experience, even though it's painful to watch many of the usual aspects of it, such as heartbreak, disappointment, or exclusion.

You cannot control your children's life experiences, nor are you responsible for the choices they make as an adult, despite what impossible-parenting rhetoric tries to convince you of. Yes, parents influence and shape the lives of their children, but you are only *one* influence on your children's lives, and your actions as a parent cannot guarantee particular outcomes. Your kids are also influenced by life circumstances, family members, and their communities. They're influenced by teachers and peers and lovers and pets. They will make meaning about who they are in the world when they have personal wins and when they experience failure and setbacks. Your relationship with your children is (hopefully) one of the most long-term relationships you will have, and like in every relationship there will be times of connection and times of miscommunication, which will be true when your children are very small and also when they are adults.

It can be easy to get distracted by trying to control your baby/babies' birth, food, health, attachment, or sleep, because these early parenting tasks demand a lot of our time and resources. But I encourage you to remember that social determinants, such as poverty or citizenship, are more impactful aspects of our children's futures. Will they experience racism? Transphobia? Do they have a (dis)ability? Those will likely shape their life more than how they were fed in the first year. I think that one of the most impactful ways for parents to protect their children's futures is to engage in social justice work to promote equity and ensure that all children are provided appropriate accommodations to remove as many barriers to success as possible. The more we work together to eliminate discrimination and ensure that the most vulnerable families have their needs met, the less responsibility we feel for trying to create the perfect conditions for *our* children alone. When we acknowledge that each generation of children needs not only individual love and support but also collective love and support, we not only contribute to protecting our children's futures, but many children's futures. This is a community-oriented way of caring for children (rather than individualistic).

So, what *can* we control? Very little, unfortunately. Which is why it's important for you to give yourself permission to separate your tasks from your children's, meaning that you are only in charge of what you are responsible for, and they are in charge of what they are responsible for. This will obviously shift over time as they take on more responsibility, but here's an example of the type of fair and reasonable allocation of responsibility: you, the parent, are responsible for preparing meals for your ten-month-old child; they, the child, are responsible for eating them. You cannot make them eat (as those of us who have fought this battle can attest) and you cannot eat for them. Assigning yourself responsibility for their eating a full meal is folly; it's ultimately out of your control and a really great way to find yourself frustrated and covered in potatoes.

You can't build your children a pathway into the life that you dream for them, but sociologists Melissa Milkie and Catharine Warner note that many middle-class parents (in particular) attempt to do this through a process called *resource guarding*, which they define as "extensive maternal labour in the service of creating a thriving child who is distinguished as unique and ... set to achieve a similar or better place in the social hierarchy compared with his parents."[1] Essentially, it's the process of trying to make sure that our children have access to as many resources, such as money, high-quality food, or living in a "good" neighbourhood, in adulthood as they did in childhood. And ideally, they would have *more* of these than we were able to offer them. It's one of the reasons many parents with post-secondary degrees push their children to get a post-secondary degree, even if their child doesn't feel ready or interested. I personally understand the pull toward resource guarding; it comes from a fear of scarcity and worry that my children won't have enough access to resources, which is why I need to constantly remind myself of what my tasks are as a parent and what their tasks are. Alison Gopnik's book *The Gardener and the Carpenter* provides a beautiful image of what it means to have permission to separate tasks.[2] She encourages parents to liken their role as a parent to that of a gardener. They can plant and nourish and cultivate a garden with intention, but how the garden will grow and develop is unknowable, just as it is with children. This is in stark contrast to the metaphor of parents as carpenters, where they are building their children by following a set of rules and instructions that guarantee a particular outcome.

The feeling that they need to control the outcome of their children's lives fuels a significant amount of anxiety for parents. Have you ever been tasked with completing a work assignment but given no authority over other project members? Having full responsibility with limited authority is one of the most stressful things a person can experience, yet many parents live this reality every day. While this is an aspect of the *invest up front* value from the culture of impossible parenting, it doesn't have to be this way. Imagine the collective weight that would be released from parents' shoulders if we could rewrite this individualistic approach to parenting, and replace it with one that recognizes the complex social milieu into which children are born. I think this would go a long way to supporting a community-oriented approach to childrearing.

Even if you're on board to let go of your perceived control over the outcomes of your children's lives, it can be hard to know how to start. It's challenging because, as we've discussed, so much of parenting involves living in multiple timelines. There's our current timeline, where we have to meet the moment-to-moment needs of our children, such as stopping them from eating that cigarette butt they've just picked up at the park; there's the near-future timeline of what they need later in the day, such as making sure you're home from the park in time for their nap; and then there's the distant-future timeline, where you're making a mental note to teach them the risks of smoking as they grow older to reduce the likelihood that they'll smoke as an adult.

I suggest to my clients that when they feel overwhelmed or anxious about this kind of problem solving, they should figure out which timeline the current problem is happening in. Once they know, they can apply some strategies to manage their feelings. I often have them start with the question "Is this something I need to deal with right now?" If the answer is yes, then jump into action! If the answer is no, then ask if there's anything you can do now to support yourself in a future timeline, or if *future you* can deal with it. Developing a relationship with future you can be a powerful tool, because you can assign responsibilities to them to address potential problems that you can't currently address. For example, if you feel anxious about your baby being a future smoker because they tried to eat a cigarette butt in the park, then don't stop the anxious thought at the worst moment, where you're imagining finding your child smoking with their friends at age twelve. You don't get a lot of control over whether or not your children try smoking. Instead, take a moment to play the scenario through with a focus on your strengths and resilience to get through it. Remind yourself that you aren't actually experiencing that moment right now, and trust that *future you* will have the capacity to handle it *if* you ever have to live through that moment. Then allow it to be *future you*'s problem in that future timeline.

Sometimes we don't have faith that our future selves could handle our worst-case scenarios, and we can find ourselves stuck in a thought loop about them. While it can feel difficult to stop ruminating about potential issues, we can't pre-process experiences by anxiously imagining every worst-case scenario. But we can waste a ton of energy pre-suffering about what may or may not happen. We can easily find ourselves trapped in an imaginary terrible experience that isn't actually happening to us in the current moment. For example, I had a client who was very concerned about how they would manage going back to work after maternity leave, even though it was still months away. For the times when she found herself in an overwhelming fantasy of being too tired to effectively do her work tasks and then being called out for it, we practised the mindfulness skill of coming back to the current moment. We also worked on cultivating a strong sense of her resilient future self who would be able to cope with any obstacle when she returned to paid work. Although the worrisome images of the future never stopped popping into her head, she was able to learn how to work through them.

I won't pretend that difficult experiences won't happen in your future, but I will assure you that you only need to live through them when they're actually happening. Every painful or traumatic moment has a beginning, a middle, and an end, and playing them out in advance in your head on repeat won't make it any less painful when you get there. Thankfully, you only need to survive it once.

Permission to Feel Negative

It's very possible that someone, often someone with adult children, has told you to enjoy every moment while your kids are young. I think this is one of the most anxiety-provoking pieces of advice you can give a new parent.

You absolutely do not need to enjoy every moment. In fact, research suggests that our happiness goes down during the years that we have young children, increasing only when we are out of the grind years.[3] This suggests that parenting may be something you enjoy more upon reflection than in the moment, which makes sense because many parts of parenting are thoroughly unenjoyable. Getting screamed at by a two-year-old because you cut their sandwich into triangles instead of squares? Not that fun, really.

You have permission to grieve your old life, for as long as you like. You get to be frustrated about your lack of freedom, and about how you wish you could go on vacation. Or be angry at your partner for not being supportive in the way you imagined them to be. You are also allowed to have a mood disorder and be sad and anxious. It's common for parents to not like being on parental leave and miss paid work and it's common for parents with high-needs babies to feel disappointed about their experience of early parenting. I encourage you to name, and to own, the parts you don't like. That doesn't mean that you *like* these negative feelings, it just means that you accept them and give yourself permission to feel the full range of human emotions.

In 2018, reproductive psychiatrist Alexandra Sacks popularized the term *matrescence* in her successful TED Talk, which resonated with many new parents. Sacks defines *matrescence* as the bio-psycho-social transition of becoming a mother and compares the experience to the bio-psycho-social transition of becoming an adult through adolescence.[4] Both transitions, Sacks argues, are huge identity challenges that include significant hormonal shifts (particularly if you gave birth) and a lot of emotional processing. Much like our teen years, there is a lot of awkwardness involved in early parenting — but we don't normalize this awkward transition for new parents like we do for teens. Instead we tell them it's beautiful and to enjoy every moment. Can you imagine saying that to a teenager who started menstruating for the first time and is caught with an obvious leak in gym class? Neither can I.

One significant aspect of matrescence is maternal ambivalence, which is often described as the push and pull of mothering. "Sometimes you'll feel pulled toward your baby's needs and your identity as a mother, and sometimes you'll want to push it all away," says Sacks,[5] which I think applies not just to mothers but parents of all gender identities. Maternal ambivalence honours the fact that motherhood is a mixture of both good *and* bad experiences, and that this is totally normal and expected.[6] I would even suggest that feelings of ambiguity and ambivalence are only the tip of the iceberg, because the experiences of early parenting are much more expansive than just good *or* bad or good *and* bad. There are so many contradictory emotions that emerge while a person is developing their parental identity, and not just in the postpartum years, but also as part of the ongoing experience of parenting. It's normal to feel a strong sense of connection, sadness, joy, fear, pride, jealousy, or grief, sometimes simultaneously. Because parenting is messy, beautiful, complex, fun, and challenging, sometimes simultaneously. It gets to be all the things with all the feels!

When I'm working with my clients to give themselves permission to feel negative, we often do an exploration of their internal parts.[7] We are all composed of many internal parts, each of them serving a particular self-protective role. Consider a statement like "Part of me wants to go to bed right now and part of me wants to stay up and keep watching Netflix." This combination of internal parts creates our own unique Internal Parenting Team that I like to imagine coming together at a board meeting to discuss issues related to parenting. I like to get to know my clients' Internal Parenting Team, so we often draw a table and start to identify each member of the team one by one.

Here are some of the parenting parts I have met throughout the years:

The Perfectionist: This part is often critical. It points out all the things you're doing wrong and how everyone else does them better and more easily. Its protective function is to encourage you to engage in self-reflection about your role or behaviours as a parent, but unfortunately it chooses criticism as the pathway to do so.

The Heart: This part is filled with love and awe for your children. It didn't know it was possible to love someone so much and finds it a little overwhelming and such a privilege. It is often a lovely part that helps you build relationships with and enjoy your children.

The Screw-Up: This part feels like it's hopeless at learning how to parent, and often gives up and wants others to come and rescue it from its failings. This part brings awareness to the possibility that you don't have enough (or the correct) help or supports in place.

The "Stop It": This part knows that things are hard but doesn't want to be a downer, so it keeps telling all the other parts to shut up and get over it. Although it's a harsh voice that could use some self-compassion, it also helps you with emotional containment and keeps you moving forward to get everything done in the day.

The Screamer: This is the part that just stands up at the meeting and starts screaming. It tends to show up when it feels like there's danger everywhere and no one is taking things seriously, and it helps us take action.

The Grieving Child: This part is often your inner child who is coming to terms with the fact that your parent(s) went through a lot to raise you — or coming to terms with all the ways in which your parents didn't support you in childhood. It needs you to be tender as it processes the past.

The Policy Writer: This is the part that creates all your internal rules of how you think you should behave or feel as a parent. It then records them and makes sure that you are following them, and it often chastises you if you aren't following them correctly. Its function is to bring clarity, awareness, and accountability to how you want to show up for your children and what kind of experiences you want them to have.

The Researcher: This is the part that doesn't feel confident about your parenting decisions or doesn't know what to do when you face a challenge. It propels you to seek out information and solutions, which is sometimes helpful and sometimes makes things more confusing.

The Tired Parent: This part doesn't care about much — or anything — anymore. It's exhausted from life and wants it all to go away. This is an important part that shows up when you're in need of more sleep, rest, or downtime.

While these are some commons ones, it's worthwhile getting to know what your personal Internal Parenting Team looks like. Take some time to draw out each part, and even personify them with names (this makes it way more fun). This way you can start to build a relationship with each of them and learn how they work as a team. Get to know what it's like when each of them is present. Assume that they each have a purpose or a function. Ask them what activates them, or what they're trying to protect you from, so you can get a clear sense of what they need you to know. And then ask yourself who you want to be in charge of the internal parenting meetings. Often the loudest part will want to be in charge, but that doesn't mean that they make the best facilitator. I think the best facilitators are our wise parts or our compassionate parts. You can also develop new internal parenting parts and invite them to the meeting if it feels like there's a leadership gap.

Permission to Take Up Space

Finally, I would love for you to feel as though you have permission for your needs, wants, and desires to take up space. Lots of space. In the next chapter I outline some strategies for negotiating ways that each family member can get their needs met, but I want to conclude the chapter on self-permission with a call to action. Once you've gotten more comfortable with knowing, naming, and allowing what you want, it becomes easier to make it happen. Give yourself permission to ask, or even to just do what you want. I've had several clients express frustration that they are the default parent and need to ask their partners to watch the kids so they can go out, while their partners don't ask permission — they just announce their plans. I often encourage these clients to see what happens when they use their partner's strategy. Instead of "Can you watch the kids while I run to the bank?" try saying, "I'm going to run to the bank. You are fully in charge of the kids." Often their partners don't even notice the change, but it can feel very empowering for my clients.

If you aren't quite ready to express what you want, but find yourself feeling frustrated by the tension between what you want and what feels possible, try practising radical acceptance by saying yes and giving permission to your current circumstances. I learned this from a client who felt overwhelmed while trying to put her baby to sleep, as her child kept squirming and crying and scratching her as she tried to nurse, doing anything other than sleeping. As she felt the feelings of frustration and being trapped rise in her body, she stopped resisting them and started allowing them by saying yes in her head to everything that she was experiencing:

"Yes, I do want my baby to go to sleep."
"Yes, I do want to sit on the patio and have a drink with my partner."
"Yes, I do hate this moment."
"Yes, I do feel very frustrated."
"Yes, I do feel resentment toward my baby."
"Yes, all of these things are happening."

By allowing her experience to unfold and allowing her feelings to be self-validated, she was quickly able to come to terms with the situation and cope until the baby fell asleep.

Try saying yes to that which you can't control. It will oddly feel like you have more ability to cope.

TEN

FAMILY-CENTRED PARENTING

Your choices can be right for you but not necessarily
the best choices for other people. Why? You are not
other people.

— Emily Oster

The culture of impossible parenting centres children's needs, wants,
desires, and experiences as the cornerstone of family life, and
typically it's the primary parent who's responsible for figuring out
how to meet all these needs. We can trace the popularization and normalization of child-centred parenting to the rise of its sister ideologies:
intensive mothering and attachment parenting. Child-centred parenting is often touted as the progressive alternative to adult-centred parenting, whereby parents take an authoritarian approach to childrearing,
set clear rules, and exact punishments when behavioural expectations
are not met. Adult-centred parenting loves phrases such as "children
should be seen and not heard" or "be careful not to spoil your baby."

The shift to child-centred parenting coincided with the mass rise of
mothers entering the paid workforce, followed by the overall acceleration
of everyday life. Currently, time is our scarcest resource and providing

compassionate, undivided attention to anyone is challenging.[1] It makes sense that parents who desperately love their children adopt a child-centred parenting approach; how better to demonstrate your love than by giving your children your scarcest resource — your time and attention. Many parents of young children interpret *constant accessibility* to their children as quality time and a marker of good parenting.[2] But I invite you to challenge this belief and instead understand that this perceived need to be always available to our children is a by-product of the culture of impossible parenting, which prioritizes sacrifice, investment, and magic making. When parents aren't as readily available for their children as they imagined they would be, they tend to feel guilt for having biological, emotional, or economic needs that create barriers to their availability, such as needing to get adequate sleep, have alone time, or put their children in daycare so they can make money or have time off from the work of parenting. This guilt can quickly lead to parental burnout, where parents complain of feeling drained of energy; they crave rest but are unable to enjoy it because there's too much to do, and they feel overwhelmed by their long to-do lists.

Parenting isn't like other jobs. It's unrelenting. At our paid jobs, there are protective labour laws that limit the hours we can work and ensure we get bathroom and lunch breaks. But parenting work doesn't have a guaranteed end of day, and even when children are asleep, the hum of repetitive chores such as laundry and tidying calls to us, leaving us with very little leisure time. All families operate by developing a unique and complex internal organization that determines who does what, establishes the roles and responsibilities that are expected of each family member, and creates traditions and routines, which I call your *family systems*. Unfortunately, most families don't have enough resources or support to create child-centred family systems in a way that also protects their physical and mental health. Instead, they operate with a constant deficit, as the needs and desires of the children begin to trump every other need in the house. It's no wonder that research on mothers whose lives are significantly child-centred found them to be less satisfied with their overall lives.[3] Child-centred parenting also assumes that children have no internal resources such as adaptability or resilience, but that's both untrue and unhelpful. Children have historically been expected — and have been able — to adapt to a wide variety of life circumstances. The work required to survive and thrive as a family has always required creative solutions. The recent pandemic has made this clear for many families, with children often adapting more easily than their parents!

I call the process by which families come up with creative solutions to meet the needs of each member *family-centred parenting*. Family-centred parenting offers an alternative to child-centred or adult-centred parenting, because rather than organizing the family systems around the needs of *some* family members, it organizes them around the needs of *all* members of the family. This means that everyone is responsible for communicating their needs and the family is responsible for negotiating and then responding to those needs. This also means that sometimes each family member's needs are prioritized, and sometimes they are delayed or unable to be met. For example, babies communicate their need for eating or diaper changes at night through crying, and this interferes with parents' biological need for sleep. Some families negotiate these needs by sharing night-parenting duties, either with partners, family, friends, or hired help, to maximize parental sleep. This can be done a variety of different ways. One is a shift-work strategy, whereby one parent is on duty from, say, 9:00 p.m. to 2:00 a.m. and the other parent or support person is on from 2:00 a.m. to 7:00 a.m. Another approach is to have each parent or support person take turns parenting for entire nights. Other families opt to night wean or use sleep-training strategies to encourage their babies to sleep through the night (or at least wake up less often). There are many respectful solutions to night parenting, yet in many families, night parenting falls almost entirely to one parent, particularly if that parent is exclusively nursing. This leaves one parent with extreme sleep deprivation and puts their physical and emotional health at risk. And this could go on for years! The reluctance to view parent work as real work because it's unpaid contributes to this imbalance, with many primary parents in two-parent households agreeing to do night duty because their partner "works," which reinforces the belief that paid work is more important than parent work. And yet, in my clinical experience, this night-parenting agreement doesn't often change when an at-home parent returns to paid employment.

"I DON'T WANT TO BE SELFISH"

Family-centred parenting doesn't ignore the needs of the children; instead it considers their needs in tandem with parental needs. My general suggestion is that if a family system doesn't work for one person in the family, then it shouldn't be acceptable for anyone in the family. Living with other people always requires a certain amount of compromise, and most of us can pragmatically agree to something that isn't our first choice, but that we can see best meets the needs of the other people we live with. I have found that in families where one parent is struggling with their mental health, very often they have unintentionally found themselves enmeshed in family systems that don't work for them. Usually this parent is the primary parent, and it's often one who identifies as a mother in heterosexual relationships. There are many reasons for this, but the one that comes up the most is a fear of being selfish.

Selfishness has a bad rap, especially for women, because part of being selfish means not being considerate of (or not noticing) the needs or wants of others, which is something that women are expected to do. While it's undoubtedly important to notice and make space for others, it can be equally important to practise self-preservation. Selfishness also means prioritizing your personal needs and wants over others', which is not always a *bad* thing. I think selfishness in parenting needs a rebranding, which is why I encourage clients to experiment with the concept of *intentional selfishness*. Intentional selfishness means that there are times when prioritizing your needs and wants over others' *should* be the goal, and that you make that decision with purpose and intention. Essentially, cultivating a spirit of intentional selfishness involves setting boundaries around how much of your time, energy, and resources you can give away, recognizing that you have limits, and that sometimes it's your turn. When everyone gets to be intentionally selfish at times, and it's equitably balanced, it can benefit the whole family.

Part of what makes it so challenging to be intentionally selfish is that the culture of impossible parenting has overemphasized the aspects of parenting that require connection and dependence between parent and child, and devalued the parts that call for autonomy and independence.[4]

Everyone in the family deserves the opportunity to explore their relationship between connection and autonomy, including young children. Both you and your children need to have the experience of autonomy so that you create a sense of self outside of each other.[5] There are significant costs to losing your sense of self, such as martyrism, family enmeshment, resentment, or rage. Without the ability to identify and respond to your own needs, it's almost impossible to be fully compassionate with your child.[6]

The question of how much connection and how much independence children need from their parents is an ongoing debate. The line between the primary parent's right to independence and their children's right to continuous care is blurry because the process of becoming a parent (more so for mothers) so often transforms people from autonomous subjects to community objects whose actions are constantly observed and analyzed by the public.[7] This is why I believe so many people who identify as mothers feel a profound sense of identity loss when they become a parent for the first time; they grow confused about where their personal identity ends and their maternal identity begins. Far too often we discuss early parenthood as if its goal is to exclusively benefit the child, with little regard to the experience or cost to their parent.[8] We hyperfocus on the romantic concept of *mother-baby dyads* and overlook the impact of the entire family system on children. The risk of overemphasizing mother-baby dyads is that it assumes that the needs of the baby are the same as the needs of the primary parent, which is not always true, or it positions the needs of the baby against the needs of the primary parent, which creates a win-lose scenario. This is why I think it's critical to position the needs of the entire family unit at the centre.

CREATING YOUR FAMILY-CENTRED PRINCIPLES

How do you begin the process of becoming family centred? Values mapping allows you to get clear about the things that are important to you and learn more about what is important to the other people in your family. I encourage you to explore your core family values using this tool.[9]

Family Values Mapping

Begin by doing some brainstorming with some key questions about your past, the present, and the future.

Past: Take a few minutes to recall your strongest memories from your own childhood. Why do they stand out? What parts of your family of origin did you internalize? What aspects of your childhood do you want to continue with your own children? What aspects do you want to be different with your family?

Present: Analyze what you've already learned about who you are as a parent. When are you the most joyful and present with your kids? When are you the most overwhelmed and frustrated? What are some of your favourite family moments? What moments do you wish you could change?

Future: Imagine that your children are adults with their own children, and they invite you to talk about parenting with them. What advice would you give them? How do they remember you as a parent? What are you proud of? What do you wish for them as they learn how to parent their own children?

Once you have brainstormed and made some notes, notice if there are any themes in what you reflected upon. Do most of the memories have to do with being outside doing something totally new? You may value *family adventures*. Did you imagine that your children remember you as always being there for them, in the same way you felt about your parents? You may value *consistent support*. Review the list of common values below and mark the ones that seem connected to your brainstorm or any that really resonate with you. My list is not exclusive, of course, so add any values that feel significant to you.

COMMON VALUES

Accountability	Discretion	Humility	Self-control
Accuracy	Diversity	Independence	Selflessness
Achievement	Effectiveness	Inquisitiveness	Self-reliance
Adventure	Elegance	Insightfulness	Sensitivity
Altruism	Empathy	Intelligence	Serenity
Ambition	Enjoyment	Intuition	Service
Assertiveness	Enthusiasm	Joy	Simplicity
Balance	Equality	Justice	Soundness
Belonging	Excellence	Leadership	Spontaneity
Boldness	Excitement	Legacy	Stability
Calmness	Expertise	Love	Status
Carefulness	Exploration	Loyalty	Strategic
Challenge	Expressiveness	Making a	Strength
Cheerfulness	Fairness	difference	Structure
Commitment	Faith	Mastery	Success
Community	Family	Openness	Support
Compassion	Fitness	Order	Teamwork
Competitiveness	Focus	Originality	Temperance
Consistency	Freedom	Positivity	Thankfulness
Contentment	Fun	Practicality	Thoroughness
Contribution	Generosity	Preparedness	Thoughtfulness
Co-operation	Goodness	Professionalism	Timeliness
Correctness	Grace	Prudence	Tolerance
Courtesy	Growth	Quality	Tradition
Creativity	Happiness	Reliability	Trustworthiness
Curiosity	Hard work	Resourcefulness	Truth
Decisiveness	Harmony	Restraint	Understanding
Dependability	Health	Results	Uniqueness
Determination	Helping	Rigour	Unity
Diligence	Honesty	Security	Usefulness
Discipline	Honour	Self-actualization	Vision

Next, write all the values you identified during your brainstorm in column one ("Initial List") of the Values Map (see below). Once you have a big list of values in column one on the Values Map, start to narrow down the list. First rank them in order of importance to you, then rewrite your top-ten most important values in the second column of the Values Map. Now try to narrow the list even further by ranking the ten values in column two in order of importance, and write your top-five values in column three.

Here are some questions to help you rank your list:

1. Which of these values feel the most vital to you?
2. Which of these values feel critical to model for your children?
3. Which of these values feel like an integral part of who you want to be as a parent?

VALUES MAP

Initial List	Top 10, Ranked	Top 5, Ranked
Intelligence	Intelligence	Freedom
Freedom	Freedom	Goodness
Usefulness	Usefulness	Leadership
Exploration	Thankfulness	Simplicity
Thankfulness	Goodness	Making a Difference
Growth	Leadership	
Goodness	Assertiveness	
Leadership	Simplicity	
Joy	Making a Difference	
Assertiveness	Helping	
Simplicity		
Making a Difference		
Helping		

Once you have your final list, I encourage you to make this the measuring stick you use to take stock of how you are doing as a parent. Instead of striving to meet the values of impossible-parenting culture, strive to hold yourself accountable to your personal values. Now that you have a list of what you personally value, you can use it to fight back against feelings of parenting guilt.

One of my favourite aspects of values mapping is that everyone's final list is unique. Part of what contributes to parenting judgment is holding others accountable to our own values, usually without being aware of these values or being able to explain why they are important to us. Imagine how parent shaming would change if we were able to communicate what's personally important to us, without expecting others to have the same values list as we do? And what if we were open to learning about what's important to others? I suspect it would completely change the landscape of parenting comparison, because we would approach each other with curiosity rather than commentary.

To learn more about what values are important to each individual family member, walk everyone through this process independently at first, and then compare your core values together. Sometimes you will realize that you have very different goals. My partner, Janna, highly values personal responsibility and hard work, while I value fun and kindness, and sometimes it can feel like those values are at odds. Neither of us is wrong, but it often requires us to get creative in how we balance everyone's values. By doing this work, we have gained a deeper understanding of why we act the way we do, of each other's parenting strengths, and of each other's triggers, so that we can celebrate and honour everyone's unique contributions to the children.

If you and your other family members have values that feel very misaligned or even contradictory, it may be helpful to create a framework for how you will approach and resolve parenting and family decisions.

I really like design consultant J Li's *Medium.com* article about the *Decide 10 Rating System*, which is a decision-making framework that explores how important the outcome of a particular decision is for each person involved.[10] Li created it for couples, but you could also use it with older children, co-parents, or family members. Here is the rating scale that Li uses, with adapted examples for perinatal families. I encourage you to adapt this and make it your own.

10. "This is so important, the relationship is at stake."

Example: I want to have a child.

9. "This is a turning-point critical event for me and I just need you to drop everything and help me."

Example: I want to do the cognitive behavioural therapy for insomnia protocol, but I would need you to do all the night parenting until I am sleeping regularly again.

8. "This is important for my wellbeing in some way. It's important enough to put things down and [would] potentially (but not always) be a significant favour."

Example: I'm too sick to watch the children alone today, so please take the day off work so I can recover while you look after them.

7. "I really want/need this and am willing to spend everyday social capital to make it happen. Do it for me as a casual favour?"

Example: I know you think professional family photos are silly, but I found a community photo session that is affordable, and I'd really like us to do this.

6. "I would love to do this and will provide the energy/momentum/ engagement boost to make it happen."

Example: I would love to go for a walk tonight but it's kind of dark and I don't want to go alone. I'll change the baby and get them loaded in the stroller if you'll come with me.

5. "Yes, if [you] want to go for this as much as I do, let's do it."

Example: Sure, apple picking sounds super fun this weekend. Let's do it.

4. "Mm, I could be chill with going along with this, but I'm not as excited so somebody else will have to drive the energy."

Example: I don't want to make two cakes just to have a cake smash at our baby's birthday, but go for it if you really want it and I'll take photos.

3. "I wouldn't do this on my own, but it's not going to hurt me so I will if it's important to you."

Example: I'd rather sign the kids up for swim classes on Mondays, but if it's really important for you to be there too, we can do it Saturday mornings.

2. "I don't like this idea at all, or this will actually cause me moderate harm/inconvenience, but it's recoverable or I can grit my teeth and live with it. I will only do it if the benefit to you significantly out-weighs the harm to me, since we're a team."

Example: I don't want to spend $1,500 on a doula, but I'm not the one giving birth so we will do whatever you want.

1. "This will cause me substantial harm/inconvenience. It's only something I would do if it's an emergency."

Example: I don't feel ready to go back to paid work yet, but I will if it is the only way for our family to survive financially.

0. "This is fundamentally damaging, and I would never do it unless the relationship itself is at stake."

Example: I disagree with you about immunization choices.

To use the Decide 10 Rating System to make a family decision, have each family member write down the number that best corresponds with how strongly they feel about the proposed idea. If everyone has mid-range numbers, you can likely negotiate a decision easily. But if it becomes obvious that you are deadlocked in opposite positions, you may need to explore alternative solutions or even need some professional support to come to a resolution.

AUTHENTICITY OVER ACCURACY

Of course, we aren't always going to follow our own parenting values. We're human, and humans make mistakes, or they have trauma responses or any other number of things happen that make things not always work out the way we want. This will absolutely happen in parenting, which is why parenting also requires a healthy dose of self-compassion and permission to make mistakes, instead trying to master the performance of "the perfect parent." I've heard the phrase "I want to give my children a childhood they don't need to recover from" and I think it puts an unnecessary and impossible amount of responsibility on parents. We will all experience a certain amount of relationship and family trauma in our lifetime, but rather than living in fear of it or being hypervigilant about never making mistakes with our children, I encourage you to accept it.

There is value in the imperfectness of parenting, as suggested by pediatrician Donald Winnicott in his concept of the *good-enough mother*, or, as I refer to it, the *good-enough parent*.[11] In chapter six, I discussed how the work of parenting is distinct from the relationship we build with our children, which we have a lifetime to explore and which will go through many growth and pain points. By embracing the concept of being good enough in our parenting, we are free to build an authentic relationship with our children, rather than a performative relationship where we are both trying to follow a set of conflicting rules. Winnicott reminds parents that authenticity in parenting is more important than getting it right, saying, "Good-enough parents can be used by babies and young children, and good enough means you and me. In order to be consistent, and so to be predictable for our children, we must be *ourselves*. If we are ourselves our children can get to know us."[12] Once we take the pressure off ourselves to figure out the "right" way of parenting, we can get to know our children and let them get to know us — flaws and all. Just like any relationship, there will be times of closeness and connection, and times that feel clunky and distant. You will work as a team *and* you will work against each other. You will irritate each other *and* you will laugh together. You will hurt each other's feelings *and* you will learn how to repair the emotional harm caused.

What's even more reassuring is Winnicott's suggestion that children actually *benefit* from parental mistakes and manageable parental failures.[13] Children have a lot to learn about what's okay (for example, get permission before touching other people) and what's not okay (for example, don't hit people) in the world, and it's helpful to learn those boundaries in a compassionate environment, even if the moments they learn those lessons are fraught with annoyance or irritation. If we have tension, feel angry, or have a fight with our partner, we generally don't conclude that we're bad partners. Ideally, we process what happened and try to find a resolution. So why do we worry that we're bad parents after a disagreement or frustration with our child? Why can't that also be an opportunity for modelling accountability and conflict resolution? Doing so can help children learn about their own emotional regulation and soothing, and it fosters independence and resilience.[14]

Obviously, I'm not referring to childhood abuse or neglect because that is never okay and requires serious support and intervention. Thankfully most parents aren't abusive or neglectful, and I believe Winnicott's insistence that the majority of babies and children are raised by good-enough parents.[15] I hold on to that idea when I remember my most shameful parenting moments. In a state of desperate exhaustion and frustration, I have raised my voice at my crying babies and put them in the crib too aggressively. I try to believe my younger son has accepted my apology and forgiven me for the time I told him to "shut the fuck up and don't let go of me or I will beat your ass so bad you will never sit again." That gem came out during a panic attack while we were riding a

Sea-Doo together in Florida. We had found ourselves far from shore in shark-infested water and my son's cavalier attitude only heightened my panic. I still can't understand why my fear that I couldn't keep him safe translated into threats of violence every time he let go of my waist to look more closely at the swarming bull sharks, but I couldn't stop myself from threatening to kill him if he fell into the water. It was particularly painful because it violated my core value of kindness, but it was impactful enough that I have never again sworn at my kids (despite the many moments while raising a preteen and a teen when I have certainly sworn at them in my head!).

I wish that we didn't have to outline all the ways in which it's good for us to be human with our children, because whether or not it's good for them, *it just is*. In fact, research suggests that healthy parent-child relationships only maintain mutual and simultaneous connection about 30 percent of the time, with ruptures and repair to that connection happening the rest of the time.[16] Parents are going to be messy, flawed humans with their children because humans are messy and flawed. We are also fiercely protective, inventive problem solvers, and rich in love and compassion. We are perfectly imperfect. It's healthy to make mistakes, and it's normal to find comfort in that fact. It's okay to embrace your humanity and allow yourself to stop trying to override it with perfectionist strategies.

FAMILY HOT SPOTS

Before I explain family hot spots, I want to do a quick overview of how the nervous system works, because it feels like an important part of perinatal mood that doesn't get discussed enough. There are two parts of our nervous system that I want to focus on. The first part is our sympathetic nervous system, which turns on in response to threats.[17] Some threats are "high stress but time-limited," such as almost getting into a car accident, while others are "low stress but chronic," such as having a boss that you don't like but have to work with. When we feel threatened physically, emotionally, or socially, our sympathetic nervous system kicks into gear and puts our body into either flight, flight, or freeze mode to help us survive; our heart beats faster, we pump cortisol and adrenalin, and our muscles tense.[18] Once the threat subsides, it's important to discharge all the stress hormones from our body by turning on the second part of our system, the parasympathetic nervous system, which allows us to rest, recover, and heal from the intensity of the threat; if we don't release the stress it can become chronic and make us unhealthy or feel miserable.[19]

Caring for young children can be very activating for the sympathetic nervous system, in particular because of the way crying makes us want to jump up and fix whatever is making our kids cry. I was incredibly sensitive to my babies' cries and felt like my body was on fire when they weren't easily soothed. I would be quickly moved to tears or anger by the level of discomfort in my body, and I was always desperate for them to stop. I would hold them and mutter swear words and we would cry together, sometimes for a very long time. Eventually, when they'd stop crying, I'd curl up into a ball and frantically rock myself while slowing my breath until my nervous system calmed down. As they got older the noise from whining, toys, and loud children often left me feeling dazed and overwhelmed, not to mention the agitation I felt from living in a constantly messy, chaotic environment. And it wasn't that my children were doing anything unusual. They were just being busy, active kids that were curious about the world. It was just that I'm sensory-sensitive and my nervous system found all the stimulation to be too much. I still feel this way when we do family events at places that have loud noises or large crowds, such as fairs or amusement parks or busy malls. My poor nervous system just doesn't like multisensory input. Sensory overload is one of my hot spots that I need to manage.

Another common reason for sympathetic nervous system activation in the postpartum period is relational stress conflict, with kids, partners, friends, or family. It's normal for each of us to have *hot spots*, or particular issues or situations that we find very activating, which cause our nervous system to freak out and leave us feeling emotionally dysregulated. Psychiatrist Dan Siegel calls this *falling out of our window of tolerance*, meaning we all have a range of emotional ups and downs through the day that we can self-soothe and regulate on our own, but we also have limits, and some experiences are too much for us to emotionally process when they're happening. We can fall outside of what feels possible for us to tolerate, sending us spinning into a state of hyperarousal (fight/flight/high freeze) or hypoarousal (low freeze/fully shutting down). It's normal for us to feel sad or angry when we feel like someone is stomping all over one of our core values, so values mapping can help each family member identify their hot spots. For example, if *respect* is one of your core values and it feels like your child is behaving disrespectfully toward you, you're likely going to be triggered by it! Sometimes you may be able to regulate easily, but other times you may not, depending on what else is affecting your nervous system in that moment.

WORKING WITH YOUR NERVOUS SYSTEM

Knowing your own hot spots is helpful, but it's just as important to know how you respond when you get activated. Does your heart start to race? Do you find yourself ruminating about what just happened? Do you feel like your body gets flooded and then powers down? With a better understanding of *why* you get triggered and *what happens* when you get triggered, you can design some support strategies to help you take control of your nervous system and feel more grounded. This could be something as simple as taking a break from the trigger and focusing on your breathing. When my kids would scream when I put them in their car seats, I would walk really slowly to the driver's side and collect myself before getting into the car, and then hum or sing while I drove, which can help stimulate the parasympathetic nervous system (the *rest and digest*, soothing part of your nervous system). It can be helpful to create family systems that limit our exposure to triggers when we're having a tough time coping with the day-to-day, but triggers are often unavoidable, so it's critical that we learn how to support ourselves through them.

I usually suggest that parents do two things once they've become activated. The first is to ground themselves, so they can get back in their window of tolerance. There are two popular grounding strategies that can offer relief: the *54321 Sensory Awareness* technique and the *Body Scan*.

54321 Sensory Awareness: A Technique for Coming Back to the Here and Now

Name **five** things that you can see in the room around you.
Example: Chair, dog, shoe, cup, book.

Name **four** things that you can feel.
Example: Feet to the floor. Skin to shirt. Ring on my finger. Sofa supporting me.

Name **three** things you can hear around you.
Example: Clock ticking on the wall. Refrigerator humming. Dog snoring.

Name **two** things you can smell around you.
Example: Fresh cut grass. Burning candle.

Name **one** thing you can taste.
Example: Cinnamon gum.

The Body Scan: The Practice of Tensing and Then Releasing One Part of Your Body at a Time

1. Sit, lie down, or plant your feet to the floor. Close your eyes if it's helpful.
2. Start by tensing your feet, hold for three seconds, and then let them go.

3. Tense your calves, hold for three seconds, and then let them go.
4. Tense your thighs, hold for three seconds, and then let them go.
5. Tense your butt, hold for three seconds, and then let it go.
6. Tense your abs and lower back, hold for three seconds, and then let them go.
7. Tense your shoulders, hold for three seconds, and then let them go.
8. Tense your arms, hold for three seconds, and then let them go.
9. Tense your neck, hold for three seconds, and then let it go.
10. Tense your face, hold for three seconds, and then let it go.

Keep repeating this sequence until you feel your body relax.

Once you're grounded, you want to complete the stress cycle by flushing out the stress hormones from your body and turning on the parasympathetic nervous system. The Nagoski sisters' research offers some easy things you can do at home to help with this:[20]

- **Exercise:** It doesn't take much! You don't need to head to the gym. Running up and down the stairs a few times, having a family dance party with Beyoncé in the kitchen, or taking a brisk walk for ten minutes all count.
- **Breathing:** I know. It's really annoying to be told to breathe when you're activated. But slow breaths do help signal to your body that the threat is gone. Try counting your breaths and see if you can double the time it takes you to exhale than inhale. For example, if it takes you two beats to breathe in, see if you can release the breath in four beats.
- **Social engagement:** Engage positively with the people around you. Smile at a stranger, say thank you to the mail carrier, or call a friend and tell them all the things you love about them.
- **Laughter:** Start telling a story that makes you laugh every time you tell it, or watch that YouTube clip that made you laugh so hard you almost peed that one time.
- **Touch:** Cuddle, kiss, nurse — anything that involves being affectionate with people you care about. If you're feeling "touched out" from too much touch, skip this one.

Alongside identifying family hot spots and learning how to expand your window of tolerance, it can be helpful to improve your conflict-resolution skills. Most of us don't feel that well-equipped to repair riffs with the people we love. Some people are conflict avoidant and make their needs small so they don't upset others. Others are prone to anger, and they know they can scare people but don't always know how to hold back. Parent rage is often the result of a silence/violence continuum, where we suck up a lot of frustration for a prolonged period of time only to reach a tipping point and act disproportionately angry about a minor situation because we've been stuffing down our anger. Then we feel ashamed of our behaviour and re-resolve to not show our rage, which leads us to go back to silence and hide appropriate frustration responses to day-to-day irritations. If you feel like your relationship to conflict or anger is confusing or concerning, it's worth getting some support in gaining some confidence with these skills. And if you suspect you have complex PTSD or a significant trauma history, I highly recommend getting professional, trauma-aware support because there are many aspects of parenting and family dynamics that can be very triggering.

PARENT ISLAND

I do also recognize that part of what can cause stress in our family systems are external influences that extend far beyond how we organize our individual families, such as financial demands that lead to long work hours, and confusion about how to simultaneously work full time and parent full time. Not having enough hours in the day or enough help to meet the daily demands of parenting are real problems; having enough resources to keep the family system running smoothly can be a serious challenge. Our family economic system was historically designed to encourage one parent to stay at home full time and have the other work full time, on the assumption that this would allow middle-class families to flourish. But the entire landscape of work life has changed dramatically in the last fifty years, with very few structural changes to support working families. Family supports such as paid parental leave, part-time work that pays a living wage, access to affordable high-quality child care, and more resources for at-home parents would be a significant part of the solution. While many activist and advocate groups are working hard to change these systems, in the meantime it's even more important to design family-centred strategies at home. Within these strategies, we also need to find ways to care for ourselves, which is why the next chapter will dig deep into reconceptualizing self-care.

ELEVEN

SELF-PARENTING

Mommy needs:

~~Wine~~

An end to the white supremacist, patriarchal, capitalist system that makes modern motherhood so dehumanizing that self-medication is both aspirational and expected.

— Graeme Seabrook

Self-care has become an incredibly popular phrase in the parenting community. And for good reason, because not only are parents tired, as discussed in chapter five, but most of us also live in a state of burnout. Ann Douglas, a prominent Canadian parenting writer, talks at length about parental burnout and the many challenges of work-life balance. With almost 70 percent of parents working outside the home and what she calls our "total work culture" that demands employees be available for work communication outside of office hours, Douglas says that time pressure has become the norm for many families.[1] It's not just physical fatigue that parents are battling, it's also mental fatigue and a general sense of overwhelm. There's just too much to do in any given day, week, or month.

It's understandable that parents are looking for solutions to burn-out, and the answer many of us are given is to increase our self-care. Unfortunately, the rhetoric of self-care is a grossly inadequate response that often only adds to the care duties of already exhausted parents. Allow me to explain. I think we can all agree that the demands of paid work and the demands of child care and household work have expand-ed in recent decades. Today we have more work-related travel, more emails, longer hours, longer commutes, and less job security (and there-fore more pressure to constantly perform) than ever before. Parents are likewise expected to do more today than simply keep their children alive and, ideally, fed. They are expected to invest in their children so that they can thrive in every area of their life. The result is an entire generation of exhausted parents with too much to do, and there has been little analysis and not enough socio-political pressure to challenge the structures that create our day-to-day mental and physical fatigue. Instead what has emerged is a barrage of messages reminding parents, and mostly femme parents, that they need to *take care of themselves*. The self-care narrative that has developed from this is hyper-feminized and usually focuses on beauty rituals such as manicures/pedicures and bubble baths, or exercise such as hitting the gym and running. In more recent years there has also been pressure on the overwhelmed to avail themselves of co-opted spiritual practices and teachings such as yoga and meditation. This can increase emotional burden and tension, par-ticularly if the teachings were co-opted from *your* culture or religion because it's not particularly restful or rejuvenating to be told how to engage in these practices in a misunderstood or inauthentic way.

I call this *prescriptive self-care*. It's the type of self-care that emerges from a combination of marketing and well-meaning advice, but I have a big problem with it. Usually prescriptive self-care has a financial or time cost that feels very expensive to my clients; it feels a little like get-ting a prescription for a medicine that they can't afford while being told that their mental health can't *not* afford it. The rise of doula care, night nannies, meal-delivery services, dog walkers, and babysitting apps that feel like Tinder has created a new economic market that capitalizes on parental fatigue. Why challenge or try to solve the problem of systemic parental overwhelm when it's so readily profitable? There is, of course, nothing inherently wrong with purchasing prescriptive self-care services. Many families use these services as a means of survival and protecting their mental wellness. But because they're definitely not accessible to all families, these coping strategies end up doubling down on systemic inequalities. What this looks like is when BIPOC and low-income women make complex arrangements for someone else to care for their families because they have been hired to support a middle/upper-class, often white, family.

One of my biggest concerns with the rhetoric of prescriptive self-care is the way in which it sets parents up for guilt and shame. The logic of prescriptive self-care says that if we're fatigued or drained, it's because we aren't *caring enough* for ourselves, making it a personal deficit issue rather than a by-product of the culture of impossible parenting. Instead of placing responsibility for parental burnout on the socio-political economic systems that make working full time and raising kids full time so difficult, we tell parents it's their fault for not hitting the gym hard enough. I cringe every time I hear someone talk about parenting self-care by referring to the phrase "Put on your own oxygen mask first." This metaphor, borrowed from airline emergency-procedure demonstrations that direct parents to put on their own emergency oxygen masks before putting masks on their children, overlooks the much more significant detail that the plane is plummeting to the ground! The culture of impossible parenting works to crash families, so blaming parents for not being able to engage in prescriptive self-care feels misguided at best. What I sometimes see in my practice is that self-care winds up being another item on my clients' to-do list, which they then fault themselves for not getting done. The best indicator that you are adhering to prescriptive self-care culture is the presence of the word *should*.

"I know I *should* meditate before bed, but I really wanted to see how *Orange Is the New Black* ended."

"I know I *should* go to the gym, but I just don't have the energy."

"I know I *should* write in my journal, but I never know what to write."

Any time you find yourself caught in a "should," take it as a signal to check in with yourself about what you really need. It's likely a sign that you're craving some time or space for yourself — but you have total freedom in how you achieve that, and what works for you may be different from what works for others. You don't need to feel compelled to follow any of the suggestions from what marketing consultant Kelly Diels refers to as the *female lifestyle empowerment brand*, which is a marketing narrative designed to sell you products and services and *not* a support in learning how to care for yourself.[2]

#WINEMOM

Perhaps the most obvious marketing narrative geared to selling products as self-care to parents has been the creation of *mommy wine culture*, where marketers sold women on the idea that wine could be a way for mothers to cope with the daily grind and frustrations of parenting, much to the criticism of sober marketing specialists such as Alana Nugent. Nugent argues that the trend of using alcohol to cope with the demands of impossible-parenting culture has been strategically sold to mothers as part of a very profitable marketing strategy to increase alcohol sales among women. And it seems to be working: the absolute number of women who drink has risen on a global scale.[3] But wine is not the solution for getting burnt-out mothers the *rest* they are craving. Nugent suggests that the marketing of alcohol specifically to mothers subtly discourages them from holding their partners accountable for their responsibility to their children and management of the household. In this sense, "mommy juice" (a marketing phrase to describe drinking wine while parenting) becomes both a mother's motivation to power through her epic on-duty hours of child care, and her coping mechanism for overwhelm, boredom, and fatigue once the children are in bed. All of this is why there's a rising resistance to alcohol being so casually tossed around as the solution for the stresses of motherhood.

The critiques of mommy wine culture are valid: mothers are the subjects of crafty marketing, consuming alcohol is not recommended when you have depression or anxiety, and it has a negative impact on women's health. Yet for many parents that I know, specifically mothers, alcohol use is an easy and relatively cheap way to relax and have fun during a time in their lives when they don't have access to their historical stress-busting activities.[4] Support for the use of alcohol as maternal self-care has been wrapped up in an "I deserve this!" attitude that's perpetrated through often humorous depictions of mothers struggling (and sometimes failing) to hold off on wine-drinking until 5:00 p.m., as seen on Netflix television shows such as *Workin' Moms* and *The Letdown*. I think the "I deserve this!" sentiment also speaks to a desire for parents to hold on to an exclusively adult part of themselves, which can get easily lost in the demands and hyper-responsibility that come with caring for young children. For many people, alcohol represents freedom, lightness, and letting go of stress, so it's understandable that for some parents drinking becomes an act of rebellion against the repetitive nature of parent life.

Which is why I feel very conflicted about the use of alcohol as a way to rest and de-stress. There was a time in my life where I would have argued that a glass or two of wine each night was critical to my survival and mental wellness, because it gave me a guaranteed way to turn down the volume of the brain chatter that was vigilantly making lists and keeping track of the needs of everyone in the house. As the kids got older, parenting became easier and I was able to share the household work in an equitable way with a new partner, so my stress levels decreased and my evening wind-down with wine and Netflix became unnecessary. While there are lots of great reasons to reduce or eliminate alcohol, I am hesitant to conclude that all parents, especially those who identify as mothers, need to give up their nightly glass of pinot if it feels supportive for them in this phase of life. Instead, what I will suggest is that parents don't need more behavioural policing. Assuming that there's no medical concern or compulsive behaviour, parents need to have the space to make deliberate choices around drinking. If it feels like another *should*, as in "I *should* skip the wine tonight because I don't want people to think that I'm trying to be a wine mom" or "I *should* have a glass of wine at book club because I don't want people to think I'm boring," it's a signal to hit pause and do a closer analysis of that thought.

FROM SELF-CARE TO SELF-PARENTING

So, if prescriptive self-care isn't the solution and self-medicating with alcohol isn't the solution, what are burnt-out parents supposed to do? Part of the solution is to cultivate a practice of *self-parenting*. Unlike prescriptive self-care, self-parenting isn't just about cultivating luxurious experiences, taking breaks, or finding ways to have fun (although this could certainly be a part of it, if you want it to be). It's the practice of parents taking care of themselves in the same way they would their children. Parenting a newborn(s) requires making sure your baby/babies sleep enough, eat enough, and poop enough. Self-parenting is no different, because it assumes that all parents are entitled to meet their own biological needs.

For example, I'm going to assume that you don't let your kids go without eating or hang out in poopy diapers for very long. I also imagine that you think strategically about naps and energy levels before leaving the house with your kids, and that if you're out and they have a fatigue meltdown you go home or organize a way for them to have a nap (even if they don't choose to nap). Parents are generally skilled at not only meeting but anticipating their children's physical, social, environmental, and emotional needs most of the time. And yet so many parents of young children struggle to meet even their most urgent biological needs, such as ensuring they get enough water or calories in a day or poop when their body tells them to.

I know that meeting your own biological needs with young children around is not always simple, but I highly encourage you to make it non-negotiable, even if it involves setting your fussy baby down somewhere safe while you go to the bathroom or to grab a snack. I once had a client that I did home visits with, and I started every session by making her a snack and bringing her water, because she was so hyper-attentive to her high-needs baby that she would not eat or drink anything during the day while her partner was at work — and working twelve-hours shifts! It is very difficult to feel grounded and attentive when you're dehydrated and hungry.

Once you've found a way to meet your daily biological needs, self-parenting is composed of four nurturing cornerstones: Rest, Play, Boundaries, and Ritual.

Rest: Given how critical sleep is for our mental health, it's really quite unfortunate that there isn't a way to get our kids, or ourselves, to sleep on command. Despite this lack of control, it is certainly worth getting creative about ways to maximize sleep, and it's equally important for parents to find opportunities to rest their bodies and their minds. That's *not* the same as protecting time to try to sleep, because that is a straight-up biological need. Rest is about protecting wind-down time, just like you would give your kid(s) some time to play quietly before you tuck them in.

Many clients lament about the difficult choice at the end of the day, when the kid(s) are asleep and the daily housework is done (done enough, anyway), between resting, usually by watching television or reading, or going straight to bed. While they're exhausted, going to bed immediately robs them of wind-down time, spending time with their partners, or connecting to the non-parent parts of themselves. It's critical for parents of young kids to have time when they are not "on duty" and aren't needed to attend to anyone or anything, so that they can have time to daydream, create, relax, and just do whatever they want in that moment. Having your partner take the children to the park so that you can mop the floors uninterrupted does not constitute rest! Often rest time gets combined into chores, such as watching television while folding laundry, which does not feel as restful as watching television while curled up with a blanket and a hot tea. So if you're going to rest, *really* rest.

Play: Adults need to play, too! It's important to break up work and rest with fun. What it means to play is unique to each of us, but ideally it means having something to look forward to. Sometimes this coincides with having a break from your kids/family, such as a date or a night out with friends. It might involve something that takes up a lot of resources, like going on a vacation, but it doesn't have to. You can absolutely integrate play into your day-to-day, although it may look really different from what fun looked like before kids. It could mean going to the park with your two-year-old and running through the splash pad with them, or taking your six-month-old to a Stars and Strollers movie and enjoying your favourite Marvel character on the big screen. There are no rules about how to integrate more play — it just involves seeking joy. I've had clients reread the entire Harry Potter series, start playing video games again, and even have a weekly group phone call with friends while watching *The Bachelor* so they could gossip and rant about the show during the commercials.

If you feel like you've lost your sense of play, try making a list of all the things you used to love to do as a child, and then revisit them, which could result in you joining a team sport or going camping or baking desserts with a loved family member. If you're feeling really depressed and nothing feels like fun, pick something that used to bring you joy and do it anyway. Sometimes when we do the opposite of what our depression is telling us ("stay in bed and don't reach out to anyone") we surprise ourselves by feeling a bit better.

Boundaries: Whenever I try to explain what's meant by boundaries, I like to borrow from Brené Brown's definition: boundaries are simply an internal understanding and external communication about what's okay and what's not okay for us.[5] Yet setting boundaries is far from simple for many of us. Often, we struggle to communicate them because we don't have an internal knowledge about what is okay and what is not okay for us. Many parents, particularly mothers, have trouble tuning in to their own internal sense of yes or no because of impossible-parenting messages that tell us sacrifice is a demonstration of love. But there are usually clues when your boundaries have been violated, such as feeling angry, resentful, or overwhelmed, which is why it's useful to pay attention when those feelings show up. Even if we do know what our internal boundaries are, it takes bravery to express our needs and keep people accountable. Saying no can be really hard, particularly if you have a history of saying yes and prioritizing the needs of others above your own, because they can be confused or hurt by your no. And finding the bravery to set (and hold) boundaries takes from our emotional energy stores, which is why it often feels easier just to say yes or do it ourselves. Even so, I would encourage you to experiment with putting your (very limited) energy into boundary setting, as it can lead to a greater sense of peace and authenticity. And this absolutely includes setting boundaries with your children!

Rituals: I generally stay away from the language of *routines* for parents with newborns and young babies, because postpartum life is often chaotic and how we spend our time can feel out of our control. Instead I suggest that every parent build a sense of the daily rituals that help them feel like they're caring for themselves. Often these are pretty boring. Go outside every night after dinner, either for a walk or just on the apartment balcony to feel the sun or moon on your face. Even if you've been up all night, set a time that marks the start of the day, such as 6:00 a.m. or 7:00 a.m., and create a ritual around changing out of your pyjamas as soon as the clock hits that time. Use an elastic band to attach your mood medication to your toothbrush and take it every night when you brush your teeth. You don't need rituals for everything, but they are important to help you feel a sense of order in your life, and rituals become extra important when you're feeling very depressed. Spend a few moments and write down the five things that, when done daily, make a big impact on your day. Next, create a simple and easy ritual around each of them (the simpler the better). Finally, ask the people on your support team to help you implement these practices.

FOUR SQUARES OF SELF-PARENTING

Once you're able to identify the differences between prescriptive self-care and tending to your physical and emotions needs in a loving, parental way, you can identify what might *actually* help you feel cared for. Often, these are simple things like "I just want to be alone in my house for a few hours," or "I just want enough time to shower and have a hot coffee in the morning." One tool that many parents find helpful is the four squares of self-parenting, which is designed to help you become more familiar with current strategies of self-parenting and let you brainstorm new ones. Simply draw a big square and divide it into four smaller squares. Label and fill out each section with the headings below and then keep it somewhere handy for those extra-hard moments.

People I Can Reach Out to for Help

In this section, make a list of all the people that you can call upon for support. It might be helpful to categorize them into three groups: (1) Emotional, (2) Physical, and (3) Informational.[6] The first group includes people that can offer you emotional support or the people you're comfortable sharing your feelings with. Often, they know the right thing to say or are really great at helping you to calm down or at making you laugh. The second are people you can rely on for physical support, such as watching your kids or dropping off dinner. They may not be great at talking about hard feelings, but they're awesome at running to the store for you. The third are people that you trust to give you good informational support. So much of parenting involves wading through conflicting or unwanted parenting advice and it can be hard to wrap your head around it all. Often these people are professionals, like your doctor or pediatrician, but they can also be wise parent friends or family members. Once you know who your people are, tell them that they made the list and let them know that you're going to be leaning on them.

Self-Talk

You can refer to this section as mindsets, affirmations, internal scripts, or anything that highlights how you talk to yourself during hard times. Some people love to use classic phrases, such as "I would never be given anything I can't handle." Others like to use pop culture references, such as Kimmy Schmidt's mantra, from the eponymous television show, that "a person can stand just about anything for ten seconds, then you just start on a new ten seconds. All you have to do is take it ten seconds at a time." I've had some clients find solace in naming distorted thinking patterns, as in "I'm catastrophizing — where is the evidence to support this thought?" and others who turn to mindfulness one-liners, such as "This is just a moment in time and it will pass." It doesn't matter what self-talk you use, as long as you find it helpful. If you aren't sure where to start, try asking friends and family members what kinds of self-talk help them through tough times and see if anything resonates. If it does, borrow it!

Coping Through Tough Moments

These are all the things that help sustain you when you feel like you're not coping well. The good thing about this section is that there is no such thing as *bad coping*. I often see *should*s sneak in here; clients will say something like "I should probably go for a walk," to which I'll ask, "Do you like going for walks?" and will often get a response of "Not really." These strategies aren't meant to be stretch goals. Ideally, your coping mechanisms will be the things that you already know work, and by writing them down you are simply bringing more intention to them, as well as making them as safe as possible. I've seen things on this list such as "take ten slow deep breaths," "throw eggs at the garage," or "rip out the pages of old books while screaming into my pillow." The things you would not include on this list are things that harm you or things that you are actively working to change. For example, if you historically shopped online as a way to self-soothe and you're working hard to find other ways to calm yourself, you would not list that among your coping strategies. I find that coping strategies for anxiety often involve movement, of your breath or of your body, because anxious energy wants to be moved, while depressive strategies are gentler and more loving, as depressive energy wants compassion. You goal is to generate a list of things that help you get back into a place where you feel grounded and able to regulate your emotions, so get creative about what helps you connect to this space.

The More I Do, the Better I Feel

This is the section where clients often list things that we generally know are good for our mental health, but can't necessarily (or aren't necessary to) do all the time. Things like "spend time in nature" or "go out with my friends" or "do my physiotherapy exercises" belong here. It's not uncommon to see things that could be categorized as prescriptive self-care in this list, such as baths, journaling, or exercise, and that's okay! When you aren't operating from a *should* place, these can be wonderful activities to engage in, if they resonate with you and you find them supportive. Once this list is complete, strive to build these activities into your days, with lots of self-compassion if you don't always get to them. If they start to feel prescriptive, you can simply swap them out for something else.

MANAGING PARENT GUILT

One of the biggest obstacles to self-parenting is parent guilt, because in the culture of impossible parenting, any time a parent prioritizes taking care of themselves, they risk compromising the best interests of their children (either consciously or unconsciously).[7] If meeting your owns needs, wants, and desires causes you to feel guilt (meaning you feel that you've done something bad) or shame (meaning you feel that *you* are bad), it could be that you're measuring yourself or your child against impossible standards. I want to gently remind you that taking time to care for yourself will not prevent your children from meeting their full intellectual or emotional potential, because there is no such thing![8] The idea that a "perfect" childhood produces a more complete or fully realized adult is a delusion that robs joy from both parents *and* children. As mentioned in the previous chapter, the relationship between parent and child is rooted in synchronistic flow, meaning that it's healthy to have both connection and independence from your children.[9] While independence from your children can feel emotionally challenging at first, it can be helpful to remember that maintaining a sense of self and learning how to share the work of parenting with partners, family, or paid caregivers will benefit you and your children.

In the early 2000s, I completed my sociological graduate thesis about how social policies shape the construction of good/bad mothering identities for women in the Canadian prison system; it involved many interviews with previously incarcerated parents. Feelings of guilt and shame about not being good enough were significantly tied to the internalized construction of *bad mothering identity* for many of the women I interviewed, which I had suspected would come up as a theme. Years later, when I started offering social work counselling to a much broader population of parents, I was struck by how consistently the themes of guilt and shame came up. In fact, guilt and shame seem to be a reliable part of parental identity for parents being held and/or holding themselves to impossible parenting expectations. What's most interesting is that the types of things parents feel guilty about usually don't seem like actual offences to most outsiders. They often include things like "I feel so guilty about putting the baby in daycare but I had to go back to work" or "I feel so guilty that I had a C-section." Many parents feel guilty about things that they cannot control, and that others would interpret as logical or practical.

I find that parent guilt comes from one of two places. The first is when parents fail to adhere to their own sense of parenting values, as we examined in the previous chapter. For example, I once worked with a parent who had a deep core value around honouring community, and they were riddled with guilt over moving across town during their pregnancy because their baby wouldn't be able to see the other children in her community as often as they would like; they worried that as their child got older, they wouldn't have a sense of belonging. Their work was to come to terms with the limitations of accessing their old friends and neighbours and seek out ways to connect with local parents to build a new sense of community.

The second place I see parent guilt emerge is when a parent feels they are failing to measure up to someone else's parenting values, whether that "someone else" is a single person or an entire culture. I lived this myself when my children were younger. I hated taking them to the park. It was always too hot or too cold, it bothered my allergies and cranked up my anxiety, and there were often gross bugs. But I felt guilty if I didn't take them every day, because the park was literally across the street from our home. Did it really matter if I didn't take the kids to the park every day? No, it didn't, but I had internalized the message years before that kids needed to play outside in parks. These seemingly innocuous ideas, such as "kids need parks," can sneakily erode our sense of parenting confidence, making us feel like we aren't following the rules of good parenting. On the days when you find yourself feeling guilty, take a moment to assess whether you're guilty of violating your own principles or external principles. If the guilt is coming from somewhere external, try to let it go by reminding yourself that you only get so much emotional energy, and you need to protect it for the things that really matter. Once I let go of the park guilt, I was able to find all sorts of fun ways to play with the kids that adhered to my parenting principles. And we got to stay in our bug-free house and not have the sunscreen fight.

However, if you find that you've violated your own parenting principles, then I encourage you to *be* guilty, rather than feel guilty. If you *are* guilty, you can do something to rectify the situation, versus trying to push away guilty feelings. If you suspect you might be guilty and have caused harm, the following questions can help you move from feeling guilty to making amends.[10] Be sure to put a cap on how long you will punish yourself — there isn't a crime in the criminal justice system that doesn't have a sentence associated with it, and it should be no different for your internal crimes!

1. What crime are you guilty of?

    Example: I am guilty of ignoring my baby's cries during our walk because I thought they would fall asleep, but they were crying because they had a giant poop, and now they have a diaper rash.

2. What is the punishment for this crime?

    Example: I feel awful. And I did have to clean up a giant poop without enough wipes and it somehow got in my hair, so that wasn't fun.

3. What is the sentence?

    Example: I'll let myself feel bad about this until tomorrow. I'm going to be extra attentive to the baby all night and then make sure that I pack extra poop gear the next time we go out. And if I'm trying to walk them to sleep and they're crying hard, I'll check on them.

You also may not feel a lot of guilt or shame, but that doesn't mean you aren't impacted by parenting expectations. Some parents share with me that while they don't have a strong internalized sense of guilt about engaging in self-parenting, they worry about how their actions (or inaction) will be received by others and whether they could be accused of being a bad parent. I'm noticing that on a collective scale, parents are growing increasingly fatigued by persistent, tense feelings of competition or judgment about their parenting decisions. We are tired of being judged and we don't feel like judging others! While it requires bravery and self-compassion to model self-parenting from within the culture of impossible parenting, it's equally possible that the people whose judgment you fear will see you as a model for a new, less hostile parenting culture.

RE-PARENTING YOURSELF

Self-parenting isn't just about finding ways to take care of yourself. It's also a way to give yourself the type of parenting you wish you had received as a child but didn't necessarily always get. In many ways, becoming a parent is an opportunity to re-parent yourself, as you become much clearer about what your parent(s) went through trying to raise you.[11] This may fill you with compassion and awe, or it may fill you with grief to realize all the needs you had that weren't met, but I think for most of us it's a combination of the two. Self-parenting requires you to observe your own emotional needs and notice gaps in the care or emotional intelligence or regulation you're experiencing, so you can learn how to address your own needs as an adult.[12] Becoming a parent is a time of significant change and growth, and an opportunity to change in ways that are irreversibly beneficial to your sense of self.[13] It might help to view facing challenges in your day-to-day as an opportunity to learn more about yourself, rather than as a struggle *against* your faults and flaws.[14] Until we are able to parent ourselves effectively, it's often a struggle to parent our children in the ways we would like to. The more we tend to ourselves, the easier parenting feels, because we're modelling the values we want to give to our kids, such as kindness, boundaries, and self-compassion. And even if our kids never notice all the loving values we are modelling for them, it feels good for us — and that's enough.

TWELVE

BE LESS ALONE

Imperfections are not inadequacies; they are reminders
that we're all in this together.

— Brené Brown

I find many social interactions painful. I've worked hard over the years
to cultivate a part of me that I call my *public representative* that can have
conversations with strangers or acquaintances. This is the part of me
that I think is the least weird and awkwardly manages to make small talk,
although far too often I still find myself unintentionally steering conversations back to my analysis of *Naked and Afraid* (my favourite reality
show), because other than the politics of parenting, how to survive without the luxuries of modern life is basically the only thing I like talking
about. Social work counselling is the perfect job for me because it allows
me to mostly listen, to set up clear boundaries and role expectations, and
to know that people want to be around me because they pay to be there.

I didn't have any parent friends for quite a long time. My older child
was five when I first became friends with someone who also had kids
the same age as me. I share this because I understand the challenges of

finding your parenting village, despite the popularity of this advice to postpartum parents. This chapter isn't going to give you all sorts of advice about signing up for baby music classes or how to start a playgroup. If you're a person who gravitates to those things, I encourage you to explore those avenues and build a village that feels good for you. For the rest of us, this chapter is dedicated to being less alone when you feel that there are significant barriers to resolving isolation and loneliness as a parent.

WHERE IS THIS SO-CALLED PARENTING VILLAGE?

I hear references to "the village" a lot when discussing new parents. This concept of a parenting village has gone through many iterations, but it usually falls somewhere between pre-industrial images of women giving birth in the woods and then sitting around with other women breastfeeding each other's babies, and images of country women bringing new parents casseroles and disciplining each other's children. This back-to-the-land mentality crops up in a variety of social areas, most recognizably in the domains of childrearing and food (take a quick look at Pinterest trends if you aren't sure what I mean). As we feel the deep impact of cultural shifts to individualism over collectivism and as we realize that the rise of technology has not fulfilled its promise of more leisure and efficiency, but instead has created an economy that demands that we work harder, produce more, and never feel like we have enough, it makes sense that we long for a return to authenticity and naturalness (whatever those are). The result has been an idealized fantasy about "simpler times." But these fantasies overlook the labour and resources it takes to raise children and run a household,[1] which was a lot when you had to grow your own food, make your own clothes, and manage seven children. We made homemade tofu at our house recently, and it was a lot of work. We soaked the soybeans, made soy milk, then made tofu from it. It took over a day from start to finish. While I felt like a total rock star and demanded praise for my industriousness, the whole family likely would have benefited more from buying it from the store and then spending the afternoon playing cards together.

When we imagine this idyllic parenting village, we overemphasize the aspects that we long for, such as family and friends nearby to help. Because our current economy requires that parents raise families close to their paid work, but not necessarily close to their extended families, our personal "villages" often lack the types of resources and security that multi-generational families enjoy. Often, the images of the "parenting village" centre around a *Leave It to Beaver*–style image that omits the high maternal and infant death rates, class disparities, and egregious human rights violations that have featured so strongly throughout history.

That sad truth is that the kind of village most of us would ideally have for our child/children is gone. I'm not sure that it ever truly existed in the way we wish it did. While I've heard references to a *modern-day parenting village*, usually that involves hiring services (which is a great option if you can afford it) or leveraging online parenting communities, which doesn't feel like a well-rounded solution. Thankfully, other conceptual models are emerging. Gabrielle Griffith, a full-spectrum doula who specializes in postpartum sex and relationships and has a focus on supporting queer and BIPOC families, doesn't refer to the village when working with clients, but instead guides them through cultivating what they call *compassionate and conscious collective care* (CCC Care). Parents often get vague offers of support, such as "Let me know if you need anything" that don't result in anything tangible, which is why CCC Care suggests that parents create a detailed list of what support means to them. This could be anything from taking your dog for a walk, to setting up a meal train, to keeping you company during the day (or night!).

COMPASSIONATE AND CONSCIOUS COLLECTIVE CARE

The first step to CCC Care is to get really clear about what help looks like for your family. Start by making a list of all the things that would give you a sense of relief, allow you to feel supported, and make life feel a little bit easier. Don't get distracted by whether or not you think what you're asking for is possible; the purpose of this exercise is to get clear about what would feel like appropriate help.

Once you have your list of support actions, the next step is taking an inventory of the support people in your life, to get a sense of who could offer support and what kind of support they could offer. Keep this list as broad as possible, not just limited to your mom and your best friend. Include friends you haven't talked to in a while, co-workers, neighbours, and extended family. The people we will turn to for emotional support are often very different from the people we turn to for hands-on support. For example, you might call your cousin and cry about how tired you are but know that they would never come over during a snowstorm and shovel your driveway, but a sibling who lives close by might if you asked.

Once you have a sense of who you can turn to, *ask them* if they would be willing to support you in very specific ways. That way you can negotiate what's possible and state your expectations, rather than hoping they notice that you need help. Here's what it might sound like:

> "I'm having trouble remembering to take my meds in the morning because I'm so tired. Could I text you every morning after I've taken them, so I have some accountability while I build a new habit?"

> "I find some of the afternoons really lonely. Could I call you on really tough days?"

> "It's really challenging for me to take the baby to the doctor on the bus. We have a few appointments coming up over the next month. Are you able to drive us to any of these?"

If it feels difficult to ask directly, it's perfectly okay to send a mass email or ask someone you trust to organize your support team on your behalf. When asking, it's important to make sure your requests include three questions: (1) Are you able to help?, (2) What can you do from this list?, and (3) When can you do this?

The last step in building CCC Care is following up and holding people who said yes accountable. I totally understand that accessing your community can feel overwhelming. Belonging to a community generally comes with rules of conduct and expectations, such as being easy to get along with and not taking up too much space, which is sometimes difficult to live up to when you are suffering from a PMAD. It can feel risky to show up in social spaces with our authentic mood, and we worry about experiencing criticism or rejection. Or worse — we may ask for help that never comes. I know someone who experienced this when they reached out for help with their PMAD, and while it was painful to realize that their community was unreliable, they said that once they had processed the frustration and embarrassment of having friends and family not follow through on their commitments, it became obvious what relationships were worth investing in going forward. It shifted their intrapersonal relationships in a positive way.

FAMILY AND FRIENDS

Families of origin (meaning the people who raised you), whether yours or your partner's (if you have one), are complex. There are some of us who have wonderfully supportive relationships, for whom family members are also the primary source of friendships. If you have that, it's special and I hope you cherish it. And if they live with you or close enough to help with the day-to-day child and household maintenance? That's basically magic.

Alas, many new parents have difficult relationships with some or all family members. You may adore your family of origin but feel tense with your partner's family (or vice versa), or you may adore your own family while your partner does not. Families can be a source of great pain, abuse, or loss. If that feels familiar to you, it's normal to feel sad, angry, or jealous about the lack of family support available to you. You may feel this extra deeply if you have parent friends who are well supported by their family members. Often we have to grieve the loss of family, sometimes for the second or third time, when we see what we're missing and feel the loneliness of not having parents looking out for us in the way we would ideally want.

Thankfully, family of origin is just one way to be in a family system. You can opt to create a *chosen family* of people who accept you and look out for you in the ways you wish your family would.

It's common for our friendships to go through dramatic changes after we become parents. We can feel very out of touch with our child-free friends, who often operate on very different schedules and can never fully understand the grind of parenting. It can be painful and awkward if you have friends that want to have a baby but are having a difficult time with fertility, especially if they have suffered a loss. How do you tell someone who's working so hard to become a parent that you're finding parenting hard? And if you do have friends with children, it can be surprisingly difficult to coordinate plans, given that they're navigating their own set of family dynamics.

If you're feeling lonely or unsupported, it's likely not rooted in poor intentions from the people who care about you. Maybe they're also managing the best they can and don't have anything extra to give, or maybe you just haven't asked (or haven't been specific with your requests, which is why the support action list is so helpful).

Also, if you have the energy, it's worthwhile asking the people in your life if there's anything you can do to support them. Not only because it models what you want from them, but also because it feels good to support other people, and hanging out in someone else's problems can give you a reprieve from your own. (And it solidifies that community orientation to raising children that I am such an advocate of.)

SEEK OUT PARENT FRIENDS WITH PURPOSE

If you're in the market for new parenting friends, it's worthwhile to check out spaces that are intentionally designed for new parents, but it's more helpful to choose activities that *you* like, rather than what you think you should do for your baby. If you hate working out but love politics, you likely won't find your parent-people at a stroller fit class, but you might find them at a political protest. Make a list of activities that you really love and see if you can seek out opportunities to engage in them, child or children in tow. Don't be afraid to try out lots of different activities, and be gentle with yourself because, similar to dating, it takes time to find the right people.

It can also be helpful to seek out support groups for parents with PMADs. Not only because it's a great form of therapy, but also because you might more easily relate to parents going through a similar experience. Also, support groups usually provide snacks and child care!

If there are physical or emotional barriers to connecting with people in person, there's an increasing number of online support groups, which are often free.[2] You can also meet local parents or parents with similar interests or parenting philosophies to you on websites like Facebook or Reddit, or on standalone sites. These are great because you can often lurk and get a sense of the people and the unspoken rules of the group before posting. Sometimes it's enough just to read others' posts and know you aren't alone with your feelings. And it's comforting to know that there are others up feeding babies at 3:00 a.m., when it's dark and you feel so alone in the world.

A NOTE TO MY SOCIALLY ANXIOUS FRIENDS

If you're particularly socially anxious, know that you are *my* parenting people. It can be helpful to reframe social interactions as a quest to find people that you like, rather than trying to make yourself likeable to others. Having kids around the same age is often not enough to build a connection, so you may need to dig for points you have in common. When I'm going into social situations where I have to meet new people, I always make a list of things I can talk or ask about, such as "I'm looking for a new show on Netflix. Have any recommendations?" or "Been anywhere interesting on vacation recently?" People love to be asked about themselves, so if you get stuck, try to get curious about who they are. If all else fails, exit the conversation and try again with someone else.

Meeting new people is difficult, and sometimes it can leave you with a *vulnerability hangover*, which is a concept from Brené Brown's research about shame and vulnerability.[3] This occurs when we've opened up a little too much, a little too fast, or to someone that wasn't able to hold a vulnerable part of us. It happens to everyone from time to time, and it's just a sign that the person you opened up to isn't a safe person to be vulnerable with. If you find yourself ruminating over a conversation, feeling like you've disclosed too much of yourself, try imagining multiple possibilities for why the conversation felt uncomfortable, rather than making up a story that you are unlikeable. For example, let's say that you talk openly about your struggles with PPA with another parent you meet at a drop-in group and they become uncomfortably quiet and find a reason to end the conversation. It might be true that the person thinks you're a total weirdo, but it's just as possible that they related to a lot of what you said but got awkward because they aren't comfortable talking about their own mood, or that they were thinking of a friend who also has PPD/A and they were worried about them. You might not be able to convince yourself of an alternative story, but it's worthwhile to make space for the possibility and allow for multiple narratives about what happened. Thankfully, talking openly about perinatal mood is rapidly gaining more acceptance and coming out of the shadows.

You may not find forever friends in your quest to seek out parenting friends. Media images and the *make every moment magical* value from impossible-parenting culture want to sell us on the idea that we need to have a parenting squad, but it's actually rare to find one, and it can't be forced. Sometimes it happens over time and not in the first few years of parenting. I like leveraging author Tom Rath's *Vital Friends* framework for conceptualizing friendship, which suggests that there are a wide variety of types of friendships, each important in their own way.[4] Rather than look for a parenting group that you feel gives you a sense of total belonging, often it's easier to look for a few specific types of friends. And it's okay if you form temporary friendships that fizzle out over time. Here are a few types of friendships worth looking for:

Activity Partner: This is someone you share a similar interest with. It could be someone you like walking with, going to baby classes with, or meeting up for coffee. This might be a superficial friendship that doesn't go very deep. The goal is just to have some enjoyable company.

Identity Inspiration: There are a lot of different types of parenting labels, such as attachment parents, tiger parents, unicorn parents, etc. The formation of your parenting social identity can be confusing and has both benefits and costs. It's true that the world of parenting subcultures can feel divisive, because they focus more on how we are different than on how we are the same, which can lead to judgment or a sense of superiority. More often than not we don't fully align with all the values of any parenting sub-culture group, so it can feel overly simplistic to assign ourselves a group label. But when our parenting identity is first forming, feeling a part of a particular group can be an important anchor and confidence building. It feels similar to exploring teenage cliques in high school. There's comfort in knowing that you're a jock or band geek, because it provides instant access to community and a deepening sense of self. Yet as we grow and have more experiences, we expand our social identities and realize that being a band geek is only one part of us (most of us do, anyway). You likely no longer identify as a jock, but as someone who loves to play sports. Finding someone whose parenting style you admire can be helpful in shaping your own identity until yours feels fully integrated.

Normalizer: This is the friend that always makes you feel a little better by saying "Same here!" when you share a challenge you're going through — not in a way that feels competitive, but in a way that makes you feel less alone.

Venting Buddy: Sometimes it feels great to rant and complain! This friend never judges you for letting it out and will often join you in saying "This part of parenting sucks so bad!" Ideally this friend is also funny and able to share venting space. You can limit time with them if it starts to feel too negative or toxic.

Answer Master: This is your friend who's a seasoned parent, or at least a little bit ahead of you, who knows a lot about what's normal. They are the one you turn to when your kiddo gets their first tooth or diaper rash and you aren't sure what to do.

Wisdom Seeker: This is the opposite of the answer master. This is a friend whose kiddo is a little younger than yours, who you get to give support and advice to. It can be helpful to realize how far you've come and how much you know about parenting.

What I like about the approach of finding certain types of helpful friendships, rather than look for a lifelong parenting crew, is that you don't need to solve every intrapersonal relationship issue in the first few years of parenting; the goal is just to be less alone. I suggest you play with the types of friends that you would like to have in your life, and limit time with any that don't feel supportive right now. Anything that helps alleviate loneliness is worthwhile.

THIRTEEN

FINAL THOUGHTS

Where there is love and inspiration, I don't think you
can go wrong.

— Ella Fitzgerald

A friend of mine once shared a story from a personal development program she attended, and I think about this story at least once a week as I reflect upon my own parenting and work through my own guilt, disconnection, and repair with my children. One of the activities of this program was to pull up a participant and have them publicly work through a long-standing personal issue where they felt stuck. The woman who was selected shared that she had struggled with disordered eating and body image since she was a child, and she wanted to heal her relationship with her body. The life coach running this activity helped her identify the first moment that she felt that her body and her eating was a problem, and she recalled being a young girl happily eating a sugary cereal. Her father walked into the kitchen and asked, "How much do you weigh?," got the answer he needed, and then said, "Stop eating that cereal" as he walked out of the room. In that moment her young mind concluded that there was a problem with her weight and that she could influence it through her eating choices. That connection plagued her for her entire life.

The coach encouraged this woman to call her father and confront him with this memory and the impact it had had on her. When she got her father on the phone, he initially had no recollection of the event. After some probing, he finally said, "Oh yes! I remember. I was buying the entire family skis for Christmas and needed to know how much everyone weighed so I could get you the right size. And you were eating my favourite cereal and I wanted to make sure there was still some left for the next day. I didn't know that bothered you so much. I wish you'd have said something earlier."

I don't know what meaning that woman made from this moment of clarity with her dad. I hope she found it healing. But this story impacted me very significantly in a few ways. The first is that it made me realize how futile the task of "not damaging" our kids is. I really believe that parents who are reflective and intentional (which I already know you are, because you're reading this book) can create strategies to prevent their children from being negatively impacted by family life in the ways that they felt they were in their own childhoods. For example, if you were bothered that your parent(s) talked about sex in an embarrassing or shaming way and it left you with an inner belief that sex was dirty or wrong, you might try to compensate by creating an environment of openness about sexual discussion, even if it's hard and uncomfortable for you. Yet there can be moments of parenting that feel neutral or even good for you that you later learn had a negative impact. I've seen this play out in my own life. I prided myself on shielding my first-born child from the details of how their father treated us in the first few years of their life (which was very negative). In an effort to protect my child from feeling rejected or in-fluence their feelings toward their biological dad, I didn't disclose this history. I truly thought this was the best strategy. But when my kiddo was thirteen and some of these details emerged circumstantially, they were very angry with me for hiding that part of their personal history. We worked through it together, but it caused harm to our relationship in a way that I didn't anticipate, and which was the opposite of my goal.

The ways in which our family roles, environments, and interactions will negatively shape our children is largely unknowable and can often result from innocent oversights or from trying to protect them, as in my example. They can also be the unfortunate result of circumstances beyond our control, such as having to move frequently for work, or personality conflicts, such as an introverted, sensitive child being raised by loud, direct, extroverted parents. What's missing from the discussions of parenting, particularly parenting infants and young children, is an acceptance of the fact that a certain amount of relational trauma between parents and their children exists for everyone, because all human relationships have harmful interactions. I don't think it's possible to be in a long-standing relationship with anyone — friends, family, lovers, co-workers — without some insensitive, painful, or confusing moments together. Which makes me question whether we always need to refer to it as trauma, or if we need a range of words to describe the painful parts of growing up. Much like how I differentiate between birth and reproductive *trauma* and *grief*, sometimes I think what people are referring to when reflecting on painful parts of their childhood is *grief* rather than trauma, meaning that they are sad or disappointed about what happened. And what makes it extra hard is that we don't get a do-over and have to find a way to live with hurts that weren't our fault.

To be clear, I am *not* talking about trauma from childhood abuse, cruelty, or neglect, but rather the impact of our normal and unexpected life experiences, as well as complications that arise from parenting children while trying to meet conflicting demands. We lose our temper with a squirmy kid who's fighting a diaper change and getting poop everywhere not because we want to scare them, but because it's disgusting and they're making it hard for us to get out the door and get to our appointment on time. We don't ignore our children's pleas to play with us while we scroll on our phone because we hate engaging with our children, but because we're exhausted and craving rest. And we don't leave them crying with an emergency caregiver they don't know well because we don't care about their needs, but because they're sick and we still have to go to work. I sometimes liken our relationships with others to our relationships with our overall health. We all have a unique starting place with regard to our health, as we are born with a certain amount of genetic health variability and levels of ability that we don't have a lot of control over, in the same way we don't get to choose who raises us or our life circumstances as children. Our individual health will continuously change over time, with many ups and downs — just like relationships — and while we have some idea about how to support it (e.g., stay hydrated) and what hinders it (e.g., don't live with chronic stress), everybody responds differently to these different variables in both the long and short terms. Imagine if we could shift from analyzing all the ways in which parents mess their children up to a culture where it was normal and expected that we would *all* need to analyze the impact of our life experiences and how they shaped us. I try to do this with my own children by talking openly about how I think we all benefit from therapy, and how it's okay to process our relationship with others. And if they need to confront me about pain I've caused, I am committed to hearing it and working through it with them so we can move into a deeper relationship together. This shift to normalizing would create a way for both parents and children to acknowledge that while everyone is both negatively *and* positively shaped by their family of origin, parents are also not wholly responsible for the entirety of their children's life experiences. It would also create the possibility for adults to not only reflect on their childhoods, but also to redefine their relationship to their families of origin and make any necessary changes or adjustments. Let's not forget that humans are resilient!

I suspect that the hardest part about the residual pain we carry from our own childhoods is when nobody acknowledges it or takes responsibility for it. When parents are so focused on not making mistakes, we can miss the importance of repair in relationships, which I think is more important than not making a mistake in the first place. Partially because mistakes are inevitable, partially because there are multiple ways to respond to our kids and it's not possible to know which one is the best, and partially because the family can be a safe place for children to learn that you can have stress in your relationships and still be loved and accepted. I wonder what would have happened to that woman at that coaching program if she had felt it was safe to speak up to her dad earlier and tell him the impact his comment had on her, rather than letting it fester and grow into a painful personal narrative.

Many of the parents I work with who are deeply entrenched in child-centred parenting often had difficult relationships with their own parents and are very afraid of recreating those experiences for their own children. They so badly want to give their children all the safety or positive reinforcement they felt their childhood was lacking. These parents often do substantial research about infants' and children's mental health, and they strive to parent through research alone, instead of parenting through a combination of research, personal values, self-compassion, and intuition. This combination is what I refer to as your *informed parent gut*, meaning that you have intentionally analyzed parenting choices and responses through what you think you know, what you want, and what feels right for you. Parenting through research alone often creates a fearful experience that includes significant amounts of guilt and anxiety. These parents often benefit greatly from working through their early life trauma and grieving the childhood relationship that they never had with their parents. It's equally important to bring awareness to the fact that they are *not* their parents, and never could be, because they have already done, and continue to do, the personal reflection work to change those historically problematic dynamics. It's simply not possible to resolve your historical family injuries by rigidly following the "rules" of good parenting with your own kids. In these cases, it's important to work at healing your history, rather than trying to make up for your parents' mistakes. It's painful. It's uncomfortable. And it often requires professional support.

MY DREAM FOR YOU, DEAR PARENTS

We have gone a lot of places together throughout this book. The Perinatal Mood Framework provided a base to understand the complexities of perinatal mood. We named the problematic links between the sociological aspects of parenting and the individual mental health experiences of parents, and we unpacked the ways in which the pressure

205

and performance of "good parenting" can devastate our perinatal mood and put marginalized parents unfairly at risk for community judgment and interference. I've argued that there are many ways to connect and deepen our relationship with our children, and that *you and your child* get to be the experts on that. We identified pain points and outlined the ways that our perinatal mood can be shaped by our parenting experiences with (or without) fertility, birth, sleep, work, relationships, food, and our own bodies.

And then we turned to hope and healing. We *can* recover from PMADs and develop a solid grounding in postpartum resilience. The pathway to this is unique to each parent, and I have suggested that radical self-permission, family-centred parenting, self-parenting, and being less alone are important pillars in your exploration of what helps. I have also claimed that the pathway forward can't just be about meeting our own support needs but must include meeting the support needs of *all* parents.

This book has also invited you into a new way to work with parental mental health. Because of the culture of impossible parenting, all parents need mental health support, with some of us needing more than others. I hope you feel invited into a call to action for changing the way we think about parenting in general. My goal is for the impact of parenting identity on our moods to be reimagined so that we recognize its inherent contradictions and challenges. It's not the experience of raising children that negatively impacts mental health; it's trying to parent in this culture that is causing so much suffering. As we work together to shift the culture from one of overwhelm to one of support and encouragement, I believe it will become easier to access the pleasure of parenting more frequently. Clearly there are parts of parenting that are incredibly joyful and connective, which is why so many of us grow our families beyond one child.

What is my dream for you, dear parents? So much compassion that it fills your whole self, overflows into your families, defines your communities, and provides allyship to the most vulnerable and marginalized among us as we advocate for sustainable positive change.

AUTHOR'S NOTE

T hings have changed quite a bit since I wrote this book. I had finished editing it in early March 2020 and had travelled to Austin, Texas, to take a break and catch my breath, only to find myself flying home soon after arriving because of increasing COVID-19 concerns. When we got back, everything was different. While we quarantined for two weeks, I watched as most of the world shut down bit by bit until it came to a standstill. Like most social workers, I shifted my practice to working online and spent the days hearing similar stories of parents who were really scared. They were scared about mass unemployment or getting sick or how the hell they were going to parent their children when they felt like they were barely holding it together. It was hard to hold space for my beloved clients because I was scared, too, and soon it became a ritual to finish my last session and walk directly to the liquor cabinet for a Scotch and a cry.

It felt important to add a note about the impact of the pandemic on parents with young children. As I write this, we are now three months into social distancing and things have become strangely normalized, which I suppose is reflective of humanity's ability to adapt. It feels very much like the pandemic has created a "before time" and an "after time," with only a fuzzy image of what the future of normal looks like. I don't know that there is anything that feels normal about family life right now, because the landscape of parenting in Canada has changed so dramatically. Although in the "before time" parents had often said they wished for a slower pace of life with more time with their family, they certainly didn't want it like this! In many ways, the pandemic has created even more barriers in the areas most impacted by impossible-parenting culture because social distancing with young children, particularly while working, doesn't feel sustainable. I'd like to return to the areas of birth, sleep, relationships, and bodies, and touch on the impact the pandemic has had on each one.

BIRTH

Being pregnant during the pandemic has left many of my clients feeling very out of control. Most prenatal appointments have been moved online, yet pregnant people still find themselves venturing out of the house for ultrasounds, lab work, or other in-person appointments. Needing to go to the hospital is particularly scary for those who are high risk/immune compromised or who live with a high-risk/immune-compromised person. Access to termination and loss support has also had sudden added barriers. Parents are terrified by thoughts of birthing alone, or unthinkably, having their babies separated from them after birth (when they do not want this). Within my community, I have heard stories of parents not being able to visit or nurse babies in the NICU, or pregnant people suddenly switching to home birth because they were so scared of the hospital, even though they desperately wanted access to an epidural. One community member, who had to birth without her partner (he had a cough) and was instead attended by a nurse in full personal protective gear, shared the trouble she was having in processing the birth. She felt both traumatized by the experience while simultaneously like she was incredibly resilient for birthing without emotional or physical support. Debates between those who argue "public-health protocols trump all" and "no one should ever be forced to birth without their chosen support" created significant tension within the birth professional community. While I understand the arguments of both sides and how incredibly complex medical decisions are during the pandemic, I also anticipate a new bucket of birth trauma directly related to birth and reproductive experiences impacted by the pandemic.

Those undergoing fertility treatment were also suddenly impacted by the pandemic shutdown. I have spent hours processing deep disappointment with those who still do not have a date for when they can reattempt IUI or IVF. Some have given up and are grieving that their family will never be what they had dreamed of. Similarly, many parents with newborns or who are on parental leave are also processing the loss of the postpartum experience they had planned. Most have been unable to have family or friends meet their babies and have lost the support they were relying on. There has been a lot of sadness for those who were anticipating this time to be joyful.

SLEEP

The impact of the pandemic on sleep has mostly been in the form of insomnia, with many parents sharing that they are struggling with racing thoughts about money or illness, and that these thoughts are keeping them up at night. Regardless of sleep, the one story that seems to be true for all parents right now is that they are so incredibly tired. This is for many reasons, but one of the most significant is that child care vanished overnight; as if the sudden dismantling of community wasn't bad enough, it was compounded by limitations on taking kids outside to run or play or enjoy the sun. This has been especially hard for parents living in high-rise buildings or those who don't have access to a yard or green space. Many parents have shared that they are suddenly quite worried about their children's behaviour, as their children have stopped napping or sleeping like they used to or are needier than ever. This has created a lot of tense households, with kids who have meltdowns multiple times throughout the day being cared for by exhausted and stressed parents that have little patience for managing these meltdowns, and who don't have the ability to take a break or call in extra support. It's not surprising that I've had a sudden spike of former clients asking to come back to see me because they are finding it almost impossible to cope. Many parents are beating themselves up emotionally for how irritable and frustrated they are with their children and have trouble remembering that the decisions made to increase public safety were made so fast that they weren't designed with sustainability in mind. We were originally told it would be only a few weeks, and what we are experiencing now are the understandable negative mental-health impacts of what it is like to try and parent like this for months at a time.

Parents who are essential workers have additional stress related to finding emergency child care and concerns about bringing COVID-19 into their homes, but some of the most exhausted parents I've talked to are those that are trying to work from home without child care. What is even more intense is that many of these parents were also expected to start home-schooling their children at the same time — an idea that makes sense on many levels but that is also loaded with barriers. The most obvious one is that it simply isn't possible to work full time and home-school children at the same time, particularly when you have more than one child and not enough access to computers (if you even have computers and internet access, which was required for switching to online learning). Another barrier, which I can personally attest to, is that depending on the grade your child is in, home-schooling is humiliating for parents because suddenly your children realize that you can't do middle-school math or conjugate verbs in French. I'm in awe of how teachers do this all day, especially those who are also parents and have to try and teach their own children after distance teaching all their students.

RELATIONSHIPS

Socially distancing with a partner has created a lot of mixed responses for clients. Some people love it and are so grateful to have someone to share the load with, particularly if their partner is newly unemployed. One client felt very validated when her male partner, who had never been at home full time with their kids, came to her in tears, admitting that he hadn't known it was so hard to parent full time; he wanted her to know that he thought she was amazing. But this certainly isn't every family's experience, with many couples claiming that they are fighting more than ever before. When both parents are working from home there just isn't any time to miss each other, and it's not normal for us to spend this much time with *anyone*, even our most loved people. We are getting on each other's nerves and running out of things to talk about because we are together so much. Tragically, I also recently learned from a friend who works in the field that domestic violence rates have gone up 400 percent.

Many articles have come out about the cost of the pandemic on mothers in heterosexual relationships, because for many families it has been quite high. Some women have quit their jobs because of the overwhelming demands of trying to work and parent without child care or because their partners simply announced that because they earn more money, their work should be prioritized. The mental load of primary parents has increased substantially with one parent doing most of the "worry work" for the house. This person keeps up to date with the public health advice (e.g., makes everyone sing the happy birthday song while they wash their hands); decides what the family's level of risk is going to be (e.g., going to the grocery store versus ordering groceries online); or takes on pandemic specific tasks (e.g., making homemade masks or sanitizing door handles). This adds up to a significant amount of extra work!

Finally, families with essential workers have different stress because although they aren't spending endless time together, the additional risk and exposure that comes from going out into the community is scary. How families are managing this is negotiated in different ways, but each way comes with its own unique set of relationship challenges. Some parents are concerned that their partner doesn't take enough safety precautions or that their boss isn't doing enough to keep them safe. Others resent that their partners get to leave the house or feel abandoned because they made the painful decision to move out during the height of the pandemic to keep their family safe. It's been tough whether you are with your loved ones all day or not.

BODIES

One of the hardest parts of the pandemic is that we have become afraid of our bodies. Any cough or slight rise in temperature sends most of us into alarm, especially for essential workers who live with a deep fear of spreading COVID-19. Most of us aren't able to support our bodies in the same way as we did before because it's harder to get a long hug or pain treatments or to work out. There have also been health consequences for those who did not become ill with COVID-19 but had important surgeries and medical procedures put on hold. Cancelled cancer treatments, organ transplants, and MRIs are just a few of the lesser seen body costs related to the pandemic.

I've noticed many of us reaching to drugs and alcohol as a way to distract, soothe, or try to manage boredom, only to have the frequency of use then become an additional stress. In the past three months, a few clients have asked me whether I think they are alcoholics, hoping to be assured they are not. The rise of disordered eating thought patterns is concerning, even though so many of us have gained weight over the last couple of months that the phrase "the COVID nineteen" (a play on "the freshman fifteen") has emerged to normalize the experience. A loving reminder, friends, that you are allowed to gain weight and that your weight does not equate with your worthiness.

Of course, some of you reading this will have been diagnosed with COVID-19 and lived through the experience, and possibly trauma, of both surviving it and giving it to others. I've heard that the guilt and internalized shame of those who have had COVID-19 has been one of the toughest parts, because even though parents are aware that it's not their fault they contracted the virus, they nevertheless feel the public stigma associated with a positive diagnosis.

IMPACT ON MENTAL HEALTH

Obviously, there has been a significant impact on parental mental health. Parents seem to be going back and forth between trying to make the best of it and then experiencing an existential crisis about life as we know it being over. Most of us have been bombarded with depressive feelings and confusing, anxious feelings while we figure out how to assess the risks associated with this new reality. This is not helped by the frequency of trauma stories and images being produced by the media, with terrifying stories of the worst-case scenarios of what COVID-19 can do. Despite the better outcomes for children with the virus, most parents are deeply worried about their children's safety. And even if parents haven't felt too personally impacted by the pandemic, many still feel deeply ungrounded, which is normal when going through massive social change at a rapid pace. Overall, parental mental health does seem to be getting worse, with many parents describing severe burnout. I think that the true cost of the pandemic on mental health will not be fully understood until we feel safer from the virus itself.

Interestingly, some of my most anxious clients are coping the best and those with compulsive anxiety behaviours, such as cleaning and hand-washing, are enjoying that these behaviours went from being a problem they are told they must work on to a social norm. One client opened our session by joking, "Well, well, well! Looks like we're all washing our hands one hundred times a day now!" which really highlights that the symptoms of mental illness have to be understood in context. What is considered normal mental health reflects what our community agrees to be normal, and this shifts over time, just like parenting norms do.

I know that not all families are impacted the same way and that parents can have widely different experiences depending on access to resources. Some people have suffered a lot during the pandemic. Thousands lost loved ones to the virus. Many more were unable to sit bedside to care for sick family members. The stress of unemployment, losing a small business, or working without child care is excruciating. Racial inequality has continued through the pandemic. Many members of our Chinese communities experienced overt racism because the virus was first identified in China, and our Black communities are grieving hard because of widespread anti-Black violence. And while violence and racism always have a negative impact on mental health, the pandemic makes social action and trauma processing extra difficult because it creates more challenges to organizing community actions, and protesting becomes additionally risky with such a contagious virus.

WHAT HELPS?

I'm not actually sure what helps. Sometimes nothing helps because there is so much grief and loss being experienced by families. And unfortunately, there isn't much to do about grief other than to figure out how to hold it, and holding it feels bad. What I can share are some simple tips that sometimes help. I've been sharing these with many clients because we don't know how much longer this is going to be or how many times we are going to be asked to socially isolate over the next few years.

- Anchor in self-compassion and self-validation. Pandemics suck. It's okay to be scared. It's okay to be tired. It's okay to not be at your best.
- Recognize that there isn't a lot in your control right now. Rather than plan for the future, try to focus on what you can control in the present, even if it's just making sure you change from pyjamas to sweatpants every morning.
- Ask yourself how you want to feel during the pandemic. Safe? Connected? As normal as possible? Then set your life up to move towards that feeling by asking, "Will this bring me further or closer to feeling the way I want to feel?" If obsessing over social media updates doesn't make you feel safe, take a break.
- You don't have to use this time to learn how to bake or garden or take on a new workout routine. If it feels good, go for it. If it feels like a "should," really consider if it's adding to or hindering your mental health.
- Please, please, let go of screen-time guilt. It's okay if the PAW Patrol team becomes your other co-parent right now.
- See if you can identify your internal "pandemic part" so that you can build a relationship to it. Pandemic parts I have met so far have been "the panicker," who worries about getting sick every

time they leave the house; "the existential crisis," who feels over-whelmed by all the hurt in the world; "the take charge boss," who self-soothes through creating systems and protocols; and "the minimizer," who doesn't understand what the big deal is. Your pandemic part has a protective function and it's helpful to know what need it's trying to have met.

- Come back to the question "Is there anything I can do about this right now?" and practise the art of not-knowing. Remember that if someone had told us at the end of 2019 that soon everything would be cancelled and we would have to line up for groceries while wearing gloves and a mask, most of us would have spiralled with anxiety. But here we are doing it, even though we don't want to.

I want to end on a positive note because things are certainly not hopeless. As much as I have been noticing the hardship of the pandemic, I have also seen a lot that brings me hope. Since schools and daycares have closed, there has been more public conversation about the workload and mental health of parents, which is highlighting how much needs to change. Communities have rallied around each other in socially distant ways, such as buying supplies for those who don't feel safe leaving the house or creating online check-ins. And I've seen so much compassion between parents as they reassure each other their kids are going to be okay.

With so many parents trying to give themselves — and others — per-mission to be a "good enough" parent right now, it feels like an oppor-tunity to make "good enough" parenting a permanent cultural norm. So, now I have a new dream for you, dear parents. My COVID-19 dream for you is that you honour all that you have lost, while holding on to gratitude for all that you have. I think that this ability to host contra-dictory emotions will guide us as we settle into a new era of parenting.

ACKNOWLEDGEMENTS

I had *a lot* of help putting this book together. It takes a village not only to raise a child, but also to write a book! My beloved clients, you are the ultimate teachers. I also want to express a giant thank-you to everyone who agreed to be interviewed: Laura, for your infinite wisdom on bodies; Laurie, for holding my confidence when I can't; Bianca, for everything you have taught me about birth (and life!); Brittany-Lyne, for being the most compassionate midwife I know; Stephanie, for changing everything I thought I knew about infant sleep; Summer, for giving me permission to stay fat; Tynan, for opening my eyes to the complexities of postpartum intimacy; Alana, for helping me solidify my personal narrative about alcohol; and Gabrielle, for deepening my understanding about what it means to provide support that lands.

I also want to offer sincere gratitude for the people who helped me figure out how to get my thoughts onto paper. Caroline, this project would still be an idea in my head without your brilliant editorial eye and thorough feedback. Victoria, your editing pushed this project forward and masterfully found a way to develop all the underdeveloped ideas. And Jess, your editing transformed my academic rhetoric into something that people can read!

This book would not exist without Dayna's kind "you should write a book!" encouragement, so thank you for that! Mindy, your hilarious validation kept me grounded in the early years of parenting, and

I couldn't have made it through without you. Natalie, huge portions of this book feel like a documented version of our shoptalk. I can't express how much I owe to you for your thoughtful critique and for helping me become a better social worker.

Finally, thank you to Janna and the kids, who graciously let me tell our family's stories. And for allowing me to escape family and household responsibilities so I could write. And for being my family. I like you all so much.

* * *

I mentioned a lot of people and ideas in this book, but this is only the tip of the iceberg! I bet you want to learn more, and I want to make that easy for you. Please check out these resources for lots of great information.

Chapter Four

Laurie Sanci, yourbestlifewithoutkids.com
bebo mia, bebomia.com
Natalie Grynpas, gardenavenuetherapy.com
Trystan Reese and Biff Chaplow, biffandi.com

Chapter Five

Stephanie Kishimoto, sleep-parenting.com
Joeyband, joeyband.com
Yoga: For information about practising yoga within the context of cultural appropriation, read the article "Yoga and the Roots of Cultural Appropriation" by Shreena Gandhi and Lillie Wolff, kzoo.edu/praxis/yoga

Chapter Six

"Why I Want a Wife," by Judy Brady Syfers: wsfcs.k12.nc.us/cms/lib/NC01001395/Centricity/Domain/10659/I%20Want%20a%20Wife.pdf

Tynan Rhea, tynanrhea.com
Julie and John Gottman, gottman.com

Chapter Seven

Victoria Millious, ca.linkedin.com/in/victorianivamillious
Brittany-Lyne Carriere, facebook.com/QueerBirthToronto
Summer Innanen, summerinnanen.com
Virgie Tovar, virgietovar.com
"The Operational Guidance on Infant Feeding in Emergencies,"
    ennonline.net/operationalguidance-v3-2017

Chapter Eight

Elisabeth Schüssler Fiorenza, hds.harvard.edu/people/
    elisabeth-schüssler-fiorenza
Postpartum Support Toronto, postpartumsupporttoronto.com

Chapter Nine

Tara Brach, tarabrach.com
Kristin Neff, self-compassion.org
Kelly McGonigal, kellymcgonigal.com

Chapter Ten

Dan Siegel, drdansiegel.com

Chapter Eleven

Alana Nugent, ca.linkedin.com/in/alana-nugent-4b274aa8

Chapter Twelve

Gabrielle Griffith, facebook.com/yourqueerdoula

NOTES

Part 1: Naming

1. Karen Kleiman, *The Postpartum Husband: Practical Solutions for Living with Postpartum Depression* (Bloomington, IN: Xlibris, 2000), 40.

Chapter Two: The Perinatal Mood Framework

1. Joyce Venis and Suzanne McCloskey, *Postpartum Depression Demystified* (New York: Avalon Publishing Group, 2007).
2. J. Guintivano, M. Arad, T.D. Gould, J.L. Payne, and Z.A. Kaminsky, "Antenatal Prediction of Postpartum Depression with Blood DNA Methylation Biomarkers," *Molecular Psychiatry* 19 (2014): 560–67.
3. Oscar Serrallach, *The Postnatal Depletion Cure* (New York: Hachette, 2018), 36.
4. Alex Korb and Daniel Siegel, *The Upward Spiral: Using Neuroscience to Reserve Depression, One Small Change at a Time* (Oakland, CA: New Harbinger Publications, 2015), 15.
5. Korb and Siegel.
6. Scott Anderson, John Cryan, and Ted Dinan, *The Psychobiotic*

Revolution: Mood, Food, and the New Science of the Gut-Brain Connection (Washington, DC: National Geographic Partners, 2017).

7. Karen Kleiman and Amy Wenzel, *Dropping the Baby and Other Scary Thoughts* (New York: Routledge, 2011), 45–50.

8. Korb and Siegel, *The Upward Spiral*, 185.

9. Linda Clark Amankwaa, "Maternal Postpartum Role Collapse as a Theory of Postpartum Depression," *The Qualitative Report* 10, no. 1 (2015): 21–38.

10. Amankwaa.

11. Amankwaa.

12. Amankwaa.

13. Amankwaa.

14. Amankwaa.

15. Sharon Hays, *The Cultural Contradictions of Motherhood* (New Haven, CT: Yale University Press, 1996).

16. Linda Rose Ennis, "Intensive Mothering: Revisiting the Issues Today," in *Intensive Mothering: The Cultural Contradictions of Modern Motherhood*, edited by Linda Rose Ennis (Bradford, ON: Demeter Press, 2014), 5.

17. Madeline Walker, "Intensive Mothering, Elimination Communication and the Call to Eden," in *Intensive Mothering: The Cultural Contradictions of Modern Motherhood*, edited by Linda Rose Ennis (Bradford, ON: Demeter Press, 2014), 223.

18. Charlotte Faircloth, "Is Attachment Parenting Intensive Mothering?," in *Intensive Mothering: The Cultural Contradictions of Modern Motherhood*, edited by Linda Rose Ennis (Bradford, Ontario: Demeter Press, 2014).

19. I. Bretherton and K.A. Munholland, "Internal Working Models in Attachment Relationships: A Construct Revisited," in *Handbook of Attachment: Theory, research, and clinical applications*, edited by J. Cassidy and P. R. Shaver (New York: Guilford Press, 1999), 89–111.

20. Bretherton and Munholland.

21. Bretherton and Munholland.

22. Bretherton and Munholland.

23. "What is Attachment Parenting?" Attachment Parenting Canada, last modified 2008, attachmentparenting.ca/about .html.

24. Diana Divecha, "Why Attachment Parenting is Not the Same as Secure Attachment," *Greater Good* magazine, May 2, 2018, greatergood.berkeley.edu/article/item/why_attachment_parenting _is_not_the_same_as_secure_attachment.

25. "What is Attachment Parenting?"

26. Faircloth, "Is Attachment Parenting Intensive Mothering?," 181.

27. Faircloth, 187.

28. Walker, "Intensive Mothering, Elimination Communication," 233.

29. Hays, *Cultural Contradictions.*

30. Tatjana Takseva, "How Contemporary Consumerism Shapes Intensive Mothering," in *Intensive Mothering: The Cultural Contradictions of Modern Motherhood,* edited by Linda Rose Ennis (Bradford, ON: Demeter Press, 2014), 222.

31. J. Lauren Johnson, "The Best I Can: Hope for Single Parents in the Age of Intensive Mothering," in *Intensive Mothering: The Cultural Contradictions of Modern Motherhood,* edited by Linda Rose Ennis (Bradford, ON: Demeter Press, 2014), 270.

32. Judith Rich Harris, *The Nature Assumption: Why Children Turn Out the Way They Do* (New York: Touchstone, 1998).

33. Johnson, 272.

34. Johnson, 274.

35. Johnson, 274.

36. Johnson, 273.

37. Johnson, 272.

38. Faith Galliano Desai, "Transpersonal Motherhood: A Practical Holistic Model of Motherhood," in *Intensive Mothering: The Cultural Contradictions of Modern Motherhood,* edited by Linda Rose Ennis (Bradford, ON: Demeter Press, 2014), 327.

Chapter Three: Impossible Parenting

1.   Kim Huisman and Elizabeth Joy, "The Cultural Contradictions of Motherhood Revisited: Continuities and Changes," in *Intensive Mothering: The Cultural Contradictions of Modern Motherhood*, edited by Linda Rose Ennis (Bradford, ON: Demeter Press, 2014), 97.

2.   Melissa A. Milkie and Catharine H. Warner, "Status Safeguarding: Mothers' Work to Secure Children's Place in the Social Hierarchy," in *Intensive Mothering: The Cultural Contradictions of Modern Motherhood*, edited by Linda Rose Ennis (Bradford, ON: Demeter Press, 2014), 68.

3.   Milkie and Warner, 69, 75–76.

4.   Lisa M. Mitchell, "Better Babies, Better Mothers: Baby Sign Language and Intensive Mothering," in *Intensive Mothering: The Cultural Contradictions of Modern Motherhood*, edited by Linda Rose Ennis (Bradford, ON: Demeter Press, 2014), 196, 206.

5.   Mitchell, 199.

6.   Linda Rose Ennis, "Intensive Mothering: Revisiting the Issues Today," in *Intensive Mothering: The Cultural Contradictions of Modern Motherhood*, edited by Linda Rose Ennis (Bradford, ON: Demeter Press, 2014), 334.

7.   Solveig Brown, "Intensive Mothering as an Adaptive Response to Our Cultural Environment," in *Intensive Mothering: The Cultural Contradictions of Modern Motherhood*, edited by Linda Rose Ennis (Bradford, ON: Demeter Press, 2014), 32.

8.   Brown.

9.   Tatjana Takseva, "How Contemporary Consumerism Shapes Intensive Mothering Practices," in *Intensive Mothering: The Cultural Contradictions of Modern Motherhood*, edited by Linda Rose Ennis (Bradford, ON: Demeter Press, 2014), 219.

10. Takseva, 220–21.

11. Brown, "Intensive Mothering as an Adaptive Response," 33.

12. Madeline Walker, "Intensive Mothering, Elimination Communication and the Call to Eden," in *Intensive Mothering: The*

Cultural Contradictions of Modern Motherhood, edited by Linda Rose Ennis (Bradford, ON: Demeter Press, 2014), 236.

13. Takseva, "Contemporary Consumerism," 223–27.

14. Helena Vissing, "The Ideal Mother Fantasy and Its Protective Function," in *Intensive Mothering: The Cultural Contradictions of Modern Motherhood*, edited by Linda Rose Ennis (Bradford, ON: Demeter Press, 2014), 108.

15. Vissing, 108.

16. Kristen Abati McHenry and Denise Schultz, "Skinny Jeans: Perfection and Competition in Motherhood," in *Intensive Mothering: The Cultural Contradictions of Modern Motherhood*, edited by Linda Rose Ennis (Bradford, ON: Demeter Press, 2014), 302.

17. Vissing, "The Ideal Mother Fantasy," 107.

18. Vissing, 107.

19. Vissing, 114.

20. Susan J. Douglas and Meredith W. Michaels, *The Mommy Myth* (New York: Free Press, 2004), 6.

21. Jennifer Senior, *All Joy and No Fun* (New York: HarperCollins, 2014).

22. Lorin Basden Arnold, "I Don't Know Where You End and I Begin: Challenging Boundaries of the Self and Intensive Mothering," in *Intensive Mothering: The Cultural Contradictions of Modern Motherhood*, edited by Linda Rose Ennis (Bradford, ON: Demeter Press, 2014), 53.

23. Amankwaa, "Maternal Postpartum Role Collapse."

24. Simone Vigod, Lori Ross, and Stephanie George, "Promoting Wellness. Extending Our Reach" (lecture, Perinatal Mental Health Conference, Burlington, ON, October 24, 2019).

25. Sondra Medina and Sandy Magnuson, "Motherhood in the 21st Century: Implications for Counselors," *Journal of Counselling and Development* 87 (2009): 90–96.

26. Medina and Magnuson.

27. J. Lauren Johnson, "The Best I Can: Hope for Single Parents in the Age of Intensive Mothering," in *Intensive Mothering: The Cultural Contradictions of Modern Motherhood*, edited by Linda Rose Ennis (Bradford, ON: Demeter Press, 2014), 268.

28. Christi L. Gross, Brianna Turgeon, Tiffany Taylor, and Kasey Lansberry, "State Intervention and Intensive Mothering," in *Intensive Mothering: The Cultural Contradictions of Modern Motherhood*, edited by Linda Rose Ennis (Bradford, ON: Demeter Press, 2014), 170.

29. Llesenia Anguiano, "A Psychoeducational Support Group for Latinas with Postpartum Depression Raising Children Within the Welfare System" (unpublished grant proposal, California State University, Long Beach, 2011), pqdtopen.proquest.com/pubnum/1499230.html.

30. Melinda Vandenbeld Giles, "From 'Need' to 'Risk': The Neoliberal Construction of the 'Bad' Mothers," *Journal of Association for Research on Mothering* 31, no. 1 (2012): 112–33.

31. Johnson, "The Best I Can," 268.

Chapter Four: Birth

1. L. Hadfield, N. Rudoe, and J. Sanderson-Mann, "Motherhood, Choice and the British Media: A Time to Reflect," *Gender and Education* 19, no. 2 (2007): 255–63.

2. Laura Carroll, *The Baby Making Matrix* (London: Live True Books, 2012).

3. Carroll.

4. I use brackets around "dis" to highlight that what it means to have an ability or disability is impacted by the social model of disability.

5. Allison McDonald Ace, Ariel Ng Bourbonnais, and Caroline Starr, eds., *Through, Not Around: Stories of Infertility and Pregnancy Loss* (Toronto: Dundurn Press, 2019).

6. Michael Lista, "A Doctor's Deception," *Toronto Life*, July 24, 2019, torontolife.com/city/greed-betrayal-medical-misconduct-north-york-general.

7. Lista.

8. *WHO Recommendations: Intrapartum Care for a Positive Childbirth Experience* (Geneva: World Health Organization, 2018), 1, who.int/reproductivehealth/publications/intrapartum -care-guidelines/en.

9. Rebecca Dekker, "The Evidence on: Erythromycin Eye Ointment for Newborns," *Evidence Based Birth*, November 12, 2012, last modified August 3, 2017, evidencebasedbirth.com/ is-erythromycin-eye-ointment-always-necessary-for-newborns.

10. Dekker.

11. Ashley Ashbacher, "Women's Experiences of Birth Trauma and Postpartum Mental Health" (Social Work masters clinical research paper, University of St. Thomas, St. Paul, MN, 2013), 2.

12. Ashbacher.

Chapter Five: Sleep

1. David Richter, Michael D. Krame, Nicole K.Y. Tang, Hawley E. Montgomery-Downsand, and Sakari Lemola, "Long Term Effects of Pregnancy and Childbirth on Sleep Satisfaction and Duration of First-Time and Experienced Mothers and Fathers," *Sleep Research Society* 42, no. 4 (2019): 1–10.

2. Ann Douglas, *Happy Parents, Happy Kids* (Toronto: HarperCollins, 2019), 175–76.

3. Douglas, 175.

4. Alexandra Sacks and Catherine Birndorf, *What No One Tells You: A Guide to Your Emotions from Pregnancy to Motherhood* (New York: Simon & Schuster, 2019), 230–31.

5. Verinder Sharma and Dwight Mazmanian, "Sleep Loss and Postpartum Psychosis," *Bipolar Disorders* 5, no. 2 (2003): 95–105.

6. T.B. Strouse, M.P. Szuba, and L.R. Baxter, "Response to Sleep Deprivation in Three Women with Postpartum Psychosis," *Journal of Clinical Psychiatry* 53, no. 6 (1992): 204–6.

7. Emily Oster, *Cribsheet* (New York: Penguin Press, 2019), 181.

8. Oster, 181.

Chapter Six: Relationships

1. Arlie Hochschild and Anne Machung, *The Second Shift: Working Families and the Revolution at Home* (New York: Penguin Group, 2012).
2. Javier Cerrato and Eva Cifre, "Gender Inequality in Household Chores and Work-Family Conflict," *Frontiers in Psychology* 9, no. 1330 (2018): 7.
3. Kelly Sullivan, "Sleep Duration and Feeling Rested are Differently Associated with Having Children Among Men and Women," *American Academy of Neurology* 88 (2017).
4. Sullivan.
5. J. Lauren Johnson, "The Best I Can: Hope for Single Parents in the Age of Intensive Mothering," in *Intensive Mothering: The Cultural Contradictions of Modern Motherhood*, edited by Linda Rose Ennis (Bradford, ON: Demeter Press, 2014), 269.
6. Johnson.
7. Ellen Cole, Esther D. Rothburn, and Janet M. Wright, *Lesbian Step Families: An Ethnography of Love* (New York: Routledge, 1998).
8. Emily Oster, *Cribsheet* (New York: Penguin Press, 2019), 277.
9. Glenda Corwin, *Sexual Intimacy for Women: A Guide for Same-Sex Couples* (Berkeley, CA: Seal Press, 2010).

Chapter Seven: Bodies

1. Centers for Disease Control and Prevention, "Weight Gain During Pregnancy," last modified January 17, 2019, cdc.gov/reproductivehealth/maternalinfanthealth/pregnancy-weight-gain.htm.
2. Centers for Disease Control and Prevention, "More Than 3 Million US Women At Risk For Alcohol-Exposed Pregnancy," last modified February 2, 2016, cdc.gov/media/releases/2016/p0202-alcohol-exposed-pregnancy.html.

3. Judith J. Wurtman and Nina Frusztajer Marquis, *The Serotonin Power Diet* (New York: Rodale, 2006).

4. Emily Oster, *Cribsheet* (New York: Penguin Press, 2019), 68.

5. Oster, 68.

6. Kristen Thompson, "Yes, Breast IS Best, But It's Time to Retire That Phrase Once and For All," last modified January 23, 2019, todaysparent.com/baby/breastfeeding/yes-breast-is-best-but-its-time-to-retire-that-phrase-once-and-for-all.

7. Linda Gionet, "Breastfeeding Trends in Canada," Statistics Canada, last modified November 27, 2015, 150.statcan.gc.ca/n1/pub/82-624-x/2013001/article/11879-eng.htm.

8. Linda Gionet.

9. Oster, *Cribsheet*, 69.

10. Country Jung, *Lactivism* (Philadelphia: Basic Books, 2005).

11. Oster, *Cribsheet*, 6.

12. Oster, 6.

13. Oster, 70.

14. Oster, 86.

Part 3: Healing

1. Emily Nagoski and Amelia Nagoski, *Burnout* (New York: Ballantine Books, 2019), 81.

Chapter Eight: Recovery

1. Stephanie Knaak, "Having a Tough Time: Towards an Understanding of the Psycho-Social Causes of Postpartum Emotional Distress," *Journal of the Association for the Research on Mothering* 11, no. 1 (2009): 80–94.

2. Knaak.

3. Rena Bina, "The Impact of Cultural Factors on Postpartum Depression: A Literature Review," *Health Care for Women International* 29 (2008): 568–92.

4. Bina.

5. Michael Lambert and Dean Barley, "Research Summary on the Therapeutic Relationship and Psychotherapy Outcome," *Psychotherapy: Theory, Research, Practice, Training* 38, no. 4 (2001): 357–61.

Chapter Nine: Self-Permission

1. Melissa Milkie and Catharine Warner, "Mothers' Work to Secure Children's Place in the Social Hierarchy," in *Intensive Mothering: The Cultural Contradictions of Modern Motherhood*, edited by Linda Rose Ennis (Bradford, ON: Demeter Press, 2014), 68.

2. Alison Gopnik, *The Gardener and the Carpenter: What the New Science of Child Development Tells Us about the Relationship between Parents and Children* (New York: Farrar, Straus, and Giroux, 2016).

3. Ann Douglas, *Happy Parents, Happy Kids* (Toronto: Harper-Collins, 2019), 77–78.

4. Alexandra Sacks, "A New Way to Think About the Transition to Motherhood," filmed May 2018, TED video, 5:47, ted .com/talks/alexandra_sacks_a_new_way_to_think_about_the _transition_to_motherhood?language=en.

5. Alexandra Sacks and Catherine Birndorf, *What No One Tells You: A Guide to Your Emotions from Pregnancy to Motherhood* (New York: Simon & Schuster, 2019), 197.

6. Sacks and Birndorf, 197.

7. I created this exercise drawing from Internal Family Systems and Gestalt modalities, as well as the parts model from the Coaches Training Institute.

Chapter Ten: Family-Centred Parenting

1. Solveig Brown, "Intensive Mothering as an Adaptive Response to our Cultural Environment," in *Intensive Mothering: The Cultural Contradictions of Modern Motherhood*, edited by Linda Rose Ennis (Bradford, ON: Demeter Press, 2014), 38.

2. Lorin Basden Arnold, "I Don't Know Where You End and I Begin: Challenging Boundaries of the Self and Intensive Mothering," in *Intensive Mothering: The Cultural Contradictions of Modern Motherhood*, edited by Linda Rose Ennis (Bradford, ON: Demeter Press, 2014), 56.

3. Virginia H. Mackintosh, Miriam Liss, and Holly H. Schiffrin, "Using A Quantitative Measure to Explore Intensive Mothering Ideology," in *Intensive Mothering: The Cultural Contradictions of Modern Motherhood*, edited by Linda Rose Ennis (Bradford, ON: Demeter Press, 2014), 152.

4. Basden Arnold, "I Don't Know Where You End and I Begin," 57.

5. Helena Vissing, "The Ideal Mother Fantasy and Its Protective Function," in *Intensive Mothering: The Cultural Contradictions of Modern Motherhood*, edited by Linda Rose Ennis (Bradford, ON: Demeter Press, 2014), 117.

6. Vissing.

7. Vissing, 105.

8. Vissing.

9. I adapted this tool from the Coaches Training Institute's personal values exploration exercise.

10. J Li, "The Decide 10 Rating System," Medium, November 25, 2017, medium.com/prototypethinking/the-should-we-do-this-rating -system-3aac062b1b91.

11. D.W. Winnicott, *Winnicott on the Child* (Cambridge, MA: Perseus Publishing, 2002), 51.

12. Winnicott, 179.

13. Alexandra Sacks and Catherine Birndorf, *What No One Tells You: A Guide to Your Emotions from Pregnancy to Motherhood* (New York: Simon & Schuster, 2019), 196.

14. Sacks and Birndorf, 197.

15. Winnicott, *On the Child*, 51.

16. Deb Dana, *The Polyvagal Theory in Therapy* (New York: WW Norton and Company, 2018), 124.

17. Emily Nagoski and Amelia Nagoski, *Burnout* (New York: Ballantine Books, 2019), 4–5.

18. Nagoski and Nagoski, 7.

19. Nagoski and Nagoski, 6.

20. Nagoski and Nagoski, 15–16.

Chapter Eleven: Self-Parenting

1. Ann Douglas, *Happy Parents, Happy Kids* (Toronto: Harper-Collins, 2019), 33, 36, 45.

2. Kelly Diels, "The Female Lifestyle Empowerment Brand. An Introduction," January 4, 2016, kellydiels.com/female -lifestyle-empowerment-brand-introduction.

3. Vladimir Poznyak and Dag Rekve, eds., *Global Status Report on Alcohol and Health* (Geneva: World Health Organization, 2018), who.int/substance_abuse/publications/global_alcohol_ report/gsr_2018/en.

4. Here I'm referring to recreational use or use with the intention to reduce stress. This does not include parents who struggle with alcohol addiction or cannot stop drinking when they want to.

5. Brené Brown, *Rising Strong* (New York: Random House, 2015).

6. This is a tip I learned from the Reproductive Life Stages Program at Women's College Hospital in Toronto.

7. Lorin Basden Arnold, "I Don't Know Where You End and I Begin: Challenging Boundaries of the Self and Intensive Mothering," in *Intensive Mothering: The Cultural Contradictions of Modern Motherhood*, edited by Linda Rose Ennis (Bradford, ON: Demeter Press, 2014), 56.

8. Virginia H. Mackintosh, Miriam Liss, and Holly H. Schiffrin, "Using A Quantitative Measure to Explore Intensive Mothering

Ideology," in *Intensive Mothering: The Cultural Contradictions of Modern Motherhood*, edited by Linda Rose Ennis (Bradford, ON: Demeter Press, 2014), 145.

9. Linda Ross Ennis, "Balancing Separation-Connection in Mothering," in *Intensive Mothering: The Cultural Contradictions of Modern Motherhood*, edited by Linda Rose Ennis (Bradford, ON: Demeter Press, 2014), 332.

10. This concept isn't one I made up myself! I learned it from a supervisor during my masters of social work placement and want to give due credit.

11. Faith Galliano Desai, "Transpersonal Motherhood: A Practical and Holistic Model of Motherhood," in *Intensive Mothering: The Cultural Contradictions of Modern Motherhood*, edited by Linda Rose Ennis (Bradford, ON: Demeter Press, 2014), 315.

12. Internal Family Systems therapy is an excellent way to do this kind of complex work.

13. Maya-Merida Paltineau, "From Intensive Mothering to Identity Parenting," in *Intensive Mothering: The Cultural Contradictions of Modern Motherhood*, edited by Linda Rose Ennis (Bradford, ON: Demeter Press, 2014), 132.

14. Galliano Desai, "Transpersonal Motherhood," 316.

Chapter Twelve: Be Less Alone

1. Marilyn Waring, *Counting for Nothing: What Men Value and What Women Are Worth*, 2nd ed. (Toronto: University of Toronto Press, 1999).

2. To find free online perinatal support groups, check out postpartum .net.

3. Brené Brown, *Daring Greatly* (New York: Averly Press, 2012).

4. Tom Rath, *Vital Friends: The People You Can't Afford to Live Without* (New York: Gallup Press, 2006).

---

adult-centred parenting, 155, 157
allopathic medicine, 133
Amankwaa, Linda Clark, 24–27, 49
anaphylactic allergies, 122
angry mom and confused dad
    model, 93
Aniston, Jennifer, 56
antibiotic eye drops, 65
attachment parenting (AP), 28–34,
    39, 130, 155, 198
    nighttime parenting, 29, 82, 86,
      157
    no-cry strategy, 30, 82
    philosophy, 28–30
    practices, 28, 30–31, 41, 82
    theory, 28–29
Ayurvedic medicine, 133

baby blues, 14, 19
Baby Einstein, 41
baby formulas, 2, 45, 113–15, 117–21
    companies' unethical practices,
      117–19

Bad Moms, 38
bad mothering identity, 187
"bad" parenting, 11, 23–24, 48–51,
    55, 189
being less alone, 191–200, 206
    collective care, 193–95
    family and friends, 195–96
    parent friends, 196–200
    parenting village, 192–93
birth, 55–74, 208–9
    Birth House, 71–74
    birthing practices, 59–65
    doula care, 63–65
    impossible fertility, 57–59
    natural birth industry, 61–63
birth and reproductive trauma, 14,
    22, 65–71, 100, 134, 203
    emotional, 68
    loss, 69–70
    nursing, 15, 69
    physical, 67–68
    sexual, 67
    structural, 68–69

birth stories, 71–72, 74, 131

Black/Indigenous/People of Colour (BIPOC) parenting, 9, 50, 51, 62, 69, 177, 193, 133, 193, 213–14

"blue jobs," 92–94

   See also paid work

bodies, 105–23, 212

   body positivity, 110–13

   nursing, 113–23

   quest for ultimate health, 107–10

Bowlby, John, 28–29, 40–41, 48

Brach, Tara, 140

brain spotting, 71, 134

Breakwell, James, 89

Brown, Adrienne Maree, 139

Brown, Brené, 182, 191, 197

Brown, Solveig, 43–44

Business of Being Born, The, 60

captain/sidekick parent model, 93–96, 98

Carriere, Brittany-Lyne, 108–9

Centers for Disease Control and Prevention (CDC), 108

Chaplow, Biff, 58

child-centred parenting, 155–57, 205

chlamydia, 65

community/collective care, 46–47, 130, 145, 147, 209

compassionate and conscious collective care (CCC Care), 193–95

COVID-19, 44, 130, 157, 207–15

   birth, 208–9

   bodies, 212

   mental health, 212–14

   relationships, 210–11

   sleep, 209–10

   social distancing, 207, 210, 215

   what helps, 214–15

CrossFit, 105

C-sections, 60, 187

DeLee, Joseph, 59–60

Diagnostic and Statistical Manual of Mental Disorders (DSM), 71

dialectical behaviour therapy (DBT), 135

Diels, Kelly, 178

diets, 38, 41, 105–10, 112, 129

   anti-diet, 112

   binge-restrict cycle, 110

   juicing, 109

   Kardashian, 109

   keto, 109

   low fat, 105, 106

   paleo, 105, 109

   vegan, 105

dolphin parents, 130

Douglas, Ann, 175–76

Douglas, Susan J., 49

doulas, 8, 51, 59, 67, 69, 70, 72, 97, 115–16, 129, 165, 193

   care, 63–65, 176

dysregulation, 76, 79

ectopic pregnancies, 69

Emergency Nutrition Network, 118–19

emotional work, 94

   See also "pink jobs"

emotions mapping technique, 112

endometriosis, 57

endurance-based mindset, 135

Ennis, Linda Rose, 42–43
epidurals, 60, 62, 67, 208
episiotomies, 60, 68
evidence-based care, 64–65
expressive arts therapy, 71, 135
eye movement desensitization and
    reprocessing (EDMR), 71, 134

family-centred parenting, 136,
    155–74
    authenticity over accuracy,
        166–68
    family hot spots, 168–70, 173
    family values mapping, 160–66
    family-centred principles, 159–66
    parent island, 173–74
    working with the nervous system,
        170–73
female lifestyle empowerment brand,
    178
Ferber, Richard, 83
fibroids, 57
final thoughts, 201–15
Fiorenza, Elisabeth Schüssler, 126
Fitzgerald, Ella, 201
free birth, 61–62, 120
free-range parents, 39, 130
friendships, 120, 195, 198, 200
    activity partner, 198
    answer master, 199
    identity inspiration, 198–99
    normalizer, 199
    venting buddy, 199
    wisdom seeker, 199

gestational diabetes, 5
gestational parenting, 18, 93

Gilmore, Lorelai, 2
Gilmore Girls, The, 2
gonorrhea, 65
good enough mother/parent, 166–68
"good" parenting, 8–9, 11, 14, 23–25,
    27–28, 33, 37–38, 46, 47, 48–51,
    84, 156, 205–6, 215
Gopnik, Alison, 146
    The Gardener and the Carpenter,
        146
Gottman, John, 102
Gottman, Julie, 102
Great Gallbladder Fiasco, The, 106–7
Griffith, Gabrielle, 193
grind of parenting, 2–4, 148, 178,
    196
Grynpas, Natalie, 62, 64, 71, 144

Hays, Sharon, 27–28, 31
Health at Every Size (HAES)
    philosophy, 109
healthism, 107
Hochschild, Arlie, 94
    The Second Shift, 94
hormonal changes, 6, 19, 76, 82, 149,
    169, 172
hormones, 19, 57, 80, 82
    adrenalin, 78, 169
    cortisol, 82, 169
    estrogen, 19
    melatonin, 19, 80
    progesterone, 19
    prolactin, 19
Hunger Games, The, 126
hyperemesis gravidarum, 108
hypnobirthing, 61

impossible fertility, 57–59

impossible parenting, 37–52

    implications for marginalized parents, 50–52

    invest up front belief, 40–43

    keeping it natural, 45–46

    making it magical, 47–48

    parental fear, 43–45

    parental identity, 48–50

    sacrifice, 39–40

    self-care, 46–48

impossible parenting culture, 6, 14, 37–52, 53, 55, 61, 76, 85, 91, 96, 103, 107, 108, 111, 122, 125–26, 128, 132, 136–37, 140, 141, 144, 146, 155, 156, 158, 163, 177–78, 182, 186, 189, 198, 206, 208

in vitro fertilization (IVF), 58–59, 209

infant sleep, 75, 80, 82–85, 217

informed choice, 63–65

informed parent gut, 205

Innanen, Summer, 110, 111

insomnia, 15, 26, 43, 76, 78, 84, 164, 209

intensive mothering, 27–29, 31, 34, 38

Internal Parenting Team, 150, 151–52

    The Grieving Child, 151

    The Heart, 150

    The Perfectionist, 150

    The Policy Writer, 151

    The Researcher, 151

    The Screamer, 151

    The Screw-Up, 150

    The "Stop It," 151

    The Tired Parent, 151

intersectional feminism, 9–10

intrauterine insemination (IUI), 58, 209

intrusive thoughts, 10, 15, 21–22, 26, 51, 71, 78, 134–35, 148

invention of light bulb, 80

invest up front belief, 40–43, 85, 108, 136, 146, 156

Janna, 3, 96, 99, 106, 137, 143, 163

Joeyband, 76

Johns Hopkins University, 19

keeping it natural, 45–46, 61, 108, 136

Kent-Davidson, Laura, 19, 118–19

Kishimoto, Stephanie, 78–85

Kleiman, Karen, 13

Knaak, Stephanie, 128

kyriarchy, 126

lactation consultants, 114–16, 118

Laditan, Bunmi, 37

Lamaze, Fernand, 61

Letdown, The, 38, 179

Li, J, 163–65

    Decide 10 Rating System, 163–66

Lizzo, 105, 110

Machung, Anne, 94

    The Second Shift, 94

making it magical, 47–48, 136, 156, 198

mastitis, 69, 114

maternal ambivalence, 149–50

maternal deprivation, 29

maternal role collapse, 24–26, 49

maternal role strain, 24–26
maternal role stress, 24–25
matrescence, 149
McGonigal, Kelly, 140
Michaels, Meredith, 49
micro-preemie baby, 68
midwives, 59, 60–62, 64, 70, 108,
    115, 217
Milkie, Melissa, 42, 146
Millious, Victoria, 107
mindfulness, 112, 148, 185
miscarriages, 59, 69, 70
mommy wine culture, 178–80

Nagoski, Amelia and Emily, 126, 172
    Burnout, 126
Naked and Afraid, 86, 191
napping, 42, 76–78, 81–82, 86, 102,
    143, 147, 180, 209
natural birth industry, 61–63
naturopathy, 118, 133
necrotizing enterocolitis (NEC), 120
Neff, Kristin, 140
nervous systems, 168–73
    54321 Sensory Awareness, 171
    Body Scan, 171–72
    hyperarousal, 170
    hypoarousal, 170
    parasympathetic, 169–70, 172
    stress-reducing techniques, 172
    sympathetic, 168–69
Nestlé, 117–18
Netflix, 150, 179, 197
Neufeld, Gordon, 83
neurotransmitters, 19–20
    dopamine, 19, 110
    gamma aminobutyric acid
        (GABA), 19

melatonin, 19, 80
norepinephrine, 19
oxytocin, 19–20, 100
serotonin, 19
Nickel, Dawn, 127
non-gestational parenting, 18, 89
North York General Hospital
    (Toronto), 60
Nugent, Alana, 178
nursing, 2, 7, 10, 19, 22, 29, 30, 41,
    76–77, 96, 100, 108, 109, 113–
    23, 139, 143, 153, 157, 208
    Breast-Is-Best campaign, 113–14
    Choice-Is-Best, 116–17
    Fed-Is-Best, 116
    Informed-Is-Best, 116
    normalizing feeding diversity,
        119–23

*Operational Guidance on Infant
    Feeding in Emergencies, The*, 119
ophthalmia neonatorum, 65
Oster, Emily, 120, 155
    Cribsheet, 120

paid work, 7, 26, 27, 31, 77, 93–94,
    148–49, 155, 157, 165, 176, 193
    See also "blue jobs"
parent guilt, 126, 186–89
parental anxiety, 44
parental authenticity, 166–68
parental burnout, 30, 126, 156,
    175–77, 213
parental identity, 6, 23–27, 43, 48–
    50, 150, 187, 199, 206
parental mental health, 6, 11, 27, 28,
    122, 206, 212–14

parenting culture, 6, 27–30, 35, 37, 38, 52, 80, 136, 189

parenting principles, 30, 188

perinatal mental health, 5, 6, 8, 13, 18–19, 126

perinatal mood, 5, 7–9, 11, 19, 23, 35, 49, 128, 132, 134, 137, 168, 198, 205, 206

Perinatal Mood and Adjustment Disorders (PMADs), 14–16, 19, 22, 26, 50, 51, 65, 89, 92, 96, 97, 100, 128, 132–37, 195, 196, 206

   attachment, 31–35

   biology, 19–20

   individual risk factors and circumstances, 22–23

   parental identity, 23–27

   parenting culture, 27–31

   thinking styles and thought patterns, 20–22

perinatal mood and anxiety disorders, 4–5, 7–11, 13–16, 19

Perinatal Mood Framework, 14, 17–35, 132, 205

"pink jobs," 90, 92–94, 156, 157, 176, 179

   See also reproductive work

polycystic ovaries, 57

postpartum anxiety (PPA), 11, 14, 15, 20, 22, 24, 43, 44, 85, 198

postpartum depression (PPD), 11, 15–17, 19, 20, 22, 24

postpartum depression/anxiety (PPD/A), 10–11, 14, 19–20, 26, 65–66, 105, 134, 198

postpartum mood disorders, 4–5, 7, 18, 89

postpartum obsessive compulsive disorder, 15

postpartum period, 3–5, 7, 20, 100, 108, 128, 129, 141, 169

postpartum post-traumatic stress disorder (PP-PTSD), 15, 65–66

(postpartum) pre-eclampsia, 68

postpartum psychosis, 14, 76, 133

postpartum resiliency, 128–32, 206

   adequate self-care, 128, 129

   feeling ready for baby, 131

   feeling understood, 130

   having enough help, 128–30

   realistic expectations, 131–32

   stress management, 130–31

postpartum sleeping, 76–78

Postpartum Support Toronto (PPSTO), 135

post-traumatic stress disorder (PTSD), 14, 71, 86, 173

practice-based care, 64–65

premenstrual dysphoric disorder (PMDD), 22

primary parent/caregiver, 3, 8, 24, 28, 32, 48, 120, 155, 157–59, 211

pronatalism, 55–57

Rath, Tom, 198

   Vital Friends, 198

recovery, 127–37

   biological influences, 133

   Mood-Managing Tool Box, 132–33

   Perinatal Mood Protection Plan, 132–33

   postpartum resiliency, 128–32

   problematic thought patterns, 134–35

recovery plans, 7, 127–37
reducing risk factors/solving
    problems, 135
resisting impossible parenting
    culture, 136–37
Reese, Trystan, 58
relationships, 89–103, 210–11
    protecting relationships, 101–3
    roommates, 90–92
    sex and intimacy, 99–101
    sharing the load, 92–99, 210
reproductive rights, 59, 121
reproductive work, 94
    See also "pink jobs"
resource guarding, 146
Rhea, Tynan, 100–101

Sacks, Alexandra, 149
sacrifice, 39–40, 96, 136, 140, 156
Sanci, Laurie, 56–57
Scary Mommy, 38
Seabrook, Graeme, 175
Sears, William, 30, 75, 82
secure attachment, 29–32, 41
selective serotonin reuptake
    inhibitors (SSRIs), 20, 100
self-care, 46–48, 128–29, 136,
    140–41, 174, 175, 176, 177, 178,
    180–83
    prescriptive, 46–47, 48, 136, 140,
        176–77, 180, 186
self-denial, 140–41
selfishness, 158–59
    intentional, 158
    mother-baby dyads, 159
self-parenting, 128, 136, 175–90, 206
    boundaries, 182–83
    four squares of, 183–86

play, 181–82
rest, 181
rituals, 183
self-permission, 136, 139–53, 206
    radical, 140–53
sensory motor therapy, 71, 134
sexually transmitted infections
    (STIs), 65
shared parenting model, 95–96
sharing the load, 92–99, 210
    co-parenting, 97–99, 103, 120
    solo parenting, 97
Shuen, Paul, 60
Siegel, Dan, 169–70
sleep, 75–87, 209–10
    coping with exhaustion, 85–87
    making decisions about, 84–85
    politics, 80–83
    postpartum sleeping, 76–80
    professional help, 83–84
sleep apnea, 80, 82
sleep associations (crutches), 79–81
sleep coaching, 79, 83
sleep consulting, 83–84
sleep deprivation/exhaustion, 6, 20,
    74, 75–79, 81, 83–87, 89–90,
    109, 130, 156, 157, 175–78, 181,
    209–10
sleep emergency, 76, 121
sleep experimenting, 83
sleep labs, 82
Sleep Parenting, 78
sleep research, 94
sleep training, 6, 32, 49, 82, 83, 85,
    102, 157
    "camp out" method, 82
    extinction sleep (cry-it-out)
        method, 32, 82

Ferber (gradual extinction) method, 82

"gradual shuffle" method, 82

social media, 38, 43, 47–48, 81, 197, 214

Sprague, Bianca, 59, 61

Sroufe, Alan, 30

status safeguarding, 42

stillbirths, 69

stress trauma, 23–26

stress-management techniques/ strategies, 20, 34, 46, 120, 130–31, 178–79

sudden infant death syndrome (SIDS), 10, 43, 78, 120

surgical birth, 64, 66–68, 100

surrogacy births, 59, 64, 119

Syfers, Judy, 93

"Why I Want a Wife," 93

talk therapies, 21–22

TED Talk, 149

Teigen, Chrissy, 17

tetrahydrocannabinol (THC), 69

Thomas, Kim, 74

thyroid imbalances, 19, 22

tiger parents, 39, 130, 198

Tovar, Virgie, 110

unicorn parents, 130, 198

vaginal birth, 62, 64–65, 100

vaginal birth after Caesarian (VBAC), 66

vaginal microbiome, 20, 41

vulnerability hangover, 197–98

Warner, Catharine, 42, 146

Watson, John B., 81, 83

Weissbluth, Marc, 82, 83

WHO Recommendations: Intrapartum Care for a Positive Childbirth Experience, 63

window of tolerance, 170–71, 173

Winnicott, Donald, 166–67

Workin' Moms, 38, 179

World Health Organization (WHO), 63

yoga, 42, 56, 61, 105, 176, 218

ABOUT THE AUTHOR

 **Olivia Scobie**, M.S.W., R.S.W., M.A., A.C.C., M.S.P., is a social work counsellor who specializes in perinatal mood, birth/reproductive grief and trauma, and parental mental health. She teaches perinatal mental health providers through the organization Canadian Perinatal Mental Healing Trainings. Olivia is also the founder and executive director of Postpartum Support Toronto, a not-for-profit that provides therapy and solidarity for new parents having a tough time adjusting to life with a baby. With two loud kids and one old dog, she believes in good Scotch, telling your story, and supporting families through difficult times.